HEALING THE DEEPEST WOUNDS

Life-Giving Lessons from My Journey with Rectal Cancer Stage II/III

KINERET SHERMAN

HEALING THE DEEPEST WOUNDS

Life-Giving Lessons from My Journey with Rectal Cancer Stage II/III

Kineret Sherman

Published by New Voices Press
75 West End Avenue, Suite C19H
New York, NY 10023
212-580-8833
917-841-1843

The author of this book is not dispensing medical, therapeutic, or psychological advice or prescribing the use of any techniques or practices as treatment for physical, medical, psychological, or spiritual issues or any other type of issue. The author's intent is only to offer information of a general nature to help you in your personal development. If you use any of the information in this book, neither the author, publisher, nor other representatives will be liable for damages arising out of or in connection with the use of this book. This is a comprehensive limitation of liability that applies to all damages of any kind. The use of this book implies your acceptance of this disclaimer.

Library of Congress Cataloguing-in-Publication Data
Published by New Voices Press
ISBN 978-0-9883591-7-8

1. Rectal cancer
2. Sexuality and menopause after pelvic radiation treatment
3.Mind-Body-Spirit aspects of cancer and rectal cancer
4. Self-help 5. Spirituality in cancer treatments

Book cover and interior design by Tony Iatridis, nycartdirector.com

To my parents, who gave me life, love,
and everything I needed to grow.

To Peggy Craik, for hours of editing, without
whom this book would not see the light of day.

To Dr. Shawn Steen, my surgical oncologist,
who "got me" and gave me a second chance at life.

EARLY PRAISE FOR HEALING THE DEEPEST WOUNDS

"This book is a MUST READ for anyone going through a cancer journey or anyone supporting someone going through a cancer journey. But that said, I believe it's a MUST READ for EVERYONE having a human experience. It is a wonderful body of work that will make a huge difference for people."

—Judy Nahkies, Life Coach, Three Principles Practitioner

"Kineret's book is an excellent read for everyone. If you have been recently diagnosed with cancer, it's an excellent guide. It describes in detail what to expect from the different treatments and empowers you to take control of your journey. It paints the lows and highs of the journey you are about to take in realistic colors and gives supportive tools for the best possible results.

Family members or friends of someone diagnosed with cancer will receive a deep realistic insight into what a patient is going through. It can support you in becoming a better caregiver and advocate. For everyone else, this book is a fascinating read. It's a beautifully written document describing a courageous, intelligent young woman's experience, strength, hope, and learning through life's toughest times. It shows you that no matter what you are going through, there is always light at the end of the tunnel, and if it didn't kill you, you are likely to end up stronger, smarter, and kinder with much more joy and appreciation for everyone and everything in your life.

Lastly, for the medical professionals who care for patients with cancer, it raises important points to pay attention to and shows you the importance of respecting each patient's way of dealing with the diagnosis."

— Rachel Furman is a Soul Centered Professional Coach, MA in Spiritual Psychology with an emphasis on Consciousness, Health, and Healing. She is a Three Principles facilitator, an artist, a retired pharmacist, and the author of "Cancer and Cosmetics: Combinations that Can Hurt You."

CONTENTS

CONTENTS

INTRODUCTION

It was a warm, casual, mid-September Saturday in 2015. I was forty-three years old and finished giving six consecutive Thai Yoga Therapy sessions at the acupuncture office. Yearning for rest, I hurried home, hungry as a famished wolf. I devoured my lunch and stepped upstairs to lie down on my comfy bed. Relief set in as the bed tenderly held my exhausted body. My euphoria lasted for less than ten minutes when my bowels signaled for a movement. I reluctantly peeled my exhausted body off the bed and walked to the bathroom. I was about to flush the toilet when I saw a red spot on the stool. My gaze lasered on it. It was a bloody clump, not liquid diffusing into the water.

What is THAT? I thought. I only saw blood on the stool thirteen years ago when I had amebas in Nepal. Instantaneously, my heart raced with fear, and a thought flashed, *something is wrong*. I anxiously watched the smear return several times in the following days before I went to the doctor's office. While I waited for the tests and their results, I began feeling a sucking sensation in my pelvis as if something was drawing my blood out of my body into itself. I felt unnerved.

Two months later, glaring lights blinded me when I finally opened my eyes from the drowsiness of the colonoscopy. The recovery room nurse said, "Honey, we saw a mass in your rectum and biopsied it. We're sending the sample to the lab. If it's cancerous, they'll call you soon. If it's benign, they'll get back to you in a month. And the next time you see a doctor, have someone with you." Her ominous message alarmed me, yet I hoped the mass was benign. I sent a text informing my siblings and asked them to hold off sharing the news with the rest of the family until I had more information.

Two days later, while at work, I received a phone call from the doctor's office. The doctor said, "I'm sorry to tell you that you have cancer in the rectum. I sent referrals to an oncologist, a surgeon, and a radiation oncologist. In addition, we need to stage the tumor, so I'll send you to another gastroenterologist at a different facility with an endoscopic ultrasound machine. Please get a pen and paper and write the names and numbers of these doctors. If you don't hear from their offices within a week, please call them to schedule appointments."

Boom. Shock. What kind of doctors? Wait. Adrenaline coursed through my body, and my heart pounded hard. I felt like my hands and legs melted into jello. With shaking hands, I pulled a pen and paper from my pocket and wrote the doctors' information.

Ten days later, I drank another colonoscopy preparation solution to empty my bowels. I met the lovely new gastroenterologist, and he staged the tumor with an endoscopic ultrasound. The doctor needed to know how deep the tumor penetrated the rectal wall and whether it had metastasized to a lymph node or a nearby organ (like the vagina, uterus, bladder, or prostate for a man) to know how to treat the growth.

My tumor was declared an adenocarcinoma of the rectum in situ (in its original place, not metastasized). It was 1.8 cm and went through the rectal wall, so the surgeon couldn't remove it without major surgery. It was a stage II, N0 (not in lymph nodes), M0 (no metastases). It was seven centimeters from the anus. The doctor recommended that I proceed with conventional treatments.

Conventional stage II/III rectal cancer treatments have good five-year survival statistics, especially for early stages. According to cancer.net, if the cancer is treated at stage II, only at a localized stage, the 5-year survival rate is 89%. If the cancer is stage III and has spread to surrounding tissues, organs, or regional lymph nodes, the 5-year survival rate is 70%. If cancer has spread to distant body parts, the 5-year survival rate is 15%. However, for patients with one or a few tumors that have spread from the colon or rectum to the lung or liver, surgical removal of these tumors can eliminate cancer, which significantly improves the 5-year survival rate.

I had an 89 percent chance of surviving for five years if I did conventional treatment. But I felt frightened of how the treatments would affect my quality of life. I still wanted to be able to conceive a child with a husband.

A few weeks before my diagnosis, I received an email invitation to watch *The Truth About Cancer* docuseries by Ty Bollinger. In this program, Ty interviewed people who healed from cancer without invasive means. *Wow,* I thought, *if I ever knew someone newly diagnosed with cancer, I'd tell them to watch the series.* Since I only managed a couple of episodes, I ordered the DVD set.

Two months later, I was diagnosed with cancer. The DVD set arrived on the day of my diagnosis, and I watched it carefully and took notes. A few years earlier, I read books by Louise Hay and Anita Moorjani describing how they recovered from cancer without conventional treatments. I was inspired to give my body a chance to heal with natural medicine.

I spoke with several healers about my situation. All the healers but one told me to have surgery and take out the tumor first before trying alternative therapies. I was too scared of surgery. Instead, I followed one healer's routine of cleansing the body with coffee enemas, taking medicinal mushrooms to enhance the immune system, and using a natural tumor drawing salve that I took both orally and rectally (which he was certain would pull the tumor out of my body).

My dad and stepmom paid for those initial visits with the healer and bought me a Rife machine, a device that delivers a low-energy electromagnetic frequency into the body, usually through the hands or feet. I treated myself for five hours daily with anti-rectal cancer and anti-worm frequencies. After two months, the tumor grew from 1.8 cm to 2.2 cm, and I had a gnawing feeling that my therapies weren't working.

I asked the healer to add more aggressive therapies. I also found an integrative MD who, for three weeks, administered daily IV therapies of high-dose vitamin C with laetrile, a compound extracted from amygdalin found in almond pits (some people's tumors respond to this combination). I added infrared hot sauna treatments three times a week because heat treatments can weaken tumors. I also added daily rectal ozone insufflations (a machine that creates ozone gas and shoots it through a catheter into the rectum to possibly kill tumor cells). Ozone therapy is supposed to increase oxygen levels to help fight cancer, which likes living in anaerobic conditions. I received a few IV ozone treatments. I drank more anti-cancerous teas like Camas Prairie Tea (essiac blend) and took paw-paw supplements. I did daily guided imagery where I killed the tumor. I listened to quieting meditations. I believed my therapies would regress the tumor.

Two months later, my endoscopic imaging showed that the tumor had doubled to four and a half centimeters with much-increased blood flow. Rather than submit to my efforts, the growth had become more aggressive, and I felt dispirited that my efforts hadn't worked.

My brain raced with panic; *what else could I do to heal the body naturally?* I spoke with a new friend about cannabis for cancer treatments, and she found me a reliable contact. I had never taken marijuana into my body and felt petrified about meeting this supplier at her home. But I had to find something new to halt the tumor. I bought a thirty-day supply of cannabis suppositories for $3,000 and added a nightly suppository of 1 gram of THC-CBD oil to my routine.

At first, the oil didn't affect me, but after a few days, it did. Each morning, as I went downstairs, I'd hold the railing tightly with both hands because my head was spinning from the effects of the THC. I'd slow down each step, praying I wouldn't slip and become a soccer ball rolling down the stairs. Once safely downstairs, my brain said, *Hey, make a juice.* But I couldn't; my head spun, and it felt impossible. *Hey, go for a walk,* my brain commanded, but that was impossible, too, as my spinning head made it hard to keep my balance. My brain also felt slow, like I didn't want to do much, and my emotions were calm. So I sat on the porch for several hours until the spin became manageable.

I worried that CBD would not be enough to fight cancer, so I researched several alternative healing clinics in Mexico. Several people knew about the Hope4Cancer clinic in Mexico, featured in Bollinger's docuseries. I hesitated to go there because their system had never cured someone with rectal cancer. But I was more scared of conventional surgery, chemotherapy, and radiation.

By then, the tumor measured five centimeters with plenty of blood flow. The blood flow meant the growth was gaining strength and possibly getting ready to move to another organ (metastasize). I was so anxious and panicked during those days that I barely slept. I prayed that the Hope4Cancer clinic would work for me. Family and friends donated $42,000 for a three-week stay at the clinic. Six months after diagnosis, I arrived at Hope4Cancer.

The clinic was the first place I'd been with other cancer patients. Some people came to the clinic right after diagnosis. Others were there as a last resort after conventional treatments failed to cure them. One woman spent three weeks at the clinic, but the therapies didn't help her. The clinic stabilized her enough to fly home and die with her family around her. Another woman's cancer was so aggressive that an ambulance took her to a hospital after a week and a half in the clinic. I met courageous people with cancers of all stages and types who utilized various options to ensure their survival. I felt frightened and comforted, freaked out and hopeful.

For three weeks, I underwent heat therapies (local and whole body), IV treatments of vitamin C, laetrile, and PNC-27 (anti-cancer peptide which induces tumor cell death), UV blood irradiation (kills bacteria and viruses, boosts the immune system), and learned about nutrition, detox, and emotional healing. At the end of my three-week stay, I received injections of a virus called RigVir. That virus supposedly finds cancer cells, multiplies itself in them, then breaks open (lyses) those cells. After three weeks, my tumor stayed at five centimeters and showed less blood flow than before, so I was making a little progress.

I went home and continued to take rectal suppositories of PNC-27, go to the UV sauna, and receive RigVir injections. At the end of three months on their protocol, the tumor still registered at five centimeters – but now it had increased blood flow. Increased blood flow meant that the mass was more aggressive. The clinic doctors suggested that I continue taking their medications, as it was keeping my tumor at bay. But it cost $1,800 per month, which I didn't have. What should I do next? The roller coaster ride of discouragement, fears, options, and decision-making continued.

Looking for more natural healing avenues, I found the Hoxsey Biomedical Clinic in Tijuana. I visited the clinic for one day, and took their tonic and herbs for three months. It cost $1,600. Two days later, I visited the Optimum Health Institute (OHI), a raw-food, wheat-grass drinking healing institute in Lemon Grove, California. I paid for one week ($1,450 in 2016) and received a scholarship that covered the following two weeks of their program. Since the staff took care of my needs, I relaxed. I took yoga, chakra toning, food making, and spiritual, emotional, and mental well-being classes. I loved being at OHI.

I felt encouraged when I met several people with ovarian, thyroid, and bladder cancers whose cancers disappeared by following the OHI protocol for five months while staying on the grounds. I wanted to remain on the property and be in that loving, supportive environment, but the community didn't have a spot for me. Thus, I went home. A staff member called after two and a half months and said they had space for me, but at that time, even on their food protocol, my tumor had doubled in size to ten centimeters. Some days, I bled rectally as if it were a menstrual cycle and wore a pad. Should I take a leap of faith and go there for thirteen weeks?

A radiation oncologist I consulted with said the tumor was growing around the rectum. I was also losing bowel control. I had about forty-five seconds from the first hint to get to the toilet. If I didn't make it in time, I would have a bowel movement wherever I was. Occasionally, I'd be driving and need to pull over, reach for a folded road map tucked into my car's sleeve, open it, and defecate on it. I felt hurried, stressed, unnerved, surprised by my creativity, and amused. Luckily, I never experienced pain.

I chose not to go to OHI's extended program. So what shall I do next? I read that a three-week juice fast could put a tumor into remission. After three weeks of drinking only green vegetable juices, my weight dropped to 102 lbs (45 kilos) and a size zero for my nearly 5-foot, 6-inch height. Sitting down was uncomfortable as I could feel my bones on any surface. But a computerized tomography (CT) showed that the tumor measured seven and a half centimeters. The growth might also have reached a lymph node, making it stage III. I felt encouraged that the tumor had shrunk a little, but I couldn't be on a juice fast forever, and I looked to see what else could help.

I learned of Anthony William, the Medical Medium, and read his first two books, *Medical Medium* and *Life-Changing Foods*. I was hopeful that Anthony could help me. I was disappointed he didn't do private readings anymore, but I consulted with one of his certified practitioners. She recommended a new regimen of supplements and herbs, which I took faithfully.

Two months later, the tumor had shrunk to six and a half centimeters – but it may have spread to two lymph nodes. Moreover, the MRI report stated a hardening of the mesorectal fat, which resides in the outer lining of the rectum where the lymph nodes attach. I realized that despite a slight shrinkage in tumor size, the cancer was spreading out of the rectum. I felt heartbroken, and the downward portion of my emotional roller coaster ride continued.

I needed to stop the search for the next alternative approach. Nothing I tried had regressed my tumor, and I ran out of money. In books and documentaries, other people had healed from cancer. Why did I not heal? Thoughts of failure and disappointment flooded me. Would I be able to lift a different switch in my brain and choose harsher treatments that might heal my body?

In April 2017, after interviewing two radiation oncologists and surgeons, I chose to receive the conventional treatments of chemo pills along with six weeks of radiation treatments. Then came the surgery to remove the rectum, sigmoid colon, and all the attached rectal lymph nodes. I lived with a temporary ileostomy for eight and a half months. During this time, I took chemo pills for four months. Then I had another surgery to reverse the ileostomy.

The conventional treatment for me took a year and four months. Healing from the second surgery took four years. I experienced pain, discomfort, surprise, bitterness, gratitude, and fear during and after treatments. And my body healed from every step. I am now five years after the second surgery – and cancer free. I was scared before every treatment, wondering how it would affect my body and quality of life. Even though my doctors mentioned some possible effects, I often experienced other outcomes they hadn't warned me about, primarily how radiation affects sexuality.

I'm grateful for my eighteen months of effort in healing with alternative methods. I learned much about holistic health and will transfer some relevant information to you in this book.

Aunt Susi and my third stepmom Jolanta told me to write a book about my experience as soon as I began researching alternative treatments. I didn't. Then a psychic medium, Chris Brown, said out of nowhere, "You have a book in you. It's got valid information. You need to start writing today. Every day. You won't know what the book is about at first, but in the end, it will make sense." I contacted several other psychics who repeated the same thing. I began writing in April 2017, right before I started radiation treatments.

If you're reading this book, you or your loved one is most likely dealing with a diagnosis of rectal cancer stage II or III, you have a diagnosis of any other illness, you're interested in the topic, or you're an acquaintance of mine. Perhaps you or your loved one had a similar story. Luckily, rectal cancer announces itself clearly by a bloody tissue attached to the stool. Some cancers are more insidious, so they progress more before being found.

Maybe you've seen this blood for several months but have ignored the signs, hoping it will resolve itself. Or perhaps you're contemplating what to do next, wondering what rectal cancer treatments are like and how they will affect your body during treatment and beyond. You might have questions about alternative therapies and whether they help. You might want to know if you have choices in your treatment plan. You and your loved ones are probably facing a fear of the unknown and mortality. I'll do my best in this book to support you with your questions on your healing journey.

This book offers support through my experience and the experience of others that might help you with your journey. It paints a realistic picture of how the treatments feel and how I and others healed.

Each chapter can stand alone. You can open up a chapter that calls to you, wherever you are on the journey or beyond, and receive information and support for that phase in your life. Those who enjoy reading might find the chapters supportive, informative, and inspirational. I also provide a summary at the end of each chapter. For those not inclined to read stories and want the information quickly, you can receive the information from the end of each chapter in a section called Summary and Suggestions. And you can read both to reinforce the information.

This book combines my interests in science, spirituality, and holistic health. I have a Bachelor of Science degree in biochemistry from UCLA and a Master of Science degree in life sciences from The Weizmann Institute of Science, an international graduate science institute in Israel.

In addition, I had an unexpected spiritual awakening when I was thirty, which has led me on a spiritual path for the past twenty years. I frequented meditation centers and pursued other educational opportunities. Today, I also hold a Master of Arts degree in spiritual psychology from the University of Santa Monica. I am a certified life coach by an ICF-accredited school and have taken many subsequent coach-training programs. I have gone to Byron Katie's School For The Work and Eckhart Tolle's course, School of Awakening. I work as a life coach and a spiritual care provider with two private hospices. I also have certificates in Thai yoga therapy and Reiki.

This book started as a memoir, and with a strong recommendation from three editors at a self-publishing company, it developed into a holistic self-help book. A surgical oncologist, a gynecologist, a colorectal surgeon, a life coach, and a tantra teacher graciously read different chapters of the book, and I received their valuable feedback.

Your story will not be the same as mine, and your body will heal in a way that is unique to you. You have sensitivities different from mine, and I cannot predict how your journey will develop. However, there are universal aspects of the treatments that I will discuss. I intend for the information in this book to support you on your path. My heart is with you as you embark on your healing journey. I trust you to handle your healing journey in a way that's right for you. I know that you are the authority on your path of recovery. You have strength of heart, resilience, wisdom, an inner GPS, and common sense. Your journey will be perfect for you.

With love and warmth,
Kineret

TWO ORCHARDS

Two orchards are growing inside of me:
The Orchard of Life and the Orchard of Death.
The Orchard of Life overflows with creativity, enthusiasm, and love;
The Orchard of Death is self-created by fear and thoughts of "Not enough."

The Orchard of Life is when I say Yes to life:
When I dance, write, call up friends, and go on hikes.
It's active when I initiate get-togethers, follow my heart, create activities,
Give good words, and follow my every hunch to engage and connect.

The Orchard of Death is when I say No to life:
When I don't make an effort to dance and when fear closes my heart.
It's active when I don't initiate get-togethers, when I live in insecurity,
When fear holds back my words, and when I keep people apart.

The two orchards live together, vying for attention, connection, and
fertile ground;
And I, like a leaf in the wind, am blown from one orchard to the other.
Occasionally I glimpse at a deeper buried reality inside;
This One allows the two orchards to thrive.

This deeper reality is calm and grounded,
It's the potential of infinite creativity through which thoughts of security
or fear pass.
This rich medium is the Canvas of Life.
Perhaps I'll start a new orchard there.

By Kineret Sherman, April 2016, in response to the prompt,
"What Orchard lives inside of you?"

Section I
BEFORE THE MEDICAL JOURNEY

Chapter One

DIAGNOSIS

My whole body shook during the phone call from my gastroenterologist (GI) doctor when he told me I had cancer of the rectum. I took a few moments to assimilate what I had heard before I returned to work. One thought felt relieved and logical: *Finally, I know what IT is, the daily blood smear on the stool I've been seeing and the blood-sucking sensation in my pelvis that I've been feeling for the past two months...It's cancer. I'm glad it has a name. Now I need to research what to do about it.* Another thought was in denial; *Cancer? Me? Impossible! I'm healthy. I don't get cancer; other people get cancer.* A third thought felt hurried and anxious; *I have to get going to find a solution, and when and how will I know what to do next?* And yet another thought went into panic: *Shit, don't people die from cancer?*

I imagine that a diagnosis can bring up similar thoughts for others who are newly diagnosed. Like me, they vividly remember the moment they received a (cancer) diagnosis as hormones created a slowed and heightened experience of the senses. I felt as though time stood still.

If you're newly diagnosed, you're facing mortality, and perhaps you're frightened. Maybe you've felt the activation of what trauma specialist Sarah Peyton calls the alarmed-aloneness circuit, where you know it's your journey to take alone. I acknowledge the shock of that initial diagnosis. You know your life will change but don't know how and at what impact. In addition, the initial process of gathering treatment options can be overwhelming. Are you trusting yourself to handle your journey?

I assure you that you will assimilate the information. Give yourself the necessary time to digest what you've heard. Be easy with yourself. You have time. You also have the inner resources to handle everything coming your way, even if it's to make quick decisions. I trust you'll be supported and held through this process by the right people and circumstances and that you will make the right choices for yourself. I support your discernment that is right for you.

When I realized I faced mortality, I momentarily lost interest in activities like clothes shopping or dancing. Instead, I preferred to stay home, learn about my options, and connect with my close friends and family. I told my immediate family, close friends, and bosses at work about my diagnosis. I held space for the family as they reacted with fear and concern and asked them to relax, be supportive, and trust the process.

I couldn't watch any television show or movie where people died from cancer. I'd get up and walk away. I wondered if the amoebas I got in Nepal contributed to my developing this disease. But regardless of the cause of the tumor, whether parasites, viruses, bacteria, toxic heavy metals, or toxic emotions, I accepted what was and buried myself in research.

The word cancer repeated itself in my mind in disbelief in those few days and weeks right after diagnosis. My mind couldn't wrap itself around that word. It seemed like a cancer diagnosis was happening to someone else, not me. It took several months for me to internalize that I was dealing with cancer.

In hindsight, I can tell you that a cancer journey will deepen you, and you'll receive many gifts. You will not be the same as you were before treatments. Your body will change with treatments, and some therapies will have intense sensations that may be uncomfortable and painful. However, healing might come unexpectedly through various sources. You will be amazed at the kindness, support, and love coming your way. Stay open to daily gifts. You might gain insights into life. You could deepen your understanding of the human experience. You may love more freely. You may appreciate people more deeply, including yourself.

In addition, one of the gifts of cancer is you get to see what your thought habits are doing. A cancer diagnosis will show you if you have a habit of taking life and yourself too seriously, if you have a habit of anxiety and are scared of a diagnosis, if you're more rational and take life with acceptance, or if you're humorous and glide through life with ease and a good spirit.

If you're prone to anxious thinking, you might worry about your life or death, your quality of life, the treatments you will have, the negative impact on your family, or financial and health-insurance issues. A friend experienced daily panic attacks after he and his wife were diagnosed with cancer two months apart.

I have another friend who focuses on logic and rationality. He looked up survival statistics about rectal cancer and felt hopeful about his diagnosis. He trusted his doctors and his abilities to research and find solutions. Consequently, he felt secure that treatment would cure him. And it did.

Other people use humor to cope with a cancer diagnosis. When one of my friends was diagnosed with pancreatic cancer a few months after me, she called and said, "Hey, I joined the Club!" Humor goes a long way in lightening up a health journey. And trust me; your dark humor will come out big time when you have your treatments. You will often chuckle at what you will experience living in a body.

Some people feel shame about their cancer diagnosis, and they close up. Other patients take the reins into their hands and own their journey, while some drop into a place of passivity and trust. I've also met people who deny cancer entirely. They view cancer as an energy pattern that isn't in them. They give little energy or life to a cancer diagnosis. They get treatment and live their lives fully. Other people turn to their religion, healer, or spiritual path. Everyone's different.

In addition, moving into the physical phases of your treatments might be easier from a place of curiosity. After the initial shock of a cancer diagnosis, another older friend wholeheartedly accepted her sarcoma diagnosis. She declared that she lived a healthy and full life. She assured me she was okay with cancer and dying from it. She did not want to take harsh measures to cure herself but did whatever she could to prolong her life.

She was intensely curious about what the process would be like and what she would learn from it. She adored her surgeon. She loved seeing how her body healed from surgery, how radiation helped temporarily, and what solutions she would conjure. She documented her journey with cancer through art. When her cancer spread, she courageously chose a Death with Dignity option and maintained her openness and curiosity.

I trust you to take the right perspective for you, especially if it's opening to the flow of life in any way it presents itself. In your journey, you can notice what feelings you attach to firmly. Accept yourself as you are. You are enough, and this moment is enough. You might embrace and allow all feelings, including fear, worry, anxiety, shame, humor, calm, curiosity, love, gratitude, restlessness, anger, discouragement, depression, and even panic attacks. All emotions are welcome. Despite experiencing uncomfortable feelings, you really are okay at this moment.

Isn't it interesting that each viewpoint about a cancer diagnosis produces a different feeling? And since there are different perspectives, no one perspective or feeling can be absolute truth. Perhaps no thought of fear, anger, discomfort, or discouragement must be given so much faith and attention.

I once attended a coaching call with coach Michael Neill. I was amidst a fear and anger response to someone overstepping my boundaries. I asked Michael about it. Michael inquired, "What's the nature of fear?" I described the sensations. He asked the question again about the nature of fear, not what it felt like in the body. He suggested that the nature of fear or any feeling is to come as a messenger and then move out on its own. In other words, when I see the message to own my power, speak up, stop beating myself up about it, or return to my quiet center, it's time to let go of attaching to fear. Then, the feeling is free to pass. There, it's already gone the moment my attention goes to something else.

Michael also informed me that feelings are thoughts we attach to as if they were true that are felt in the body. I prolong fear the longer I engage with the thinking that created it in the first place. And the nature of thoughts is to move until I decide to hold onto an opinion as if it's true.

Nine months into my cancer journey, my friend Colleen asked, "Kineret, are you dating?" I told her I couldn't imagine dating someone new while attempting to heal from cancer. "Cancer is not your identity, Kineret," Colleen advised me. Although cancer is a physical diagnosis, I encourage you not to turn cancer into a mental identity and not to put a label on yourself. Beware of clinging tightly to any concept that diminishes who you are.

Open-hearted and humorous Colleen met her boyfriend while dealing with cancer. He loved her so much that he supported her through it. Colleen constantly traveled when she had cancer. She didn't take her label seriously and kept living life to the fullest. Identity is made of clinging to thoughts that tell you, "I am this, or I'm not that" — and who wants to hang out there? Don't take the magnificence of who you are and reduce yourself to a concept like "I am scared, I am fat, or I am a cancer patient." I invite you to do what you need to deal with your healing and let go of the identities that reduce the greatness of who you are. You are so much more than a diagnosis.

For those of you whose mind has a habit of fear, anxiety, or discouragement, have you noticed that what you think about cancer or how much you believe your thoughts about cancer changes depending on whether you're with people or alone, or whether you're doing what you love or not? *I'm scared of cancer; I'm not scared of cancer; I can handle it; what if I can't handle it, I might die, I will live, I'm confident, I'm insecure. I'm okay; I'm not okay; I need support; I need time alone.* These thoughts can occur within one hour of each other. Which one of them is real, if any?

I can't be what my thoughts say because they come and go and contradict themselves all day long. I'm not anxious, scared, confident, or hopeful. Those are passing states. Well, if I'm not what my thoughts say I am, then who am I? Who are you?

I invite you to take a moment and allow yourself to relax. Relax some more. And even more. Take a few breaths. Give yourself the gift of slowing down. Then slow down even more.

Permit yourself to release the roles that you attach to. Allow yourself to relax around the role of daughter, mother, sister, cousin, son, father, brother, provider, worker, dancer, art maker, athlete, professional horse race better, a person diagnosed with cancer (or anything else), or caregiver to someone with a health diagnosis. Release yourself for a few moments from the labels.

Allow yourself to relax. Just breathe. Just be. Breathe in your own time, in and out, without agenda. Nothing to do and no one to be. Just breathing quietly. Allow yourself to be without putting any pressure on yourself. Just relaxing. Letting go. Notice the breath coming in and notice it going out through your nose. Notice your belly expand, then contract. Allow yourself to slow down and just be. Then slow down even more and breathe.

As you quiet down, I invite you to notice who you are when you're not attached to any concept. You may close your eyes and check inwardly. Without thoughts, is there a quiet space? A stillness? Is there a subtle, quiet aliveness, like a quiet inner hum? Is it relaxing to be no one and no thing in particular? Is it peaceful not to believe any concept right now? Is it comforting or pleasant? Is there a deeper dimension inside of you as you're breathing quietly? Is there something quiet and subtle beyond the words? If you noticed anything, it's the ever-present space of your Third Orchard.

The Third Orchard is a peaceful energy inside you deeper than any fleeting thought, feeling, diagnosis, or physical manifestation. That energy is relaxed and free. You feel whole and complete when you're in that energy; nothing is missing. You feel secure that you're connected to something other than your personality. You feel satisfied there. It's a place that feels like it exists beyond space and time.

When you're in this space, you know you'll handle your journey when you open up to your options. You realize this journey is taken just one step at a time. You know you've handled everything until now and are confident you'll continue managing your life. Consider staying with your current step.

Please pay attention when your habit of running forward with your mind is trying to figure out the next few steps and control everything. Notice that it brings you stress. Pay attention when the overthinking habit takes over. Then surrender thinking. You do it when you fall asleep each night. You just let go. You also surrender thinking hundreds of times a day when life summons you to do or relate with something else. It happens naturally. Notice your breath.

Notice if there's a quiet space beyond the words on the page. Is there space in your mind? Is there space in your body? Is there a space between the breaths? When you feel it, you become that quiet space.

The quiet space is aware. At times, it's aware of quiet. That feels calm. Other times, it's aware of thoughts, people's moods, sounds, and feelings. The awareness can focus on your habitual thoughts and bring them to life as feelings. Other times, awareness notices the sensations of your feet on the ground, buttocks on the chair, hands on the table, and fingers typing away: the present moment. You know the difference between feeling quiet, the present moment, or being caught up in a thinking habit. You have discernment.

In addition to cancer-related activities, you have a whole life. Continue enjoying it as much as possible. Do more of what you love. Give yourself rest when you need it. Doodle and color more if you like it. See your family and friends more. Play whenever you can. Garden. Take mini vacations. It's vital to balance treatments with joyful activities.

I and others who have been through this journey are with you in energy through this book. We're holding you with warmth. You are beautiful and perfect as you are. You will take your health journey just one step at a time. You really can handle whatever comes your way. You have our love and support.

SUMMARY AND SUGGESTIONS

1. I invite you to notice if you have a Third Orchard inside you. Close your eyes and let go of all the roles that you play and all the associations you have with people, places, work, diagnoses, pets, and things. Just breathe and let yourself be. You don't have to be anyone or anything in particular. Just allow yourself to be as you are, getting into the quiet. Allow this moment to be enough and you to be enough. Allow yourself to notice the incoming breath and the outgoing breath. Slowing down. Is there stillness inside? Is there a

subtle, quiet aliveness, like a soft hum, inside you? Is there a quiet space in your mind or between words and thoughts?

2. Your feelings are thoughts you are attaching to being felt in the body. Your anxiety or fear is not your situation; it indicates the thinking you're buying into about your situation. Despite having uncomfortable feelings sometimes, you really are okay.
3. Consider choosing to relax in your quiet nature more. You'll enjoy the place of relaxation. When something needs to get down, you'll do it. You have common sense and discernment.
4. Everyone has a physical challenge to deal with at some point. Now it's your time to heal from your physical challenge. It's okay. You take this journey one step at a time. You can do this. I believe in you.
5. Approve of yourself as you are right now. Accept yourself as you are. You are enough. This moment is enough.
6. You might notice that you appreciate life more and that people show up to help you. You might start to see that a healing journey from cancer brings unexpected gifts.
7. Your life is fuller than the phase of cancer treatments. Enjoy life. Do more of what you love. Take more walks and weekend getaways. Do more hobbies. Balance is essential on this journey. Be your own gentle best friend. I trust your wisdom about what's right for you. You can handle whatever comes your way.

Chapter Two

CHOICES

At the beginning of my journey, I realized I needed to decide whether I wanted to live. Doing everything I needed to live would require effort, so I had to be clear on my choice.

In my twenties, I struggled with wanting to live. I faced both family and romantic challenges. My divorced parents went on to create families of their own, and I didn't sense I belonged with their new families. Family issues, lies, emotional distancing, violence, and misunderstandings occurred in my childhood. In my twenties, I often felt pain about the lack of closeness in my relationships with my parents. I concluded that I didn't matter to them.

In addition, I felt trapped in a romantic relationship with a nice man. I made attempts to leave, but he didn't want me to. I didn't stand my ground. Instead of using my power to go and create a life that suited me better, I wished to die. I imagined ways to exit this world.With the help of two friends and my stepfather, I mustered up the courage to leave the relationship. I got involved in another romantic relationship. I chose to leave that relationship also because I couldn't find a way to make it work. I needed more relationship skills, including with myself.

I vividly remember sitting on a tropical beach in Brazil when I was twenty-five years old, gazing at beautiful clouds. I imagined the clouds were God's hands reaching toward me and taking me to the next realm. *Please take me away; I had enough pain in this life,* I silently called to God. I lived inside a wall of pain that I didn't know how to break open.

I didn't die. Instead, I hobbled through life, leaning on my pain crutch and moving from one orchard to the next, happy, devastated, joyous, or defeated. At 30, a profound spiritual awakening introduced me to the Third Orchard, the place beyond thoughts and feelings. I experienced a beautiful, loving power inside. That loving power was not the physical world reality I knew.

Fast forward to age 43, I had made headway and peace with my past and felt more hopeful, joyful, and optimistic about many aspects of my life. Then cancer appeared. I wondered if my past requests to die were fueling this cancer.

My housemates asked to sit with me one evening to hear how I felt after the diagnosis. I shared my fears of suffering or dying from cancer. I told them I felt scared that what I would choose to heal myself with wouldn't work. I divulged that I knew I needed to decide whether I wanted to live or die. For a few moments, I considered what it would be like to leave this plane of existence and the life I had created up to age 43.

Tears welled in my eyes as I contemplated that option, and I sobbed. The pain of considering choosing death at a young middle age was unbearable. Anguish showed me that I wanted to live. I wanted to own a business, experience life with a mutually loving partner, enjoy life, dance, paint, and express myself. During that emotional evening, my housemates listened and held a beautiful space for me to express my inner world of thoughts and feelings. They didn't try to change me or soothe me. They just heard me, told me they loved me, and would do whatever they could to support me. I felt deeply moved by their love and acceptance.

That day I pulled my energy together and intentionally chose to live. I decided to have a new beginning, a new start. I hoped to turn around the destructive energy pattern within me that hides from engaging creatively and intimately with this planet and disowns my power.

Readers of this book could be facing various emotional challenges that would bring inner turmoil or not. You might be in a loving, intimate relationship, a lonely personal relationship, or in no connection but seeking one. Maybe you have children and are brokenhearted over their possible loss. Or you might be grieving the loss of the possibility of carrying your future biological children because of treatment side effects. Perhaps finances are a challenge right now, and you're wondering how to work and deal with cancer. The question is, are you willing to face your challenges or not?

Some people might see cancer as a welcomed "early exit." Some people had trauma in life and had or have thoughts about life being too painful. They are ready to let go. Others feel they've led a full life and are prepared to let go. They want the dignity of their process to choose what feels right. If you don't want to live, accept yourself and your choice. Give yourself love and tenderness for your courage to be honest with yourself.

Most people will choose to continue living and do what they can to increase their chances of survival. I invite you to get clear on whether you want to live in a way that is alive and aligned for you. Is there any change that would be meaningful and fun for you? You may want to create something new, write a book, learn to crochet, paint, garden, or live a slower-paced life. Maybe you want to leave a relationship. A health journey can be a call to focus on what you'd really enjoy in life, including getting clear about doing your part to heal or not. It's your journey, and you get to have the dignity of your process.

In addition, you get to choose how to care for yourself. You'll select your doctors and your treatment options. There will be times when you will advocate for yourself. You might need to ask for what you need from your loved ones. A cancer journey can be a journey of empowerment. You can grow from an old habit of hiding from the world or yourself.

According to the World Health Organization, cancer can be caused by physical carcinogens, such as ultraviolet and ionizing radiation; chemical carcinogens, such as asbestos, components of tobacco smoke, alcohol, aflatoxin (a toxic food compound created by mold), arsenic (a drinking water contaminant); and biological carcinogens, such as infections from certain viruses, bacteria, or parasites.ii Mental and emotional toxicities can also contribute to cancer.

In a healing journey, you choose how you want to heal. Some people approach healing from cancer by studying nutrition to better fuel the body for healing and health. Others focus on reducing physical toxicity in their immediate or global environment. Likewise, some people may reduce emotional toxicity by learning to forgive themselves and others for what they've done or haven't done. Some people might cultivate compassion for themselves and others, even if their actions felt hurtful at the time. And others make no change at all after diagnosis.

The author Louise Hay says in her Cancer audio CD that even if we heal from cancer with medical treatments, if we don't change anything about our lives, cancer will return, or another disease will manifest in the body because the conditions that created the disease have not changed. The neuroscientist, researcher, and chiropractor Dr. Joe Dispenza says that if we do exactly what we did in the previous days, we'll get the same response. We are living a conditioned life, being who we were yesterday. You can step out of old habits and cultivate more aligned and healthy ones. A cancer journey can be an incentive to make the changes that will lead to more robust health and joyous lives.

Dr. Gay Hendricks teaches that physical discomforts can disappear when people move from unfulfilled to fulfilled lives. A friend told me that many of her physical ailments disappeared when she left her husband and got into a relationship with a man that she adored and who adored her. Only you know what's right for you. And only you can change your choices. You are connected to infinite intelligence and creativity. You are infinitely powerful. Own and use your power to choose a life you'd love. You have all the resources inside of you to know what's right for you and take steps towards a life you'd love.

Having a compass to what would make your life more vital and alive may help you heal more rapidly from cancer treatment. I acknowledge your magnificence and your common sense. You are the expert on your needs and inclinations. You have my love and support.

SUMMARY AND SUGGESTIONS

1. Consider sitting with a journal, a trusted partner, a close friend, or several friends and family (or in writing) and sharing your thoughts and feelings. What is going on for you with this cancer diagnosis? How are you feeling? How would you like to be supported? What are your concerns? What do you need? Accept your thoughts and feelings fully. Breathe. Allow yourself to be honest with yourself and others, to be seen as you are without being fixed. If you are going to speak with your family or friends, start by asking them to listen and not try to fix or solve anything for you. They get the privilege of listening to your human experience. They might ask how they can support you, and you get to answer.

2. Consider sitting with your journal and reflecting on your life. Write what is going well in your life. What are you enjoying? What do you wish was different? What creative endeavors would you like to engage with during (or after) cancer? What would you like to do less? Where would you like to live? What do you long for that you don't have? What are hobbies you would like to cultivate? I invite you to make a list, draw, collage, and connect to your heartfelt longings and dreams. Keep this vision in your visual field.
3. Consider taking one step toward moving in the direction of what you wrote that you wanted.
4. I invite you to reflect on whether you intentionally choose to be in life. If you want to live fully, consider standing up for yourself, advocating for yourself, accepting yourself, taking steps towards a future you'd love, and releasing attachment to thoughts that hold your full expression back. I invite you to step into your power and use it in the world. If you don't want to live, accept yourself and your choice. Give yourself much love and tenderness for your courage to be honest.

Chapter Three

BE YOUR ADVOCATE

When I first saw the bloody tissue on the stool, I went to the nearby urgent care facility. The doctor said I had hemorrhoids and gave me a prescription for hemorrhoid cream. I never claimed the medication. I had an intuition that hemorrhoids did not cause the bleeding. I didn't have hemorrhoids before and sensed something new had created them.

I returned to the doctor's office the following week. This time, I explained more of my symptoms of pressure sensations in my pelvis and asked for further testing. The doctor thought it might be something gynecological and also prescribed blood work. Everything we tested came back normal. But I was still seeing blood smeared on the stool almost daily. My housemate June asked if I thought I should have a colonoscopy. Her suggestion rang true; I went back to the urgent care facility and asked for a referral to a gastroenterologist so I could have a colonoscopy. I told the front office staff I would not leave without a referral. That colonoscopy revealed the presence of a rectal tumor and saved my life.

A year and a half later, I joined two colorectal cancer Facebook groups: Blue Hope Nation and Colontown. I read comments from several women who presented the same symptoms I had to their doctors. Just like me, their doctors diagnosed their symptoms as hemorrhoids. Some of these women did not persist in following up on testing and the referral process. Some tried to seek further testing but to no avail. A year and a half later, they were diagnosed with stage IV rectal cancer. We've kept in touch, and now, twelve years later, they live and thrive, though they've had extensive chemotherapy, surgeries, and radiation treatments.

Consider joining Blue Hope Nation and Colontown Facebook groups. You will find other people going through treatment, along with survivors and caregivers. It can be inspirational to hear the stories of stage IV patients who have been disease-free for years. The good thing about online support groups is you can ask any question about treatment options, side effects, bowel movements, or sexuality. Someone will answer, often more than one person. Then you can take the information and discuss it with your medical team about yourself.

One woman wanted me to tell you that the advice she received from those Facebook pages was worth gold, and she wished she had joined from diagnosis. Colontown also has subgroups that focus on smaller topics. When I wanted to ask about women's sexuality, I preferred asking in a women's group like "Tough Chicks" in Colontown, although I sometimes asked on both main pages.

The online forums have been helpful to me and others, and as such, we were able to advocate for ourselves with more information. But some patients don't like online support groups because there is much talk about "problems" or what isn't going well. It could scare some people to read about other patients' issues. You'd have to assess the benefits versus risks to you, as you are the one who knows you best.

Another organization, Imerman Angels, matches you with a mentor who went through the process you are about to go through.

They can also match caregivers, survivors, and other loved ones with mentors. In addition, many people find great value in attending an in-person support group. I didn't. The support group attendees offered advice I didn't appreciate. Thus, I left and have yet to return. But your experience might be supportive and informative about your treatment. I did enjoy the calming classes at the Cancer Support Community. I took their yoga, meditation, tai chi, art classes and lectures. I felt deeply moved that they were free of charge. I cried with gratitude for the generosity of others at a financially and emotionally vulnerable time for me.

A cancer diagnosis will challenge you to advocate for yourself. Give yourself permission to call your medical insurance and ask about the status of the referrals. Please don't allow fear of pestering someone or being a burden on someone to stop you from following through on your care of yourself. You matter and are essential. You are an intricate part of the web of life, and you gift yourself to the world. You are worth advocating for. Advocating for yourself is love in action. It's okay to be a persistent patient who asks for what she needs. You will get an inner prompt telling you to follow up with something. Listen to it, and please, follow up.

When doctors explain new procedures, I invite you to ask clarifying questions. Consider permitting yourself to ask all your questions, especially the silly-sounding ones such as: what's the healing like from this phase? How many patients have you treated with the same diagnosis? What is the typical response to this treatment, and what are the variations? What would you advise your daughter / son / spouse / parent to do in this situation? What are the long-term issues and side effects associated with this treatment? You're assimilating new information. It's reasonable to ask for more time, patience, answers, and slower speech. It's okay to say, "Could you repeat what you just said? I didn't get all of that."

Give yourself permission to claim your space in the world. Some of you had strong authority figures as children or were shamed and criticized, and speaking up with authority figures may feel intimidating. You may feel uncomfortable asking questions. But in the previous chapter, you considered living joyously and doing what it takes to care for important You. I invite you to own your innate courage and ask those questions.

Are you listening to your body? Are you feeling new sensations? Are you asking your doctors about them? Are you satisfied with their answers? It's crucial to keep asking questions until you find satisfying solutions.

I've seen people in their teens, twenties, thirties, and forties presenting with rectal cancer through Facebook pages. I invite you to listen to the soft and steady whispers of your inner guidance and intuition. Consider researching doctors' suggestions and checking them out with yourself, with a trusted friend, or with a family member. Consider getting a second opinion or even a third opinion. When the doctor told me I had hemorrhoids, I knew there was no plausible cause. I ate lots of fruits and vegetables, had regular bowel movements without straining, and wasn't aware of a new source of stress. I couldn't imagine what would cause hemorrhoids.

I invite you to notice you. My surgeon said, "You are the one residing in your body, and you know your body." You are the authority on how your body feels and what feels "off." You get the privilege of taking the most exquisite and meticulous care of yourself. Consider giving yourself permission to keep asking questions.

When I started radiation on Monday, April 10, 2017, I asked the radiation oncologist if I could have a protective shield. He laughed. He told me that radiation is sixty million times more potent than X-rays and that no protective shield exists. A week after starting radiation, I felt my labia and clitoris buzzing. *Why are my labia and clitoris buzzing? Is the machine radiating them?* I told the radiation technician who sent me to the radiation oncologist. Luckily, the radiation oncologist listened to me and, after examining the calculations the following day, said I was right. When his staff did their calculations, they made an error and included the area of the labia. His team re-did the calculations so the clitoris and labia were not in the radiation field.

What if I hadn't been sensitive, alert, and outspoken? I might have lost all function and sensation of the clitoris at forty-five years of age due to a medical error. It was time-consuming to check the work of doctors and office staff. But there was no other alternative but to pay attention to the effects of the treatment on my body and follow up on every sensation and referral by calling both the doctor's offices and, at times, my insurance company.

I was a single woman going through these treatments, and although friends and family accompanied me to some appointments, I went to many of them on my own. I had to advocate for myself. I trust that you will advocate for yourself.

Doctors are excellent, bright, learned people who care for their patients. However, they are still human beings. They may have a large load of patients; they may also have their issues to deal with. Doctors may be fully present or absent-minded for a moment. They might not be aware of all conventional and alternative treatment options available. It's your job to care for yourself, even at your most vulnerable. If it's frightening or intimidating for you to advocate for yourself, consider asking someone to come with you and speak for you.

Because my health insurance changed several times on this journey, I had four oncologists by the time I started Xeloda with radiation. Only my maternal grandmother had cancer in my family, so I was unlikely to have genetic aberrations. Maybe that's why none of my oncologists asked me to do genetic testing. Genetic testing reveals if you have a known gene mutation and are a candidate for immunotherapy. When I chose to be treated conventionally, I asked my new oncologist for testing. The test came back negative.

If your oncologist hasn't sent your biopsy sample for genetic testing, consider asking for it now. It could be crucial for your treatment plan, depending on whether you have any known genetic modifications. Advocate for yourself.

I met a woman with anal cancer who was treated with radiation and chemotherapy. Three years later, a tumor showed in her rectum. She mentioned that her father had colon cancer and had a colostomy bag. I asked if she had had genetic testing done. She said no. I encouraged her to ask her oncologist for it. Her results showed that she did have a known genetic mutation. She received immunotherapy and chemotherapy, and her tumor disappeared. She did not need to have surgery or an ostomy. In many institutions, immunotherapy is reserved for stage IV only; however, shop around and see if some oncologists will administer it.

When I began taking the low-dose Xeloda pills, I developed two spots on my cheeks that lit up like a skin rash. My oncologist said rashes were a normal side effect of Xeloda. But with my red hair, blue eyes, and freckles, I wondered if Xeloda was targeting precancerous lesions on my face. I saw a dermatologist who confirmed the spots were precancerous lesions and froze the sites with liquid nitrogen. After my first surgery, I took four rounds of the higher dose of Xeloda. My face lit up again in precisely those two spots. I went to a different dermatologist who confirmed it was actinic keratosis, and he treated it with liquid nitrogen and chemotherapy cream.

I am now checked regularly by a dermatologist for skin cancer. Had I listened to the oncologist who said the spots were a side effect of the chemo drug and not to worry about it, I would not have known that the rash was precancerous. And if I hadn't gotten it treated when I did, it might have developed into skin cancer.

In short, I invite you to listen to your nudges, intuition, and wisdom, even if a doctor tells you not to worry about something. If you are concerned, contact the right people and get it checked out. Keep looking until you find answers that make sense to you. Get more opinions until you are comfortable with the answers. I believe in you. You will be a different person after this journey, a more mature, humble, empowered, compassionate, and beautiful person who went through a significant challenge. I know you can do this. You are a fiercely powerful and loving being. You have the energy of life itself running through you. You are connected to a vast field of intelligence. I trust your wisdom and common sense. You have my love and support as you express yourself and advocate for yourself.

SUMMARY AND SUGGESTIONS

1. Cancer is a journey of empowerment for many patients. You get to take care of yourself. Enjoy the privilege of standing up for yourself. It might be uncomfortable at times, but that's your growth edge. You get to advocate for yourself, nurture yourself, and love yourself. Advocating for yourself is love in action. I encourage you to keep going.
2. You are a powerful, magnificent being. You have everything you need inside you to advocate for yourself.
3. Consider listening to your body. You are the one living in it. I invite you to listen to your inner nudges and intuitions and follow up on them.
4. Consider following up with your doctors' offices. If you're not satisfied with their diagnoses, ask for further testing.

5. Authority figures can be intimidating. Some doctors were intimidating to me too. But remember that doctors are people, the same as you, equal to you. If you feel any odd sensation during your treatment and are concerned about your diagnosis, please consider advocating for yourself until you get the understanding and the results that satisfy you. If you're having difficulty advocating for yourself, please ask someone to come with you and speak for you.
6. Consider following up on the referral process. Sometimes, referrals get stuck in a loop. Some staff can forget; their workload is tremendous. It's your responsibility to make sure that referrals are executed. Consider calling your doctor's office if you don't hear from them about a referral within a week.
7. If you get a nudge from inside yourself that what your doctor is saying isn't reaching the depth of the matter, consider going to a different doctor for a second opinion or a third opinion. Keep asking until you get the right people to help you. Someone will hear you.
8. You may ask for genetic testing.
9. Consider joining a colorectal Facebook group and asking questions you have before and after treatment. Other patients will give you their honest-earned opinions. Blue Hope Nation and Colontown are two Facebook pages I belong to. Some patients like Imerman Angels, where you are matched with a mentor and can have phone chats with them. Likewise, some people feel supported by a local in-person support group at a local hospital or the Cancer Support Community.
10. You have my love and support.

Chapter Four

CHOOSE YOUR DOCTORS: THEY WORK FOR YOU

Rectal cancer treatments require a team of doctors. You might have an oncologist, a radiation oncologist, and a surgeon. Most doctors are loving, knowledgeable, and caring people. It's important to feel comfortable with the doctors you choose. Are they listening to you? Do they have patience with your questions? Have you read doctor reviews before choosing your doctors?

I interviewed several doctors for every significant process. I spoke with two surgeons and two radiation oncologists. My sister had a friend who was a surgical oncologist. He offered to look up both surgeons and said both surgeons had impeccable records.

I chose doctors with pleasant demeanors who spoke to me kindly, listened to all my questions, and answered them. I chose a surgeon who "got me." Sometimes, I asked doctors' offices to speak with a patient who underwent the same process I was about to have. I asked my surgeon's office if I could talk with another female patient who had a low-lying tumor similar to mine. After checking with the patient, the office connected me with a patient willing to speak to me; chatting with her put my mind at ease.

In selecting an oncologist, I didn't take the time to interview doctors. When I began to consider undergoing conventional treatments, I had an oncologist who spoke to me with disdain for my attempts to heal my body alternatively. Although I knew his remarks came from concern for my life, I still dreaded seeing him for my appointments.

Around the same time, my brother's wife came with me to see the surgeon. On the drive back, she asked if I liked my oncologist. I said, "No, I feel scared around him." She inquired why I chose to continue under his care. She said if she had a doctor she didn't like, she would find a new one. I replied that I was part of a state HMO plan, had already switched oncologists several times, and wasn't sure how many times I could do so.

Upon reflection, I realized I could find another doctor to give me the care I wanted. I also realized that I employed my doctors. They worked for me, a paying customer. Despite their extensive knowledge about cancer and its treatment, I was their boss. I had every right to choose how I wanted to be treated by an oncologist, whether I chose the recommended treatment or not. I could choose a doctor who would treat me with dignity for my choices.

I began connecting with my power to choose. I could call several oncologists in my HMO plan and interview them. I would ask them what I wanted and needed, even if it was neutrality. I would find someone else if a doctor's choices didn't match mine.

With this more confident and explicit attitude, I called several offices and inquired about the oncologists. I made an appointment with a new oncologist, knowing I needed to interview him to see if I wanted him to be part of my medical care team.

I met with one oncologist who passed "the test." He was a gentle man with an easy demeanor. He knew I had done only alternative treatments and was changing course. I asked if he could respect my choices even if they didn't match his beliefs. I asked him if he would treat me kindly and compassionately even if he didn't approve of everything I chose. He said, "Sure. Your body is yours, and you get to decide how to treat it." I asked if he was willing to stay true to his knowledge and expertise and report findings to me in a non-judgmental manner while respecting my thoughts, intuitions, and decisions. The oncologist assured me that he would. Finally, I asked if he would be responsive to my requests and phone calls, especially about imaging, and schedule follow-up appointments with me right after imaging. Again, he replied affirmatively.

I decided to move forward with this humane and compassionate oncologist. It was crucial as I had chosen not to do the entire course of chemotherapy prescribed for a stage II/III treatment. This oncologist still treated me with dignity for my choice. However, I noticed him cutting short my appointment to meet his next patient. Because of that and the lack of warmth of his office manager, after my chemo treatments were over, I switched oncologists. My current doctor answers me patiently, gives me time to ask all my questions, and has a pleasant office manager. I've come to appreciate how vital the office staff is. Warmth and kindness go a long way.

It would help if you decided what qualities are vital for you in a doctor-patient relationship and which are secondary. You may or may not get everything you ideally want, but what is most important to you? Do you want your doctor to listen to you sensitively and answer all your questions? Do you feel like your doctor "gets you," and you're on the same page? Is it essential that the doctor have evening or weekend hours? Consider writing a list of what is important for you in your search for the right doctor. Do you want a doctor who has warmth or can cite survival statistics?

A friend of mine had a radiologist who would walk out of the exam room while she was still asking questions. The radiologist was friendly and knowledgeable but wanted to keep on schedule. My friend switched to a doctor who was not as warm and fuzzy but answered every question patiently, thoroughly, and with statistics. When she asked him what he would do versus what he would advise his sister or mother, the answers were different and gave helpful information. Even without the warmth, my friend appreciated this doctor's approach. It was what she needed.

You may live in a small town that has a limited number of specialized doctors. If so, I invite you to consider a more extensive area radius for your treatments. You are worth the drive to receive excellent medical care for cancer treatments. Some people have found that they can get chemotherapy or radiation treatments, for instance, locally, but have them overseen by a specialist at another hospital.

In some countries, you only get to choose your doctor if you are in a private healthcare system. But even in a non-privatized system, you must know that you don't have to stay with the first consultant you are sent to. You have the right to find someone with whom you resonate. It may be time-consuming, but continue to consult with doctors until you get to someone you like. It is worth the effort in the long run.

Your doctors are working FOR you. Do you resonate with them? It's essential that doctors hear you, answer all your questions, and explain matters to you in a way that you understand. You want to feel comfortable addressing any issue that might come up with your doctors. I trust you to pick the right doctors or change them. You have discernment. You are a beautiful, magical, gifted, powerful, creative, loving being who will be treated by the best doctors you can find. You have my love and support through the process of consulting with and choosing your doctors.

SUMMARY AND SUGGESTIONS

1. Remember that you employ your doctors. They are working for you. Your team is supposed to talk with each other about your treatment. You get to hire your doctors and change them until you find a great team you trust and have a good rapport with.
2. You want a surgeon with an impeccable record. Consider checking your doctors' internet reviews. I had a third-party surgical oncologist check the records of the two surgeons I considered.
3. If you feel judged, criticized, or intimidated by your doctor, there are better doctor-patient relationships than this. Consider changing your doctor. You have the power to do it. Give yourself permission to terminate treatment by a doctor who does not resonate with you. Empower yourself and find the right doctors who fit your needs. This is your journey.
4. You are strong, beautiful, magnificent, gifted, loving, creative, and empowered.
5. You have my love and support through choosing your doctors.

Chapter Five

WHAT DOES SPIRITUALITY HAVE TO DO WITH YOUR HEALING JOURNEY?

Spirituality was not a big part of my early life. I grew up as a secular Jew in Israel until I was twelve. I culturally celebrated the holidays and studied the Bible at school. But my home was not religious, and I didn't know what God was. I resonated with some prayers, like, "Blessed are You, the Lord our God, Sovereign of all, who has kept us alive, sustained us, and brought us to this time." It was a blessing of gratitude and struck a chord of truth in me. I also resonated with, "Hear O Israel, the Lord is our God, our Lord IS One."

Being a science student later in life, I realized how life is interconnected. I breathe oxygen made by plants from the atmosphere. With that gift, my body can live. In return, my body emits carbon dioxide, which plants use to synthesize sugars. Moreover, plants share some of that sugar through their roots with other organisms. In turn, those organisms serve the tree with chemicals like available nitrogen. Insects pollinate fruit flowers, and fruit grows; then, animals eat the fruit and, through their digestive system, drop the seeds elsewhere for new growth. Nature showed me that we are not individuals; we are part of a more extensive system and depend on each other to live. We are a system in which "The Lord IS One."

I also traveled in my twenties. What I noticed was how similar religions were. Religious Jews, Muslims, Buddhists, and Hindus expressed humility of the body. All cultures had a belief in something greater than the personality. In addition, wherever I went, I saw families with similar needs for work, creative expression, love, nurturing, fun, play, and raising children. I received random kindness wherever I went.

When I was thirty and traveling in Thailand, other traveler-friends urged me to meditate. I had zero interest in meditation. A friend gave me a book to read on my travels which said that if several people are telling me the same thing, it is the universe's way of communicating with me about my next steps. When the sixth person I met asked if I would attend a meditation retreat, I wondered if "the universe" was telling me to meditate. I questioned my friends until they convinced me it was a safe activity. Hesitatingly, I went on a silent ten-day insight meditation retreat. I had problems accepting some of the rules, and I argued against them. The retreat center staff told me I could follow the rules or leave. I accepted them.

At the Wat Suan Mokkh International Dharma Hermitage retreat, books, phones, or other external materials were not allowed. Reducing external distractions and focusing on meditation were of the essence.

I learned to follow my breath. I learned to slow down walking, eating, standing, and brushing my teeth: to ssslllloooowww dooowwwnnn. When I ssslllloowwed dooowwwnnn and used FULL awareness on any task with little to no thinking, I noticed pleasure, aliveness, and fullness. Nothing was missing. Everything was beautiful. I needed little food to sustain my body because I couldn't focus if I ate large meals. I delighted in communicating with others through silent gestures. We had daily Buddhist talks from a monk, and I was hooked. It all made sense.

But after ten days, I realized I still didn't know how to meditate more deeply. I had watched Maria from Spain sit with her eyes closed for the past ten days, and I had an intuition that she knew how to meditate.

"Maria, you know how to meditate, right?" I asked her.

"Yes," she answered.

"Can you teach me what you know? I've been here for ten days and still don't know how to meditate."

Maria agreed. Three additional women joined, and we moved to the main monastery. Maria gave us further instructions, which changed my life. She told us to notice the belly movements naturally caused by the breath.

Once we mastered focusing on the belly movements, she instructed us to be present for any thought arising in the mind. Maria said to give the thought a one-word name that described its kind of thought, like analyzing, fantasizing, prioritizing, naming, planning, remembering, imaging, emoting, sounding, etc. Once I named the thought, my task was to return to noticing the belly movements and wait for the next thought. When a type of thought appeared similar to what I had named before, for example, an analyzing thought followed by another analyzing thought, I was to give it a new name: "knowing," and return my focus to noticing the belly movements.

I sat with closed eyes, noticed the belly movements, and waited for a thought to arise. Then I named the thought and returned to the belly breaths. Noticing and naming each thought that arrived both surprised and delighted me. It was the first time in my life that I consciously met and labeled each thought that ran through me.

I found this process exhilarating. A thought flashed; *my thoughts are more exciting and entertaining than television because they are personal to me:* analyzing. I chuckled internally with delight. And back to watching the belly movement. What thought will I have next?

Futurizing. Music in my ears, *sounding*. Back to noticing the belly movements

I felt so thrilled and entertained by each thought, note, or image that arrived that I sat in heightened alertness and waited to greet the next one. I was like a kid who found the planet's most fascinating and amusing game. *Knowing*. The joy and eagerness to encounter the next thought overcame my whole being. A thought flashed: *This is my own movie screen, and I'm watching my personal thought movie starring me.* I felt energized by that realization. Back to noticing the belly movements. I eagerly awaited the next thought in super heightened alertness.

As I waited for thoughts in intensely focused alertness, gaps unexpectedly formed between thoughts. I experienced a profound calm and peace. I relished this silence even more than the entertaining thoughts.

The more I watched in heightened anticipation, the slower the thoughts arrived. At times, waiting in super alertness, thoughts wouldn't form. I experienced more calm, silent spaciousness, which felt freeing. It was a most glorious feeling. Sometimes I sensed energies coming from a couple of locations above my head, intending to fuse into a thought, but since I watched them intently with a focused presence, they wouldn't form; they'd move their energy out of my energy field. Thus, I waited in delighted silence for the next thought to arrive.

I sat in meditation three times a day for an hour; morning, noon, and evening. My focus was as great as my fascination was with what I noticed. Thus, I experienced longer gaps of silence and spaciousness as days went by. The silence felt deeply nourishing.

On the fifteenth day of meditation (five days after the retreat ended), I woke up early and sat in the forest alone. I awaited thoughts. Something had shifted. The conglomerate of thoughts, feelings, and memories that make up the identity of Kineret disappeared. It completely vanished. "I," as I knew myself to be, dissolved. There was no "Kineret," no "me," no "I." Instead, there was an inner energy that was loving and powerful. It was gender-less, religion-less, person-less, name-less. It was a silent, loving, impersonal energy-power and light, an "It." An It was running the show, not a "Kineret." Kineret truly did not exist.

Instantaneously there was a knowing that this was "Home." Home was nowhere external, not with anyone or anything. It was internal but was not the body. It was energy-light. It became apparent that this power was more real than anything I had ever known. The external world instantaneously became flimsy. It, too, melted and did not exist. I realized the life I had known was an illusion of the decoded signals of the organs of perception. I knew that the powerful It inside me was the real deal. I broke down crying in gratitude. I spent thirty years of pain searching for an external love and a home to belong to, not knowing it was inside.

That was the most beautiful and powerful moment of my life, the revelation of a power inside that is not the personality. Before this meditation retreat, I had no interest in spirituality or meditation. I had no notion of a power that was inside of everyone. After this incident, spirituality became my life.

But as the realizations occurred, the flimsy personality returned with fear for its life, with its characteristic sense of identity, entitlement, memories, feelings, thoughts, and pettiness, making it all about "me," attaching to wants, to a better moment than this one, to judgments, righteousness, and fear of everything. The fake personality tried to convince me that it existed as Kineret. But I had seen deeper. I remained stunned with awe, deep gratitude, and confusion about what I had experienced. I had no context for what had occurred.

I went searching for understanding. I went to spiritual centers in India, called ashrams, to seek answers. I went to yoga centers and learned that yoga means a union with the personal mind and universal mind and a cessation of the fluctuation of the mind. I had little interest in physical world reality after I reached the spiritual self. I didn't have the ambition to do anything external, including travel. I only wanted to meditate and return to the place inside that was powerful, loving, quiet, and light. I liked that peace and stillness. I frequented more meditation centers.

Since the personality that melted was back, I could see how easily it became unbalanced. My personality was reactive and acted out patterns as it did before. I wanted to learn how to live with a personality knowing what I experienced about a deeper reality. How do I reconcile the two?

I did whatever I could to continue learning about the ego personality and the spiritual nature. I went to the University of Santa Monica to study spiritual psychology. While in a group process, I was transported again to an expanded space. I had no fears or doubts for two weeks, and people's insecurity patterns seemed absurd. There was nothing to discard and nothing to fix about anyone. People didn't know who they were. They all seemed like they were sleepwalking. They thought they were their thoughts and personalities and took themselves seriously. They didn't know they were whole and didn't need anything other than who they were.

Cancer showed itself thirteen years after my spiritual insight. My intellectual mind sometimes knew It was constant and could not be destroyed. However, other times, my thoughts hypnotized me into believing I could die and that "I" existed as a person instead of a more immense, lasting impersonal consciousness. When I didn't notice each thought that ran through me and labeled it, nor noticed the gaps in between, the thoughts took hold of me, and I felt my thoughts as feelings. The body reacted as if every thought I attached to was real. I often blew with the winds of thought and emotion from orchard to orchard, not connecting with the ultimate truth that I am an immortal energy.

To ground me in the spiritual dimension, I listened to spiritual teachers Eckhart Tolle, Byron Katie, and David R. Hawkins. They merged the personal soul with the universal soul, and they've been my reminders. Listening to them helped me remember who "I" was and return to It. Being with friends and family also helped me get my mind off of thoughts. Being with pets or engaging in a hobby like dancing also kept me from being seduced by the "all about me" mind.

Beyond my spiritual experience, every society has an aspect people call spirituality. Some call it a higher power, Spirit, God, Source, nature, Jesus, reality, humanity, the Tao, or nothing. Likewise, every religion has an esoteric offshoot like Kabbalah, Sufism, mystical Christianity, and shamanism. Some people shrink from the word spiritual, while others embrace it. As a spiritual care provider at two hospices, I've spoken to people with different beliefs, from devout religious people to people who don't believe in anything. Regardless of spiritual beliefs, people take comfort in surrendering their doubts and worries.

The spiritual teacher Eckhart Tolle reminds me that everyone will be challenged in life, challenged within the family, work, and survival. You live in a vulnerable body, in a home that needs fixing, in a world where people's fear leads to greed and unrest. In addition, there's an unpredictable natural world and a society that asks for something called money to pay for life. Yet nothing external is permanent.

Sooner or later, you become humble, usually through pain, debilitating fear, suffering, or a diagnosis facing your mortality. You get to a place where you can no longer endure the pain. You realize you cannot control life, your partner, your children, your body, wars, earthquakes, accidents, pandemics, the future, or even your thinking.

At this humble juncture, you learn to relinquish personal thinking or righteousness and show up in life one moment at a time. You refocus on your health and well-being. You do what you can for yourself and the world and stop trying to fix family members. You problem-solve just what's in front of you without running forward too much in your mind. You let go of expectations that others should treat you how your mind tells you you should be treated. You learn to respect other people's yeses and nos as well as your yeses and nos.

You also come to appreciate what you have and what is good about you, your family, and life. You see that you are enough right now. You understand that now is all you've got, and the future and past are thoughts in your mind. You bring yourself to the now. You slow down. You quiet down and feel grateful that you are alive. You marvel at this planet that's abundant with life forms. You appreciate planet Earth spinning at just the right speed, situated at the perfect distance from the sun. You see what's right in yourself, others, and the world. You have more fun. You focus on what brings you joy. You start giving more for the joy of giving, contributing, and loving. You feel freer. You feel exquisite warmth and care toward yourself and others.

Some people appreciate the power of prayers or affirmations and enjoy saying them often. Prayer and affirmation have form and energy and can ripple and affect lives. Some people with a solid spiritual community ask their community to pray for them; some heal, even from cancer.

In addition, you can tap into a spiritual power that may heal you. The neuroscientist and author Dr. Joe Dispenza healed himself from broken vertebrae with the power of his mind, as he mentions in several of his books and talks. He tapped into a picture in his mind of his back in perfect condition, sustained the image for twenty minutes with feelings of gratitude, and his back snapped into place. In his advanced retreats, which he holds worldwide, people practice his process of opening their energy centers, going into the center of being no one and no thing, and then creating what they'd like. People who have attended these retreats report numerous instances of spontaneous healing from all sorts of conditions.

To relax the thinking mind, some people enjoy listening to meditation apps, mindfulness meditation classes, YouTube guided meditations, dance, hike, or working on an art project. I still like meditation, focusing on belly movements and naming thoughts.

What are your intuitions about death, life after death, a more profound power, or who you are? What gives you comfort in your cancer journey? In her book, *Dying To Be Me: My Journey from Cancer, to Near Death, to True Healing,* author Anita Moorjani shares her near-death experience from cancer. She had stage IV lymphoma and experienced organ shutdown. She left her body, saw her body on the bed, heard the doctor speaking with her husband down the hall, and even saw her brother on an airplane coming to say goodbye to her. She also met her father and best friend in spirit form. They had passed some years before. Anita realized how every person is connected to everything in a beautiful tapestry. She saw she was a part of the creative power of the divine and realized she WAS the universe, not apart from it. Her understanding of her spiritual nature expanded, and she understood that fear of disease created her cancer.

Anita's dad, in spirit form, advised her that if she chose to go back to her body, she would need to live her life fearlessly. Anita knew if she decided to go back to her body, she would heal from cancer, as cancer would not be able to thrive in her new expanded vibration. Anita returned to her body, and within five weeks, there was no trace of cancer in her body. Reading Anita's book during my cancer journey brought me comfort.

What comforts you on your journey and keeps you grounded beyond believing your thoughts? Are you noticing the present moment of your body lying comfortably on the bed, a pillow under your head, and comfortable socks on your feet? Are you noticing how relaxing the present moment is? Are you listening to your spiritual teachers, going to your house of worship, or reading comforting books? Are you enjoying your favorite activities? Are you connecting with family and friends, nature, music, art, hobbies, or pets? What uplifts your spirit and returns you to balance and well-being? The spiritual teacher Sydney Banks suggests doing more of whatever brings you peace and joy. Do more of what feels good. Focus on joy. Focus on goodness and love. It will help you with your journey.

You are more resilient, powerful, and brilliant than you realize. You have an It, are an It, and are always connected to the greater It. You're part of everything and everyone. And, the bigger It has got you. It's safe to surrender your personal mind often. Your bigger It doesn't die. It is waiting with infinite patience and love for you to return home to yourself right now, in the silence, in the quiet.

The external world is an ever-changing playground. Whatever sense of security you seek externally cannot be found there. You can find satisfaction by looking inward in the secure quiet. Even during your healing journey, It is inside of you. Come home to yourself whenever you need healing. You (It) are there to nourish yourself with love and support.

SUMMARY AND SUGGESTIONS

1. What support system keeps you grounded and humbled? Are you connecting with people or a spiritual community? Are you listening to grounding meditations, spiritual talks, or reading soothing, grounding material?
2. Are you prioritizing doing what nourishes you? Consider balancing cancer treatments with life-giving activities that restore you: being in nature, listening to music, doing art, etc. Consider giving yourself time for rejuvenating activities, even to rest and watch the trees and birds from your window.

3. Have you come to a place of surrendering the personal mind and opening to the flow of a bigger system, whether you call it nature, reality, God, spirit, It, or source? How does it help you on your journey?
4. You are more resilient than you think. You are more powerful and brilliant than you know. You have all the inner resources to move through your healing journey. The bigger It has got you. You can surrender your fears to It. It is always inside, with infinite patience and love, waiting for you to return home to yourself.

Chapter Six

HOW TO LIVE WITH YOUR CRAZY MIND ON A CANCER JOURNEY

Journal Entry: *April 7, 2017: I'm tired of being a ME, an "entity" that runs the show for "me"...that tells me to be worried, that relates everything to a ME. That's so tiresome. That fake ME is distancing itself from people right now. It doesn't want to talk or see anyone. It doesn't want to repeat the story or tell others what's painful. It wants to be left alone. And I want it to leave me alone, to be quiet in the mind, to go on walks and just relate with the flowers, plants, and animals.*

I'm tired of the internal dialog about cancer treatments. It's such a mindfuck, this process. Such a freaking mindfuck. I see the small self pushing everyone away. It's fragile, the ego, but I want to be quiet, centered, and connected to safety and joy. Then the mind takes over, relating all life experiences to "things" called "cancer" and "me." Enough already. I am tired of self, of comparing to self, of strategizing about self, of talking about self. Maybe it is time to get back to work.

I wrote that diary entry nineteen months after several attempts at regressing the tumor naturally and seeing daily blood on the stool. The tumor kept growing, and I had mind chatter about what to do next to keep myself alive. When the first imaging showed that the cancer had grown, I felt disappointment and gnawing fear. Subsequently, when the growth doubled, then doubled again in size, I experienced surprise, disappointment, acceptance, then panic. It was an internal roller-coaster of thoughts, feelings, research, and redirection.

Thought vs. Thinking

So who are we, and what is thought? We're quiet, spacious, aware energy. Thought, as the spiritual teacher Sydney Banks mentions, is a universal, spiritual energy that passes through our space. Thought is neutral and informative. Thought is always there. It comes and goes. It's a creative tool.

Thinking is an activity that your consciousness does. It is what you do with thought, how much life you give each thought, what meaning you ascribe to the thoughts, and what direction you keep thought on. It often happens without your noticing.

You use thoughts to create sketches, buildings, colors, computers, gardening, music, humor, cooking, and dance choreography. You use thoughts to find solutions. Thoughts also create internally. When you say, "I can, and I am," you feel expansive, and when you say, "I can't" or "I'm not," you feel contracted. It's the power of thought. It creates. You're always creating with each thought you focus on.

Hurried, Fearful Thoughts

When imaging showed that the tumor grew in those early nineteen months, I saw that what I did wasn't working. It's one thing for me to notice that what I chose to do didn't regress the tumor and focus on finding a different healing method. The problem for me was that until I found the next method to try, I'd run hurried thoughts through a panic-worry loop repeatedly. And since I felt what I listened to, I had days of feeling panic constantly. But is it a great approach to healing?

Coach Chana Studley mentions that the problem isn't having scary thoughts but listening to them. *I have to get this done now or as soon as possible. I have to visit six patients today, and there's a lot of traffic. I have to find a solution as quickly as possible.* Notice how you feel when you believe your hurried thoughts. You feel uneasy, tight, unsettled, and anxious. Notice the feelings and follow them. Where are they in your body? Let go of the commentary by following the feelings fully with your awareness. Does the intensity change? Just be open to following the feeling and be in your quiet.

If you've taken a more traditional approach than I did, you may feel calm and trusting with your medical journey. But even if your logic is strong, there will be curve balls on this journey where your mental balance will shift. You might want to discern whether you are over-listening to fearful thoughts at those times.

Fearful thoughts could point you to what needs to be done. Eighteen months after diagnosis, I inserted my finger into the rectum and felt two unusual bumps. They had never been there before. I knew cancer was progressing, and I needed to change to conventional treatments quickly. The fear pointed me to look in a different direction. Then I needed to stop my habitual addiction to fear.

Perfectionism and Urgency

My habitual internal commentator used to give me a daily printout of what needed to happen for my optimal survival: "Get up, brush your teeth, go for a walk, make your juice, drink the health smoothie, eat the right foods, rest, relax, do visualizations, clean your desk, do yoga, go to the sauna." On my cancer journey, my inner sergeant was relentless with everything I needed to do to be healthy.

It was an endless to-do list. I'd be exhausted just thinking about accomplishing everything on my list. I often lived in a future moment about what needed to be done. My busy-mindedness prevented me from enjoying my walk, savoring the smoothie, or slowing down enough to feel the celery with my fingers before placing it in the juicer. Coach Michael Neill uses the analogy of living with a gun pointed to your head to describe the sense of urgency, "Do this or else." And who wants to live like that?

Is there a choice in living calmer and taking things more leisurely? Once you notice the hurried feeling, you can stop attaching to the future list. Live right now; enjoy the moment right now. You and I have discernment about what is truly needed. Choose your schedule at a pace that is leisurely for you. It's saner to choose calm, balance, rest, and often do less.

Sometimes, doing less accomplishes more. When you do less, you slow down. A slower pace might lead to a quieter mind. A more tranquil personal mind has greater access to the universal mind. Wisdom allows you to see your situation clearly. And quiet allows your body to sleep and heal better. Have faith in your quiet space. Have faith in slowing down. Your quiet space is inside you; it's the space of just being. Just quiet. The space of now. The space of breathing. Try it and see how good you feel.

Shoulds and Shouldn'ts

I'm too thin. I'm too fat. I shouldn't eat any sugar. I shouldn't be afraid of cancer. I should do yoga to heal. I should make more money to pay for co-payments. I should live in a place of my own. They should be calling me more and offering help. I should be calm more often. I should have more fun. I should meditate. I should focus only on positive thoughts of seeing myself healed. I shouldn't have such crazy head chatter. I shouldn't be worried. I should be going back to work.

Did you notice how reading "should thoughts" affected your body? Did you feel the contraction in your body? Did that feel good or not? After my spiritual insight, I knew I wasn't the body. But my feelings showed me where my consciousness was still holding on to unquestioned fear as if it were valid. "Should thoughts" flooded me, fearing that what I was doing wasn't enough, that there wasn't enough money, and that I could die if I disobeyed their direction.

Often, I don't even notice what thoughts caused my fear and contraction, but once I feel the insecurity, I can accept it and make space for it. I can allow whatever experience my consciousness created. It created fear from thoughts that may or may not be accurate. It's innocent. I Breathe in. I breathe out. I accept it with love. If I'm feeling contracted and small, I might want to question if I need to do something about my "should" thoughts right now. Is it essential to address or note it immediately for the future, or do I need to drop my attachment to what I'm buying into so I can be my essential nature of peace and calm? When I drop my attachment to the commentary, I might notice that my reality is calm. The trees, grass, and furniture outside my window are calm. And so is my chair.

Underneath insecurity and anxiety thinking, there is love, quiet, peace, joy, and common sense. That space reminds you that you are enough, this moment is enough, and you can take your time and notice this moment. Your wisdom says you have inner guidance and have had it your whole life. When you get quiet enough to hear your guidance, you'll know what to choose and do from calm.

You'll realize that you enjoy calm more than anxiety. If you have choices to make, you'll understand that everyone lives in the unknown every second of every day, including on a cancer journey. You'll trust that you'll find your way with your unknown. You'll know that you can course-correct as necessary. You'll accept your feelings. You'll be compassionate with yourself often. You're doing so well with your journey.

Negative "What If" Fantasies and Anxiety

During my alternative journey, I became intimately acquainted with the voice of the negative "what if" fantasies. It would sound like, *What if you don't find a solution in time? What if the next treatment doesn't work? How do you know that it will be helpful?* Then, when I'd see the tumor grow, then double, and double again, I clung to my thoughts and felt terrified. Anxiety kept me awake at night when looking for the following healing method.

When I subsequently chose conventional treatments, new thoughts frightened me about each phase of the treatment. *What would radiation do to me? How will I manage the symptoms of treatment? What will be the aftermath? What if chemo damages my heart? What damage, permanent or temporary, would chemotherapy create? What if the surgery won't work? What if I die during surgery? What if the oncologist/ surgeon isn't careful? What if I have a permanent colostomy? What if I have a terrible quality of life after the ileostomy reversal?*

The questions were valid to consider. However, my fearful "what if" habit allowed my thoughts to rev up their speed along with the stress hormones. I was innocently attached to fear as if the thoughts were true. I forgot that I'm connected to the creative power of intelligence that finds solutions.

Fear and anxiety are what Psychiatrist Dr. William Petit, Jr. calls "love letters to me." They are the messengers that show that I'm stuck in a level of understanding where I forgot that I am an It that can never die. The love letters wake me up to see beyond my current level of understanding. When I get an anxious "love letter," I now know to follow my feeling. I notice where it is in the body. I allow it to be, and I follow to see how it morphs. Then I bring myself to just this present moment. There's only now. I was just under the attack of future thinking that occurred without my noticing until the anxiety happened and alerted me to what my thinking was doing.

If you're feeling anxious, have you taken the time to examine if the content of the thinking is accurate or if it's a scary fantasy or movie in your head? Much of the scary "what if" fantasies are not reality. You could research to be prepared, but even then, healing will be what it is, and you'll deal with it like you've done your entire life, one step at a time. Reality is you sitting on a chair or in your bed reading this book. It's you breathing. It's you having a bowel movement with or without blood on it. It's you looking at the screen before you as words appear on the page. It's your room with walls and a window. It's the photos on the wall and the plants on a shelf. It's the carpet or rug.

It's okay to stop engaging with negative "what if" fantasies beyond your research. When peace becomes more important to you than anxiety, you'll drop into a space where you are whole and complete.

You can also shift a habit of negative fantasies into curiosity. Drs. Gay and Kathlyn Hendricks suggest opening up to curiosity using the sound, Hmmm, which shifts the consciousness from critical to soft right brain. *Hmmm, I wonder what recovering from the surgery would feel like. I wonder how chemo will affect my body. I wonder what I'll learn from these treatments. I wonder how I will figure it out.* In addition, I wonder what if the fantasies were framed positively: *What if I know that I'll find a solution; what if the surgeon knows his work; what if chemotherapy will help me; what if I trust myself and my doctors to navigate this treatment?*

Resisting the Need Behind the Thought

Do you have a thought that is resisting what is happening in your life right now? While healing from the reconnection surgery, I had thoughts like, "This is too difficult; I don't know if I can handle more days like this." If I believed those thoughts, I felt discouraged and dispirited. If I noticed that the thought might be giving me information that I needed to stop pushing through the healing and rest, then life became more graceful.

I invite you to notice what's the need behind your thoughts. Do you need to rest? Do you need to take your journey more patiently and let go of your anxious thoughts? Do you need more choices by getting more treatment options? Do you need to trust the flow of life, the universe, God, or your resiliency for a solution? Perhaps watching a movie and spending time with a friend will bring out more fun? Do you need to communicate with your loved ones? Do you need to do less? Do you need a hug? I challenge you to ask for one today.

You Always Come Back to Balance

Have you noticed that you keep returning to the relaxed you without concepts? When you've been in an argument, you returned to being balanced at some point, right? You've had many instances where you've felt scared, insecure, happy, elated, creative, sad, inspired, expansive, depressed, joyous, angry, enraged, quiet, or contemplative. And yet, these states have passed, and you returned to being you. You had loving thoughts about your children or pets, felt expanded, and then returned to quiet. You had frustrated, annoyed, and worried thoughts about your children or pets and felt contracted. At some point, those thoughts passed, and you returned to balance.

Balance is your nature. The feelings pass. Moments come and go, thoughts come and go, and moods come and go. You go up and down on your healing journey, from treatment to the subsequent treatment, from orchard to orchard, and you regain balance. No matter what thoughts or feelings are present, they'll pass, and you'll return to your quiet self.

Thought Storms

Something happened one day, and my frightened and angry circuits were triggered big time. I knew better than to engage with the storm. I also knew I didn't have access to rational thinking when I gripped those thoughts. I knew to go to the porch swing and spend most of the day there. The thoughts raced through me the whole day, creating pain. I let it be. I knew I wasn't the thoughts, but there they were. I knew that thought storms always pass. The storm was there most of the day. I knew I'd feel better the next day after sleeping. I did. I felt even better two days after.

You may get caught in a thought storm when you believe fearful thoughts about an upcoming treatment or how it will affect you. A thought storm can also happen when you worry about how to pay your bills or when you need to have a scan after treatments. Likewise, it may occur when there's marital discord on a cancer journey, when your children suffer, when someone acted in a way you didn't like, or when you break up with someone, cancer journey or not.

You don't have access to your rational mind when you are worried, angry, or in a depressed-hopeless thought storm. Your bandwidth is occupied with the "worry, anger, or depression show." The thinking looks real, and you engage with it. You may not have room for perspective. It's best to let go of trying to figure things out. It will move out in time..

Your true nature is not the passing storm, even though storms pass through it. Your nature is quiet and still. It's loving, joyous, lovable, and curious. It's calm, relaxed, and trusting. It's powerful and creative. It knows that it doesn't know. It delights in surprise. It loves solving puzzles, even health puzzles. It loves to create. It trusts life. It's you. It loves making mistakes and redirecting. It loves to learn. It's the most loving and beautiful energy that exists. It's you. It's always there.

Low Moods and The Illusion of Time

Along your journey, you may experience depression, grief, or another low mood. I did after the low anterior resection surgery. You might feel down if there is a recurrence, challenging side effects, or you're having another health or emotional challenge. When you're down, you can get snappy. You might push people away because you don't want to be seen in a low mood, or you don't want to hurt them with your harsh comments. I know you don't like being in a depressed state. Often you would love for those states to pass quickly. It's as though you're projecting what you're experiencing into the future, wanting to control the grief or depression. But when you want to "get rid of" your experience, you resist it, which keeps the low mood in place.

Coach Tom Mattox relates that what helped him when he went through a period of severe depression was seeing what his mind was doing with time. He had thoughts like, "this has been going on for months" and, "this is never going to end." When he really got a feel for the fact that the past was over and was no longer relevant and that he truly didn't know the future, his mood lightened. For him, it's normal to feel down at times throughout his day. But when it's just a momentary experience, and he's not projecting it into the future and knows that it's already gone because the past is gone, it's a completely different experience than before. He knows a power in him constantly brings him back up when he goes down. It had been operating all his life, but he didn't realize that it was happening. When he saw it, everything changed. He says anyone can get a feel for this inner power.

Perspective

When I need to find a solution, I often ask my notion of a universal power or God to show me a new perspective. Then I wait for clues in my environment that give me perspective. I look to see what attracts my gaze, and I focus on it until I see something about it – maybe its shape or color – and somehow, I get an insight about how to hold the situation. I need to keep looking for it. I always get perspective when I ask for it.

Pointing your attention toward "what else is possible here" could be a more practical use of thought than ruminating on the problem.

Trying to "figure things out" might get you entangled in the thinking that created the problem. Consider letting go of trying to figure it out. Take a break. Trust that a solution is there. Pick it up again when you're relaxed. Some solutions come while in the shower or out on a walk. Trust that a perspective will be available because you've asked for it. It might not appear immediately; maybe it will show up in a day or two.

You are aware presence gifted with the tool of thought. Sometimes you unconsciously get tangled with imagined thinking, the movie in your head about your life. Be kind to yourself. Your organs of perception are externally focused on keeping you safe, making the outside world seem so real. You forget your well-being is inside of you under the thinking. You will get caught up in unhelpful thinking. I get caught up every day. But my feeling reminds me to wake up, let it be, and breathe. The more I get this and allow myself to notice, accept, allow, and stop engaging with the story, the less frightened I am of being frightened. It's a movie my thoughts are creating. Most of it isn't real and does not need attention. Then I can choose to drop into a place of more calm. The more I am willing to practice, the kinder my human experience gets.

You will get caught up in stressful thinking; then you'll wake up. Caught up and wake up. It's the human condition. I am finding my way through it. If I'm finding my way, you will find your way with yours. Remember to be kind with your human experience.

SUMMARY AND SUGGESTIONS

1. You live in the unknown every second of every day. Consider embracing the unknown of every phase of your treatment. Trust your innate resilience and your body's healing capabilities. While treatments can be harsh on the body and spirit, most people heal with patience and time.

2. Thought is universal and impersonal. Everyone has thoughts all the time.
3. Thoughts pass through you the whole day and often contradict each other. Notice how fickle they are: I'm competent, I'm incompetent; I'm happy, I'm scared; I look great, I look awful.
4. You can't be the fickle thoughts or the voice in the head. You might be the quiet you always return to between your thoughts and feelings.
5. Your thoughts can get the best of you on a cancer journey, so consider being extra kind, compassionate, and forgiving with yourself on this journey. Most thoughts have nothing to do with reality: they are scary future or past fantasies. Reality is what is happening right here and right now.
6. Your journey can flow easier when you know that you can handle everything that comes your way. You have done it your whole life. You have shown up and taken life one step at a time. You can do so during a healing journey, one step at a time.
7. When you know that thoughts are not reality, and their nature is to move, you'll allow their movement. You'll understand you don't need to control their coming and going. They will move when you stop listening to them. Common sense will tell you if you need to attend to the information or let it pass.
8. It's easy to detach from thinking. You do it often during the day and when you fall asleep.

9. When experiencing a thought storm, your capacity for a different perspective diminishes. It might be a good idea to notice the storm, accept yourself and what is happening, and stop trying to figure out a solution or take action from that state.
10. Let go of any notion of perfection that stresses you out. Do things at a pace that feels good to you. "Should thoughts" compare you to a notion of perfection. Perfection is this moment as it is. Without hurried thinking, this moment is clear. If you feel stressed, consider letting your attention move to the quiet of the present moment.
11. Focusing on the direction of a solution or a new perspective can allow creative wisdom to come through. Some people might ask a universal power for a new perspective, guidance, or help.
12. You are awareness experiencing life in a body with the organs of perception. You will get caught up in thought. Then you'll wake up and remember who you are. It's the human condition. I trust you to find your way through the process of waking up to the spaciousness of who you are.

Chapter Seven

YOU GOT THAT BEAUTIFUL FEELING

Aren't feelings amazing? Don't you love being excited about skiing, dancing, traveling, reading, and being in love? Don't you love feeling love for your family and friends? It's such a warm and gentle feeling. And how do you feel in your body when you're grateful for a safe place to sleep, your friends or family, the ability to eat, the car that drives you to your destinations, and the chair that's holding you when you sit? Isn't it fantastic?

Feelings are great messengers about how you think. Expansive feelings show you that you're focused on appreciating the goodness of life. And contracted feelings bring to your attention that something needs to be handled. You might need to speak up, figure out what you need, set a boundary, change your doctor, care for your car or body, apologize, or let go of habitual thoughts of insecurity, anxiety, or depression.

Feelings are supposed to alert and inform you, then move on. Your job is to feel, notice, let go of the messenger, and drop back into your quiet space. However, people have developed a habit of keeping the messenger and fixating on it rather than receiving the message and letting it go. The notification arrives, then you do something about it and let go. Come back to the now, to your bottom on the sofa, your feet on the ground, your breath coming in and out of your body, and your arms holding a book or relaxing by your body.

My first encounter with examining feelings happened twenty years ago at my first meditation center. I received a small, green instructional booklet upon registration at the Wat Suan Mokkh International Dharma Center. It said to follow the breath as it comes in and out with full focus. A few pages later, it suggested examining how feelings feel in the body.

I sat with closed eyes and imagined something sad. My cheeks sunk in, and a pressure formed around my heart. Sadness dragged my energy downward. Then I imagined anger. My cheeks and upper arms vibrated with hot energy, and my jaw had noticeable sensations. My heart closed, and my breathing and heartbeat increased. I felt the sensations in my body with imagined fear, jealousy, happiness, joy, and love.

None of these feeling states was sustainable. All imagined feelings increased my heart rate, changed my breathing, and created contracted or expanded sensations. All were exhausting to hold for even a minute. I realized the only sustainable feeling was a state of peace, calm, and subtle joy. I concluded it is our nature. The only thing that can pull us away from our peace is believing and holding on to a thought that goes against myself, others, or life.

I'm often asked how to stay more often in a state of peace. The spiritual teacher Syd Banks says, "Don't hear my words; listen beyond it to a beautiful feeling." In other words, sense beyond these words. You'll notice a beautiful, calm feeling. And look for it often. You've had a lovely, peaceful feeling many times throughout your day. The spiritual teacher Eckhart Tolle says words can only point to that subtle energy. He asks if there's a deeper dimension you're noticing right now that is not your thoughts and feelings. He also steers people to the space between words. Other times, he directs people to pay attention to the subtle energy in their bodies. When I follow his instructions, I feel calm and relaxed.

Notice who you are being right now. When you let go of the to-do list and your identity as a worker, parent, daughter, son, wife, partner, husband, patient, dancer, welder, biker, computer programmer, knitter, and exerciser, you might notice that you drop into a quiet space. You fall into a sense of calm and well-being. With nothing to do and no one to be, you enter a space that has a beautiful and quiet dimension. You look around the room in a slowed manner. You notice a more profound presence and resonance with everything. There's a lovely feeling of amazement at every tree, bird, lizard, and flower. This moment feels alive and abundant. Your breathing slows, and the feeling of quiet and recognition expands.

That pleasant feeling is your natural state. It's good for your nervous system and great for your health. When noticing and focusing on the dimension of quiet, you feel alert. This feeling accompanies every person. It just feels good. It feels good to be yourself at this moment. It feels nice to just be and breathe. You feel loving, relaxed, and peaceful. That is your subtle, beautiful Feeling with a capital F.

That said, humans fluctuate between being in that Feeling and fleeting human feelings.

Feelings exist for a reason. Feelings are your emotional alarm bells. When you cut your leg, you feel pain, which draws your attention to the injury so you can attend to it. And when you put your hands on a hot stove, pain draws your attention to pull your hands away. Similarly, your feelings are love letters to call your attention to what you believe. You either need to attend to the thought by making changes on the outside, or you need to stop engaging with the automatic thoughts that take you away from just being here and peaceful.

Feelings are helpful! You'll feel contracted when you experience a lack of acceptance of yourself, your body, your stoma, your experience, or the people around you. When you feel tight, it's your cue to wake up from the dream of resisting reality. Take a moment to notice the sensations in the body and breathe with gratitude that your system is working. Allow the feelings. Accept the sensations running through you. If you want, you can follow the feelings in the body and breathe. Despite having uncomfortable feelings, you really are okay at this moment.

If you want, you could soothe yourself like you would a tiny baby. *There there, my love. You got caught up in scary thinking. It's okay. The feeling woke you up. I love how sensitive you are. I love you so much. It's okay to feel everything. Give it space to be, to move, to flow. Breathe with it. You are doing so well on your path. I marvel at how courageous and resourceful you are. I appreciate how resilient you are. I love you so much and am always here for you. You are the most precious human to me. I love and adore you.*

A few days ago, I was driving to visit patients. I noticed how fast and anxious I felt. My mind was racing forward, mapping my driving from one location to the next and planning how much time I'd spend with each person to make it fit into my day, and I hadn't even arrived at the first place. Do you see how habitual minds are? They innocently attach to habits of planning and strategizing. What woke me up to what my mind was doing was when I realized that I felt anxious. Then I told myself to notice and follow the anxiety sensations. Later, I focused on being here now, feeling my hands on the wheel, enjoying the car and the freedom to drive. I also reminded myself that this moment, just this driving, was enough, and I was enough. I noticed a beautiful tree in bloom and the incredible color of the sky. I was back to being present.

Once feelings have been created by our minds, they need to be acknowledged and allowed, even during panic attacks. Right before the Covid pandemic, I was hired for two jobs. Due to the pandemic, the businesses halted to change their protocols, and I did not receive clients for several months. I had very little income, and my father offered to pay my rent. He called nearly daily to ensure I was sending more resumes. He was certain I should do more than what I did. I knew things would work out in time. But after each phone call with Dad, I created intense anxiety thinking that revved me up. I bought into his thoughts that what I did wasn't enough.

I would wake up in panic each morning with my heart racing. I tried to rationalize what was happening: "It's only my thinking. My feelings are my thinking. I don't need to pay attention to it or take it seriously." But my tactic didn't help my anxiety. I tried to think positively or ignore it, but the morning panic returned. Only when I chose to allow the anxiety to be expressed did it stop showing up as morning panic. I spoke with Dad about what would be helpful for me and took steps to keep myself in a place of calm. I trusted my inner knowing that things would change, which they did. I had to allow the expression of anxiety, not ignore it, for it to move through. It was already there. It had to be acknowledged.

Feelings are healthy. They let us know what our thinking does so we can notice the feeling, allow its expression, and wake up from the unconscious thinking that created it. Then we return to our mental health and balance, to being here now, even with diagnosed mental illness.

Coach Yael Abramson was diagnosed with bipolar disorder. Earlier in life, she had episodes, spent time in and out of mental institutions, and was on medication. Yael heard Sydney Bank's teaching that everyone is always sitting in the middle of mental health- they just don't know it. It struck a chord in her. She began listening to Syd's teachings, often called the Three Principles, about who we are and the role of thought in our experience of life. In one conference, a participant asked Dr. Bill Petit about getting off medication. The psychiatrist answered that the goal is not to get off medication but to live in the greatest peace possible. Yael dismissed his counsel.

She began weaning herself off medication, and then she felt strange. Without medical drugs, she felt angry, depressed, reactive, anxious, and with panic attacks. She acted out manic episodes. Yael didn't understand how to live with her feelings, even though she heard that thoughts created her feeling experience. She negated her feelings, saying, "It's just thought," but she had no change in behavior. After more learning, Yael realized that feelings shouldn't be dismissed. Instead of intellectualizing her feelings, she had to notice and feel the emotions created by her thoughts.

In her words: "The reason to be with feelings is that it stops my mental activity. Being with a feeling is only helpful because it's arising in me now. I allow it to be because it's here, and that's what's alive in me. I don't want to make a big deal about it. When I experienced feelings, I saw that they were not a problem but a part of life. Emotions are information about what is going on in my mind, not the truthfulness of the stories in my mind, past traumas, or future ideas.

When I saw that feelings were waking me up to what the mind was doing, I stopped resisting them and allowed them to take their course. It wasn't my job to change them. A greater intelligence moves these emotions through me, just like I put food in my body, and the body digests it without my interference. Without my resistance, the feelings know what to do. In letting go of the story, the emotion finds its own way. When I allow myself to be with the process, it brings me back home to myself."

Yael is now grateful for her feelings as messengers that wake her up to what her mind is doing. She says her feelings are her health. They serve a healthy function. When she feels unsafe, fearful, anxious, angry, or anything other than okay, she knows it's an alert to STOP and follow her feelings. She trusts a greater intelligence to bring her back to her mental health. Yael is off medication, lost fifty kilos, and befriends her emotions and mind. She knows there's mental well-being inside of her, and the way to it is to follow her friendly messenger feelings all the way Home.

There's no need to be scared of feeling a feeling. Feelings are healthy. They are your natural and healthy alarm bells to wake you up from what your mind is doing unconsciously. When you feel anything but peaceful, stop. Get into your body and follow your feeling and see it morph. It will stop your mind chatter. When you're ready, bring yourself back to the quiet now. Feel your body, notice your breath, notice the quiet in your body and the stillness of the furniture and the trees. You're back to yourself. Back to the stillness.

I wake up and notice that I'm excited to prepare healthy cookies for a group of friends. I feel delighted and energized. Another day, I wake up with a dream of disgust and feel disturbed until Coach Chana reminds me that I listened to and replayed that dream scene in my mind. Then I experience relief as my attachment naturally relaxes.

On other mornings, I might feel quiet, curious, or excited to stretch. Yet other mornings, I might feel heavy with dread or grief. Some mornings I wake up from anxious dreams. I don't even know what thinking creates my mood. It happens so fast. My feeling lets me know what thinking my consciousness is attached to. I feel the heavy grief and let it be. I accept it. It doesn't mean anything except that it is expressed rather than hidden, and I move on with my day.

I get up, put my comfy slippers on, then open the front door. A shaggy dog comes over for licks and hugs. I feel warm and loving. I look up and see the beautiful pink blossom of the apple tree flowers. I sit in the sun. I notice love, dread, awe, warmth, and beauty. I get dressed, drive to work, feel anxious and insecure, feel comfortable, and then grateful. Thoughts constantly compare me to an idealized version of me, others, or the past. They try to take me away from being present with the quiet that is right now. There's nothing to fix. I notice and let it be. I accept the minute fluctuations of insecurity to gratitude the whole day, the movie in my head.

The psychiatrist and spiritual teacher, Dr. David R. Hawkins, wrote the book *Letting Go: The Pathway of Surrender.* He highlights that when a feeling arrives, it needs to be felt and allowed its expression. Healing can happen when you allow emotions to run their course.

In the Physical Healing section of the book, Hawkins writes that when people don't feel their feelings, health issues manifest for them. He suggests that the way to feel better is to stop changing and manipulating your human experience. Allow the anxiety, the anger, the insecurity, the grief, or whatever else you are experiencing. Completely accept it and stop paying attention to any chatter or analysis about it. The feelings run out of fuel when the story stops. Hawkins also suggests employing forgiveness as a way of being, accepting, and forgiving what we do not understand about ourselves and another.

The neuroscientist, Dr. Jill Bolte Taylor, also reports that feelings run their course if you don't interfere with them. She noticed that when she had a feeling that she didn't react to, it ran its course and went through the body. Coach Mavis Karn suggests following your feelings with your mind. Allow their coming and going. Feelings are meant to move and be seen for their message, whether to do something about the message right now or to let go of attaching to the thoughts trying to control you, nature, reality, the future, or another.

When you are facing a medical imaging scan, and scanxiety comes up about what it might find, notice that it's an alert that you're caught up in your scary thinking. Your trusted feelings alert you that you are focusing on a negative "what if" fantasy. Those feelings are okay; all feelings are okay and accepted. Notice that thinking creates them, not the scan you haven't had yet. Follow the feeling. There's no need to be afraid of a feeling. Allow and follow your feelings without judgment, without trying to run away from them, fix, repress, suppress, or change them. Give them space. Have softness and gratitude. They're the brilliant messengers that awaken you from your fantasy.

Some feelings are intuitions that also arrive as thoughts, sensations, sounds, or images. These are the inner nudges of yes or no when you go out on a date with someone. Likewise, you instinctively know that you like sports, dance, or classical music. You feel a subtle joy and a giddy aliveness around those activities. You instinctively know you enjoy or dislike yoga. You know if you gravitate toward gardening, fashion, finances, or meteorology. You know. You even know which surgeon to choose. You feel it. You are connected to something greater than your personal mind.

Likewise, you know when to phone your friend or text her. You know to call your doctor's office or post on Blue Hope Nation and ask how to manage the side effects. You know. You know to choose healthy food. You have quiet wisdom that directs you where to go if you listen. Even if you ignore it, your inner GPS will keep nudging you until you listen. And you can't get it wrong because it will keep giving you signals until you hear it.

You are awareness gifted with the ability to focus on your current thoughts and feelings about the present, past, or future, your intuitions, or the innate quiet inside. The innate quiet is a blank canvas. You can stay in the space of infinite potential for as long as you like and as often as you like. It's a rejuvenating space that feels peaceful. It feels good. It feels nice. It's that Beautiful Feeling. It observes the present moment. Thoughts are the paintbrush, and your feelings are the paint. Your experience is the painted product. And yet your thoughts, feelings, and experience are impersonal products. They are states that come and go depending on your focus. You'll get caught up in your human experience often, the story about your life made of thoughts and feelings.

At some point, that nice Feeling will come around again. It will pull you back to balance, to the state of no thought. That nice Feeling is beyond words on this page. It's in the space between words. Syd Banks reminds people to "Look for a nice feeling. And go enjoy your life. Do more of what you love."

The more you find that pleasant feeling and focus on what you love doing, the more you'll choose to do more of what gets you into that space. Feeling good and focusing more on the quiet or what you love will become more effortless. It will calm your nervous system, and your healing might increase. Ask yourself, "Where is that nice feeling in me?" Then look for it until you find it. You got that beautiful Feeling. You have my love and support as you navigate your journey with your Beautiful Feeling and your helpful human feelings.

SUMMARY AND SUGGESTIONS

1. Feelings/emotions are moving states. They are not sustainable long-term.
2. You are peaceful when not attached to concepts or feelings. That's your natural feeling. It just feels nice. It's your inner energy hum of just being. Look for it. Cultivate it. Choose to go there often.
3. Your feelings show you what you're thinking; they're an alarm bell to wake you up to what you believe.

4. All feelings are allowed and accepted. You feel the ups and downs of the human experience of the effects of attaching to thoughts. Feelings give you a depth of aliveness, like colors in a painting.
5. Intuition is a feeling that knows. You know you love your hobbies. It's lovely to be in areas and people of interest to you.
6. You might look for a nice feeling. Just ask yourself, where is my nice feeling? Then wait. Do it as many times as you'd like. The more you find it, the more you'd want to drop into it.
7. You have my love and support.

Section II

THE FIRST PART OF THE MEDICAL JOURNEY

Chapter Eight

THE PORT

If you have intravenous (IV) chemotherapy as part of your treatment, your doctor will most likely recommend getting a port-a-cath, also known as a port. A port is a subcutaneously implanted device with two parts: the "docking" port and the long, thin, silicone catheter. The port is about a quarter-sized plastic or metal disc. According to WebMD, the middle part of the port has a rubber piece that holds the needle in place when you receive treatment or have your blood drawn. The thinned-tube catheter connects the port to a large vein in your body.

There are several reasons why doctors ask patients who will have multiple chemotherapy treatments to get a port. One is to minimize the poking of the arm veins. With repeated insertions, some veins close up or become harder to access. That doesn't happen with a port. Moreover, without a port, the nurses must poke you with a new IV needle each time you have chemotherapy treatments. They must also use separate IV lines for IV fluids or blood transfusions. Second, some chemotherapy is caustic and cannot be delivered through a peripheral vein. Third, Some people have veins that are very difficult to access. Fourth, it's easier for health care professionals to poke the needle through a port than a vein in your arm.iii

The port is implanted during an outpatient procedure. It takes about 45 minutes. I felt pain in the cut area when the anesthetic wore off. I felt sore for about two weeks as the place was healing. Sleeping was painful and uncomfortable for a few days with pressure on the cut side. A few days later, I could sleep on my side again when the pain subsided. You'll need to avoid lifting anything heavy for a week to allow the area to heal.

For most people, port placement is a seamless procedure. Unfortunately for me, I couldn't breathe deeply after my procedure. My port surgeon advised me to visit the ER to rule out any blood clots that might add to my breathing difficulty. An X-ray revealed that all was in order. My body required time to heal. I think we're called patients so we can have patience with our healing. After four months, I could breathe deeply without discomfort.

I had the port placed because I had three weeks of daily IV treatments of vitamin C and laetrile and, later on, another three weeks of vitamin C, laetrile, and PNC-27. I started IV treatments two days after the port placement. The needle poke through the port was so painful I almost cried. I didn't know the plastic reservoir under the skin is tough to poke through and requires a big needle and a strong jab. And I hadn't even healed from the port placement procedure. It was really trying.

If you're going to have a port, you might want to wait until it heals before you start chemo treatments. The poking might be more manageable. It will become easier as you will get used to it. But it will probably be painful the first few times a needle enters your port.

Depending on the personality and sense of adventure, people may or may not be comfortable having the port seen by others. Since the port protrudes from the skin under the collarbone like a little bump, others might see it when a person wears tight or revealing clothes. It took me a while to feel comfortable with it. At first, I didn't wear spaghetti straps, tight shirts, or a bathing suit in front of people. I was still interpreting cancer as a shock and didn't want any stranger to ask me about the port or make comments about cancer. It took me over a year to become comfortable enough to be okay if others saw it. I had my port for two and a half years. By then, I felt more comfortable getting into a bathing suit.

If you have a port, you may feel self-conscious and uncomfortable about the protrusion of the port. Allow your feelings to be there. Breathe with them. You're believing insecure thinking. You're making scary thinking seem real. Do you want to be walking around scared in the world about a protrusion under your skin? Do you want to give that thinking so much life, or do you want to enjoy your life with or without a port?

Nine months after finishing chemo and having two clear CT scans, my oncologist recommended removing the port. I was so attached to it by then that I felt scared to take it out, perhaps prematurely. Maybe I would need more treatment? I couldn't believe that my cancer episode was over and that taking out one of my "what if" crutches was safe. I asked my oncologist if he was confident this was a good time to take it out. He insisted it was. But I was afraid to take it out. I had gotten to love the sense of security from having it implanted in me, "just in case." Nonetheless, I went to an outpatient surgery where they removed the port. The procedure lasted thirty minutes. I asked my surgical nurse to photograph my port once it was out.

Healing from this procedure took roughly two to three weeks. There was swelling, bruising, and pain while the area recovered from the cut skin. The bleeding coagulated two weeks after the procedure, and I removed the bandage.

The port process was just like every other procedure outlined in this book. I felt scared and shocked at first. Then, over time, I accepted what was occurring. Then, I became comfortable with the port, and by the end, I felt sad to let my crutch go. Notice how thoughts created my contracted or expanded experience of life. The port was in me, and I either allowed myself to enjoy life with it or suppressed my joyful expression and worried about what others would say when they saw it. Notice how much content I placed on the experience of having a port. Life is precious. Consider enjoying it, port and all. Notice how much busy thinking you have about your experience. Do you want to keep buying into the busy-mindedness, or do you want to leave it and drop into relaxation and expansion instead?

You will have your journey with your port. I believe that your body will handle it well and will heal. If you're going to have chemotherapy infusions through the port, you'll be grateful for having the port and not ruining your veins. I trust you and your medical team will find answers for whatever you need. You are a resourceful being that can handle your journey perfectly. You have my love and support through your adventure with your port.

SUMMARY AND SUGGESTIONS

1. Your medical team will advise you whether you should have a port or not, depending on your treatment plan, the chemotherapy agent, and your veins.
2. Both placement and removal of the port are outpatient surgeries requiring about thirty to forty-five minutes. You'll feel pain and tenderness for a few days. Your body will need a couple of weeks to heal.

3. You may feel self-conscious about the protrusion of the port under your skin. Accept and allow the insecure thinking and feeling that you're making real. You will be comfortable with the port in a few months. Consider shortening the time of acceptance to feel freer being yourself.
4. With time, having the port will feel normal, as normal as can be, on a healing journey. The port will feel like a safety net. You might come to love and appreciate the port as another intimately connected device that helped save your life.

Chapter Nine

RADIATION WITH LOW-DOSE CHEMOTHERAPY

Journal Entry: *Friday 4/14/17: Started low-dose Xeloda chemo pills and five days a week radiation this week. So far, so good. I go on daily nature walks right after radiation treatment. I love it when I can be present and just look without the interpreting mind.*

Journal Entry: *Monday 4/24/17: The skin in the perineum area feels tender, like it's being burned with radiation, and it's only week two; I have four more to go. When I pee, the skin burns. It's time for more Aloe vera gel.*

In this phase of treatment, patients usually take low-dose chemotherapy along with receiving radiation treatments. Before radiation starts, a technician will take you to a sophisticated CT scan machine to create imaged layers of the tumor for the radiation field calculations. In addition, at this appointment, you'll most likely get three tattoo dots on your body: one on each hip and another in the center of the top of your pubic bone. The tattoo dots are for body alignment with the radiation machine. The tattoo process doesn't hurt, and the tattoos look like tiny blue freckles.

I visited the local Cancer Support Community and looked at their Buddy Book. It's a book with names and phone numbers of cancer patients who have been through different cancers and are willing to speak with others who are newly diagnosed. I contacted one woman who told me she experienced tremendous pain from radiation and could not sit on her bottom for several months after the treatment. I spoke with another man who said he only did radiation and chemo without surgery six years prior. His cancer did not return.

The radiation oncologist I chose had many years of experience and seemed knowledgeable. He looked like Santa Claus, heavy set with white hair and a big smile. I asked him about the extensive damage I had heard about from the woman I spoke with. The oncologist assured me he had plenty of professional experience and didn't use the highest dosage. No patient of his had reported such extensive damage, he claimed.

I brought up menopause. The doctor said it was no big deal. He brushed off side effects as if they were easy to deal with, "Just use hormones and creams for the sensitive areas." He gave me zinc-oxide creams and Lidocaine. He was certain of the effectiveness of radiation. I asked if there was any radiation guard, like the guards I put on at the dentist's office, to protect areas that weren't being radiated. He laughed and explained that therapeutic radiation is 60 million times stronger than a regular X-ray and that no guard could stop those rays (Actually, I received 6,020 centigray. 6,020 centigray is 60,200 millisieverts. One chest X-ray is 0.1 milliSievert. The radiation I received was 602,000 X-rays in 33 days). This knowledge scared me as routine X-rays are known to cause cancer. The radiation oncologist and I discussed the possibility of only using radiation and chemotherapy for a complete response and not having surgery.

The first surgeon I consulted with mentioned that there is a fifteen percent possibility that I'll have permanent bladder damage from radiation treatments. I asked the radiation oncologist about it, and he wasn't concerned. Luckily, I followed the Medical Medium morning protocol of drinking sixteen ounces of water with lemon followed by sixteen ounces of celery juice and a smoothie. By the time I got to radiation, my bladder was full. Years later, I would find out from other patients that having a full bladder minimizes radiation damage to the bladder.

The surgeon also mentioned the radiation treatment would render my ovaries non-functional; they would not be able to produce any estrogen, progesterone, or testosterone. The surgeon likewise informed me that radiation would damage the uterus, and I would not be able to carry a baby. He called this condition sterile. My thoughts frightened me about what I'd heard.

Before you have radiation and chemotherapy, ensure you've done genetic testing, especially if other family members have or have had cancer. Patients with a genetic mutation may benefit from a different course of therapy.

For example, one patient was diagnosed with Stage IIIa anal cancer. Thanks to the Colontown Facebook page, he read about the side effects of radiation therapy. This patient had an HPV-neg, MLH1-pos cancer, and knew that 5FU (Xeloda chemotherapy) would not be effective for him. The addition of radiation horrified him. It took five oncologists turning him down before he found his current doctor. This patient almost cried when his oncologist agreed to put him on Keytruda (an Immunotherapy drug). This patient mentioned that he is disheartened to see the number of Lynch syndrome patients on FOLFOX and FOLFIRI chemotherapy before they are allowed to get Immunotherapy.

Lynch syndrome is a genetic condition that increases the risk of different kinds of cancer. Families that have Lynch syndrome have more instances of colon, endometrial, and other types of cancer than expected. Lynch syndrome also causes cancers to happen at an earlier age.iv

I recently read an article about using Immunotherapy for a mismatch repair-deficient (dMMR) genetic aberration in rectal cancer. All twelve patients healed without radiation or surgery. Besides Lynch and Mismatch Repair, other mutations may include KRAS, PIK3CA, NRAS, BRAF, HRAS, (EGFR), AKT1, KIT, FGFR1, FGFR3,

FLT3, CDK, ERBB2, ABL1, MET, RET, and PDGFRA.v Some oncologists will not prescribe Immunotherapy even if you have a known genetic mutation if the cancer is not stage IV. Please consider the patient's comment above and keep looking for an oncologist who will prescribe Immunotherapy. You will spare yourself radiation, stoma, surgeries, and living with a challenging aftermath.

I took a course of chemotherapy using Xeloda pills, which is standard for adenocarcinoma treatments stage II/III without genetic aberrations. The surgeon informed me that low-dose Xeloda enhances the effects of radiation in shrinking the tumor. In some hospitals, patients receive low-dose Xeloda intravenously through their port, which directs the medication into the bloodstream. My oncologist explained that both methods are equally effective.

I started the pills on the first day of radiation and took them as instructed: twice a day with food for the duration of the radiation treatment, five days a week. I felt scared of the possible effects of chemotherapy on my body. I didn't know what to expect. Two days after beginning Xeloda, my sister and brother-in-law, Hanna and Mark, visited me. I showed them the four pills I reluctantly took with my two meals. Mark instinctively took the pills and made them into a happy face. His quick and intuitive gesture made me take the tablets with a smile and less fear. Thank goodness for creative and humorous family members!

I had no problems with Xeloda (5FU), but two women had severe allergic reactions to the medication. One patient wanted you to read about her experience. She wished she'd had the DNA test to determine if she was compatible with 5FU. Her body shut down. It stopped producing blood and became septic. Her family came to say goodbye when she was urgently rushed to the hospital. She survived after months of barely living. Then more side effects arrived. She lost all her hair and fingerprints. In addition, she had diarrhea and fatigue.

A specialist came up from another hospital. He suggested a DNA test which showed that she could not tolerate the full dose. When she was strong enough, they started the treatment again at fifty percent strength. The side effects were awful, but she survived it. You never know if you're allergic to Xeloda. Consider asking for the DNA test. This standard test shows if you have an incompatible gene with 5FU chemotherapy.

Regarding radiation, you'll most likely go to the radiation office five days a week at the same time each day. You'll get on the radiation table, pull down your pants to the level of the three-dotted tattoos they gave you for alignment (consider wearing stretchy pants with no metal) and converse with the radiation technician. Then you'll wait about five to ten minutes for the machine to radiate the tumor field from all angles. From my understanding, radiation starts with a larger area at first. Then as the weeks go by, the radiation field narrows until it is entirely focused on the tumor.

If anything feels suspicious, please let the radiation technician know right away. If you sense your labia, clitoris, scrotum, or penis buzzing, immediately report this to your doctor. Be aware and perhaps ask to see the calculations before radiation starts to preserve pleasure sensitivity.

I bought herbs and made an anti-radiation tea to help my body not absorb all the dangerous radiation. This tea contains equal parts of Atlantic kelp, Atlantic dulse, dandelion leaf, and nettle leaf. The recipe comes from Anthony William's books *Medical Medium* and *Thyroid Healing*—steep one tablespoon of herbs per cup of hot water. I added raw honey. The tea tasted horrible, but I made myself drink it. Some companies make anti-radiation tea blends, and you can find them online. Some naturopaths endorse baths with Hydrogen Peroxide, Borax, and bentonite clay.

Each week, I became increasingly tired after radiation. My body experienced fatigue from the radiation effects. Likewise, chemo pills weakened me. Each day I'd leave radiation and go on a hike. Some days I'd feel like I was sleep-walking from fatigue. And yet, I'd connect with nature. Exercise was one healing path still in my control. The amazing thing was that I'd go on a hike feeling exhausted. After forty minutes or an hour of being in nature, my body rejuvenated, and I felt more alert and energetic.

Each person responds differently to radiation. The tumor's exact location differs from person to person, the radiation dosage varies, and the body's sensitivity differs. Some women reported having burning sensations around the anus. I didn't experience that. Other women experienced the same sensations as I did: burning around the perineum, burning while urinating, and itching.

One woman shared that drinking cranberry juice lessened the burning while urinating during radiation and afterward as the area was healing. Yet another group of women reported painful bowel movements toward the end of treatment. Because I ate daily salads and drank smoothies and without a blockage, I never experienced painful bowel movements.

Another woman shared that the burned areas cracked and bled around her perineum. I didn't experience that side effect. Everyone reported increasing fatigue, burning, and discomfort. Another patient said she had bathroom issues because of radiation. Her rectum felt sore. She said you should tell your radiation oncologist if you get a yeast infection. I did not experience yeast infections while going through radiation.

One woman wanted you to not put on any lotions or powders before radiation. Ask your doctor about it.

Another patient wrote me that she wished she had known that just because procedures and treatments can cause side effects, they don't always happen. During the first meeting with her radiation oncologist, he said the treatment would be painful, and she would need prescription painkillers. That scared her. She never had pain throughout 28 days of chemoradiation. She experienced fatigue, discomfort, and painful bowel movements in the latter part of treatment, but she never needed over-the-counter analgesics. Her oncologist's nurse told her she would have nausea starting day three of oral chemo. It never happened. She was 68 and not in good shape. She began thinking of side effects as possible, not guaranteed.

As you see, each person's body reacted differently to radiation treatments. You will probably be uncomfortable, burning, itchy, and increasingly tired. Beyond that, I have no idea how chemoradiation will affect you. It sounds scary, but if you choose to have this treatment, I believe you can do it. You can move through this phase of your healing journey. Thousands of people before you moved through it. There will be long-term consequences to your body. Please read the following chapters.

Your body is more resilient than you know. And you are more resilient than you give yourself credit for. I support your choices. I acknowledge your depth of resolve to live and to choose therapies that are harsh and will leave permanent damage. You have my love and support for your healing choices.

SUMMARY AND SUGGESTIONS

1. Consider interviewing your radiation oncologist and ask if you can speak with a few females or males with rectal cancer who have had radiation to the pelvis. Ask them what kind of permanent and temporary damage they experience from radiation.
2. Consider having a full bladder before you get daily radiation to minimize bladder damage.

3. Consider checking the radiation field before treatment begins to ensure that the clitoris, labia, and penis are out of the radiation field.
4. One woman reported drinking cranberry juice during and after radiation treatment alleviated the painful burning while urinating.
5. Before taking Xeloda pills, consider having a DNA check to see if it is safe. A couple of women had a rare but severe allergic reaction to Xeloda and ended up in the hospital for months.
6. Before you take any chemotherapy pills, consider shaping them into a happy face or any other creative, fun design to change your mood to joy and gratitude for its healing power.
7. You may want to wear stretchy pants without metal when you go to radiation as you'll need to pull your pants down daily to the level of the tattoos.
8. You will feel burning around the perineum while urinating. You'll feel fatigued as the weeks go by. Other side effects are individual and related to tumor location, radiation strength, and body sensitivity.
9. Consider eating a high volume of fruits and vegetables, especially greens, for ease of bowel movement as radiation progresses.
10. Consider researching anti-radiation tea for its radiation-absorbing properties.
11. You are more resilient than you give yourself credit for. I acknowledge your depth of resolve to live and to choose therapies that are harsh and will create permanent damage. You have my love and support for your healing choices.

Chapter TEN

HEALING FROM RADIATION

Journal Entry *5/21/17:I finished radiation and low-dose chemo. I have vaginal discharge, so much of it, like a stream trickling the whole day. It's yellowish-pinkish and has an odor. I wear a pad; otherwise, I need to change underwear three to four times a day. I've had a low-grade headache the past few days; I feel dehydrated. Not sure if I'm taking in enough fluid.*

Saturday 6/10/17: Symptoms have changed and a whole week arrived full of pain and burning while urinating. It was so unnerving and uncomfortable that I prayed to God to stop it, to heal fast. After one week, the pain was gone. And then, I went back to itching. I am itching around the anus and all the tender skin around it up to the vaginal opening. It's worse at night when I wake up to urinate, and my hands have no control. I put on Aloe gel, zinc oxide, and coconut oil with frankincense and myrrh essential oils. It's been a week now, and it's itchy. I will talk with God tonight and request that the itching stop. It's unnerving, and I feel unsettled. I need to constantly refocus my awareness on other aspects of life and keep busy; that's my strategy, total distraction.

Healing from radiation was accompanied by inflammation and secretions. The entire region felt inflamed and required a long pad covering both openings. In addition, I had to constantly shift my position on the toilet so the urine would not touch my body and burn.

That awful effect lasted about two weeks. This effect was followed by intense, almost maddening, itching of the body around the anus and vaginal opening as the body was healing. I continued to apply zinc oxide and Aloe vera gel. Other people also applied calendula lotion. I used fresh Aloe vera leaf on the skin to heal the burn. Healing from the superficial radiation treatment took roughly six uncomfortable weeks.

Within two weeks of stopping radiation, I noticed super quick heat waves with heart palpitations. At some point, my brain realized; *It's hot flashes. No one mentioned hot flashes!* I'd have numerous hot flashes. They didn't bother me much. I'd just get hot and sweaty out of nowhere. The sensation of heat wasn't horrible compared to the other symptoms. I didn't particularly appreciate the racing heart that preceded the hot flashes.

Much more distressingly, I stopped being able to sleep. I'd lie in bed but would not fall asleep. A couple of years later, I read that the ovaries and adrenal glands are responsible for producing progesterone in the body. With radiation, there is an abrupt reduction in the levels of progesterone. Progesterone is a calming, soothing hormone that helps women sleep.

Because every health forum I listened to or visited said that healing occurs between 10 P.M. and 2 A.M., I tried different sleep aids. Low-dose melatonin (1-4 mg) didn't work. Ten to twenty milligrams of melatonin worked better. I also began taking cannabis oil under the tongue, a 1:1 THC:CBD Indica preparation for sleep sent by Jetty Extracts. I needed a good amount of sleep not to feel the burning, itching symptoms of healing from radiation, and I wanted a natural sleeping aid. Sometimes I'd take a bigger dose of the cannabis oil so my body would sleep longer, and I would have a couple more hours of respite from the sensations. I'd still wake up at night with my hands scratching the sensitive areas. I'd often wake up dehydrated after taking cannabis oil for sleep.

The process of healing from the radiation irritation around the perineum is rough. The itching and burning are incessant, almost like a poison oak rash. Remember, you can do this. You got this. You can find your way with the healing part. You've found solutions your whole life. You'll find ointments. You have wisdom, and you'll ask on the Facebook pages what others have used. You know how to take care of yourself. I promise that in six weeks or so, the itching will stop. I know it'll be maddening until then.

I will comfort you with the knowledge that it's a phase in your healing and will pass. Your body will heal. You know how to pass the time to distract yourself if needed. Play those video games. Watch those movies. Work and visit people. Take whatever you need to sleep well. It's a phase in your life that you will move through.

I wish I were with you in person to hold your hand and tell you it will be alright and that you'll heal. I wish I could tell you I understand it's rough and that I'm here for you and rooting for you. I'm holding your hand energetically through these words. I am inspired by your courage to heal and do what you need to choose life. You have my encouragement and support as you recover from this itchy phase.

SUMMARY AND SUGGESTIONS

1. Healing from radiation will take about six weeks. At first, there will be much fluid discharge from the vagina and anus. Then there will be pain with urination because the delicate skin is burned. Then, there will be about a month of intense itching until the body heals the superficial skin layers.

2. It's vital to have gels and lotions to apply throughout the day: Aloe vera leaf or gel, zinc oxide, calendula cream, or coconut oil. Consider having them in your purse and your bathroom.
3. You may or may not have hot flashes as menopause sets in after radiation treatment.
4. You may or may not have sleep issues.
5. Consider taking melatonin as a sleep aid, 10 mg or more. Check with your medical provider. Or consider taking a THC:CBD oil 1:1 or 3:1 INDICA prep for sleep. You'll need to experiment to find the concentration that works for you.
6. During the first two weeks, you will have fluid secretions as the body is healing. Make sure to drink plenty of fluid with electrolytes throughout the day to hydrate.
7. One woman shared that drinking cranberry juice during healing reduced painful urination.
8. Remember, you can do this. You got this. You can find your way with your healing. You know how to take care of yourself. You've done it your whole life. In six to seven weeks, the itching will stop. Your body will heal. Distract yourself if you need to. It's a phase in your life that you will move through. I send you my encouragement and support.

Chapter Eleven

THE SURPRISING CONNECTION BETWEEN FEMALE SEXUAL PAIN AND RADIATION TREATMENT

Journal Entry: *Friday 11/17/17: I am wondering about vaginal scar tissue today. I spoke with two women who reported painful penetrations. Why didn't the radiation oncologists inform us about the radiation effects on the vagina? Now I need to find a doctor to help alleviate the radiation treatment gynecological issues. Would I have changed the course of action knowing what I know now? Yes. Perhaps I would have insisted on having only three weeks of radiation or none.*

The surgeon scheduled the low anterior resection (LAR) surgery for ten weeks after I finished radiation treatment. Your LAR surgery might be scheduled sooner. I went on a hiking-camping trip to strengthen my body and ensure the best possible surgical outcome. I asked Toby, my friend and camping partner of many years, if he'd join me on a two-week trip to Glacier National Park. He agreed. We drove for two days and hiked from seven to nine miles most days.

One morning we were both tired from hiking. We stayed put, and Toby asked for a physical connection with me. I thought it over. We have gotten physically closer during camping trips over the years.

I agreed. The play continued, and there was sexual connection and penetration. I felt pain. What was that? I had never felt pain before with sexual intercourse. What's going on? I concluded that my body was still burned inside from radiation and perhaps the vaginal wall needed to heal. The following day we played some more; a finger went into the vagina, and I felt pain. Again I thought that the area needed to heal.

A few days after this distressing experience, my sister texted me. Her female radiation oncologist friend told her to tell me that radiation oncologists generally "don't talk about this" but that I needed to use dilators after radiation. I didn't know what dilators were. I looked online to see what they were and decided to deal with this issue after the surgery.

After I healed from the surgery, I had a consultation with a gynecologist. She said that due to the radiation, my vagina suffered relatively mild damage, with a small patch of scar tissue on the left vaginal wall. She said to expect menopause symptoms, including vaginal dryness. She suggested a procedure called FemTouch. It's a laser probe inserted into the vagina and shoots a 360-degree carbon dioxide gas stream into the vaginal canal. The resulting irritation causes minimal damage to the vaginal walls. The body then heals the minor damage, renewing the mucosal tissue and creating vaginal moisture. She said the treatment cost $700 per session, and I'd need three. I wanted to percolate on the subject and do some more research.

I learned that when a woman becomes menopausal and estrogen production drops, natural lubrication diminishes; dryness causes uncomfortable and painful intercourse. However, I intuited that dryness was not the cause of my pain. The pain seemed to be coming from a particular area inside the vagina.

Meanwhile, life orchestrated a meeting between two women with similar cancers and me. I asked the women if they had vaginal damage from radiation. One woman said that she had undergone radiation treatment after her initial diagnosis of anal cancer three years prior. Following radiation treatment, the vaginal canal closed as scar tissue grew, blocking the vaginal entrance. For the past three years, she and her husband have not had intercourse. This friend was upset that doctors didn't inform her about this potential drastic change. She felt embarrassed to ask doctors if she could relieve the situation somehow. Thankfully, she marveled that her husband had not left her after radiation-induced scar tissue had closed off a vital part of their physical, romantic connection.

The other woman experienced painful intercourse and bleeding during intercourse at times. She was upset that no one told her about how radiation treatments would affect her vagina, her sex life, and her relationships.

After these encounters, I felt shocked that my radiation oncologist did not share critical side effects information with me and that other radiation oncologists also had not discussed gynecological pain after radiation with their female patients.

At this point in my healing journey, I asked in Blue Hope Nation and Colontown colorectal cancer Facebook pages: "How are women on this site dealing with the vaginal pain caused by radiation? Has anyone tried FemTouch laser treatment?"

I received posts from angry women in reply, sharing how their radiation oncologist didn't disclose the vaginal trauma side effects. Many grieved the end of their sex life in their twenties and thirties. Older women felt no less loss. No one had tried the Fem-Touch laser; some even said it was contra-indicated for women after pelvic radiation.

The women wrote that every woman needs to use dilators immediately after radiation. Dilators are plastic or silicone vaginal inserts similar in shape to thicker candles and come in various sizes. Women are supposed to use them to stretch the vagina after radiation because radiation shrinks the vaginal canal. Moreover, in some cases, scar tissue can build up and close the vaginal canal if dilators aren't used. Women are supposed to start with the smallest size, then increase the sizes until the vagina stretches enough to accommodate the largest size dilator.

Some women whose radiation oncologists warned them of vaginal damage said they received dilators from their oncologist. Some women were referred to a gynecologist specializing in pelvic radiation damage and prescribed estrogen creams. Some women made coconut oil suppositories and used them nightly as vaginal moisturizers. Many women suggested going to a pelvic floor physical therapist for support with stretching the scar tissue in the vagina.

After reading these comments, I phoned my radiation oncologist's office and spoke with the office staff. I explained the situation and requested that the office provide me with dilators. I asked the office to help me solve the vaginal pain caused by radiation. The person I spoke with said she would talk with the doctors and return the call. I called a few days later, and after speaking with the doctors, the office staff said the office did not give dilators to female rectal cancer patients. They only gave dilators to women who were undergoing gynecological cancer treatments. Regarding vaginal issues, they advised calling a reconstructive surgery gynecologist.

Upon hearing that a radiation oncologist would not give women with rectal cancer dilators, I felt a surge of emotion. I took a breath to calm down. I explained to the staff member that the rectum is situated right under the vagina. When radiation is concentrated in the rectum, the vagina gets damaged, like gynecological cancers. She said, "I'm sorry, we just don't do that." I pressed her to ask the doctors again. When I called back within a few days, the answer was, "We just don't give dilators for rectal cancer patients." She also informed me that my radiation oncologist had retired.

I felt angry and saddened at the response I received. What was occurring didn't seem to be aware of patients' needs. I wondered if more radiation oncologists didn't tell women in the United States about possible vaginal damage.

In September 2018, I wrote and published a survey on two colorectal cancer Facebook pages: "Hello. This is for the Ladies. I REALLY need your help. I am conducting a survey about vaginal radiation effects and whether women were told about it or not. Who was told or not told about any vaginal radiation effects? If you were told, what were you told? For myself, I was not told at all that radiation would create scar tissue in the vagina, was not told about dilators, was NOT told there would be pain with intercourse as the radiation scarring hurt the nerve cells. I am wondering how many of you were told and how many were not. This is for my own understanding of what's happening in the U.S. as far as letting women know. It will also go in a book that I'm writing. Thank you so much for participating. The more data I have, the more it'll reflect on that status in the U.S. Thank you so much!!!"

One hundred women responded. About one-fourth were told of all possible side effects. I'm grateful to their radiation oncologists for being forthcoming, honest, and respectful. About five percent of the women received some information; they were told about menopause and scar tissue in the vagina but not about painful intercourse. Seven percent were women who researched, heard from a friend, or were on a colorectal forum and read about the radiation effects from other women's posts. They had asked their radiation oncologists about vaginal damage and dilators.

About two-thirds of the women who wrote to me were not informed that radiation would create scar tissue in the vagina that could adhere to the other side. They were not told this scarring would damage nerves, resulting in a permanently painful sex life. These patients were not advised to use dilators to keep the vagina stretched and the scar tissue from growing and adhering to the other side. Many reported that the radiation oncologists, men or women, dismissed and disregarded any future symptom as insignificant.

I cannot tell if this number accurately reflects what is happening in the United States. I don't know if angry women were willing to share comments or whether women who were informed were not reading the colorectal Facebook posts because they live happily and are not on Facebook pages.

I asked the women who answered if they were willing to share their comments from Facebook in my book for a more significant impact. These women permitted me to share their intimate experiences so that the women reading this narrative would not be surprised like we were. There were many comments:

Tammy from Georgia was told that she wouldn't be able to get pregnant after radiation and that she would go into early menopause. She was single for a couple of years. The first time she had sex, there was so much blood that she had to go to the ER. The doctors acted like she had done something to cause it. She did not know why the bleeding happened and felt embarrassed by what the doctors thought. No one, including her gynecologist, had told her about the scar tissue. He just said she was having a lubrication problem. She didn't know why sex was painful. She had never been told about dilators. That was five years ago, and intercourse is still painful. She says it's frustrating that many doctors don't take the time to discuss how the body will be affected by these treatments.

Jennifer was given a printout about side effects to read at her convenience. She felt she had no choice and was already nervous about what was happening. But just how severe the scar tissue was to the vagina and bowels was not mentioned. She learned about it by reading other women's stories online. She wanted to thank me for bringing this issue to the public eye.

Lisa's doctors from Oklahoma did not tell her about vaginal effects. She's livid. If she had known, she would have declined radiation. Chemo was enough to shrink her tumor for surgery.

Courtney from Virginia wrote that her doctors mentioned these issues in passing. "Oh, and yeah, by the way, you're going to need dilators because your vagina will shrink. Kthx byeeeee." End of discussion. She asked more questions. She didn't follow through with the dilators because everything hurt because of radiation, and the last thing she needed was to add more pain. Two years later, she did pelvic floor physical therapy. She was told she would have to use dilators two to three times a week for the rest of her life to have sex. She went through menopause at age 31 and has zero sex drive, so she gave up on the dilators. Her husband understands and agrees it's not worth it, but being celibate early in life is crushing.

Judy shared that her treatment was seven years ago. She was told nothing about vaginal issues, even when she complained about vaginal spotting during radiation. She felt angry when it was too late for dilators a year later, and she was diagnosed with vaginal stenosis. She uses coconut oil when she does have sex, which is rare, and her partner only fits part way. She has to be on top to control depth. It's like a hot fire poker feeling sometimes; it just burns. It's not fun anymore and not worth it. She can't have a routine pap smear; the top of her vagina is webbed and closed. It's a nightmare, and she wishes she had skipped radiation but then wonders if she would still be considered NED (No Evidence of Disease).

Kimberly wasn't told and found out the hard way. As a result, she ended up in the hospital for four days. The information would certainly have been appreciated. She's confused about how doctors could withhold this critical information from patients. She wonders how doctors think that sex won't be part of female patients' lives afterward. Kimberly is grateful for her excellent treatment, yet she believes doctors should have told her what to expect later.

After radiation, Robin now has urinary incontinence and painful sex. She rarely has the big O due to radiation damage. She is using estrogen and lube and might need a bladder sling.

Colleen imparted that knowing about the side effects of radiation is essential, especially since women are being diagnosed younger. She had to have a bladder sling, and it was never the same down there.

Kim shared that she had vaginal stenosis and a failed reconstruction surgery. She lost all sexual function at age 35.

Amanda reported that nobody told her about this issue, and her lady garden has shrunk. At 48, she hasn't had sex in more than a year because of this damage. Radiation and surgery took away her desire.

Morgan from Canada wrote that she was told nothing. She's 22 and in early menopause. She cannot have children. She has chronic yeast infections now. She hasn't even attempted sex because everything hurts, and she's six months out of surgery, eight from radiation. She has problems with her bladder.

Another Judy was told that vaginal pain would be a "non-issue" if she used the dilators after treatment. Two and a half years after treatment, she's still unable to have intercourse. She's had three vaginal surgeries to no avail. Her doctors now are firm in the belief that had she used dilators during treatment, she would not have had such unfortunate side effects. Her oncologist was adamant about not using them until six weeks after radiation, at the earliest. Looking back, her goal was to eliminate cancer and avoid a colostomy. Judy had thought that would be the worst possible outcome at the time. Now, she wishes she had seriously considered using the dilators earlier. She's lost a special part of her relationship and wishes she had known her options.

Rosemary from Colorado was not told about these side effects. She wanted to thank me for bringing this up. She didn't know it was this widespread. She thought her symptoms were rare.

April wrote that she wasn't told anything in the paper she received about the side effects. She even had to ask if it would prevent her from having kids later because even that topic wasn't addressed.

Lori from Pennsylvania wrote that she was told nothing. She's very irritated about it and had a male doctor. Thank God she has a patient and understanding husband.

Elizabeth had stage II rectal cancer at age 34. Doctors removed her rectum, and she has a permanent colostomy. She was told about fertility loss. The field of radiation was too large for ovary transposition. She was single, and unfertilized egg freezing was not yet a viable option. She was not told about the scar tissue and was horrified at the large pool of blood on the bed the first time she had sex after radiation.

She talked to her primary care doctor, who filled her in. Elizabeth was furious no one told her about the scar tissue. She mentioned that it bleeds when it's stretched and is painful. She also wished someone had discussed what happens to the cervix and uterus when the rectum is removed. Her cervix is now sunken into the space where her rectum was. To get an accurate Pap smear, she has to have a D&C (dilation and curettage) procedure. She was going through early onset menopause, and her sex drive was very low, but now it is sad not to be able to enjoy intimacy anymore. She was never told this would happen. She got dilators after complaining months after the radiation was completed. She used them for a while but had pain, so she gave up.

Tania was told she would need dilators but that it was not a big deal. She was never told about the possible terrible pain. They said it could be "sore" and to use a baby ointment, and she would be okay.

Michelle from Illinois had asked for dilators only because someone she knew had rectal cancer, and that person had not been told. Even when Michelle asked about the pain, it was trivialized. She was proactive and asked about pelvic floor therapy and dilators.

Peggy said she was never told about radiation ruining her sex life, and she's angry.

Bonnie wrote that, in fact, she still hasn't been told. Maybe because she's almost 70, they all decided she wouldn't need to know. They are now talking about the rectal scarring, which is awful.

Steph from Minnesota wrote that the radiation doctor had told her she would stop having periods and probably go into menopause. She was 43 at the time. A nurse mentioned a dilator and gave her one. Steph used it during radiation but then stopped. The nurse didn't tell her how long to keep using the dilator. Fast forward to age 47, and Steph's gynecologist said between the radiation and menopause, her insides are fried. She can barely have a Pap Smear because the procedure hurts so much. And she mentioned that her radiation oncologist was a female who had been treating this type of cancer for 20 years.

Jennifer was told nothing. She suggested that a urologist or a urogynecologist should be included when assembling a team to address rectal cancer. She is at a crossroads dealing with extreme vaginal dryness, urinary incontinence, and full bowel incontinence. She's seen a urogynecologist who seems to think if her inside parts aren't falling out of her vagina, then what she's experiencing is minor. She's had two rounds of pelvic floor physical therapy which helped with the urinary incontinence but not the bowel issues.

Cameron from California also wasn't told about any of this. She was in perimenopause. When she asked her near-retirement oncologist what impact radiation would have on her, he said she's "kinda long-in-the-tooth anyway." Cameron sandwiched seething anger on top of an already choking fear.

K from New Jersey was told nothing. The radiation stopped her periods. Three years after the treatment, she experiences zero libido and has only attempted sex twice. It's just too painful to be fun. She's grateful for her understanding husband.

M wrote that she was told nothing. They removed most of the vagina. She was told nothing about reconstruction. She found out online about that. She can't have intercourse and can't have a pelvic exam. What is left is scar tissue. She wishes doctors would be more understanding and upfront with women about the side effects of treatment.

Another Robin from Canada was not told about these issues. She found out through a friend. She had been serving on a Canadian working group to make this a key issue in colorectal cancer care for all women. Her book *The Cancer Olympics* describes her struggle to overcome the damage and medical indifference. She combated the medical indifference by insisting to the patient representative that this information be a standard of care in her province. You will laugh, she shares, the group was comprised of colorectal cancer care doctors who use the word "anus" and "rectum" easily. But when she said the word "vagina" in that meeting, one of them covered his ears with his hands!

I asked her how she overcame the vaginal damage for her own well-being. She said she used the dilator every other day and worked through the pain and bleeding. Wine helped her relax. She used a product called a Berman dilator, which is available on Amazon. It is a smooth device with graduated sizes, so a woman can start small and work up. It has a gentle vibration, which increases blood flow to the tissues. Robin was able to restore caliber using it. She graduated to "natural methods" after six months. She is happy to advocate on this issue. She has even done a YouTube about it, to which many women responded with tears and gratitude for the truth https://youtu.be/tDmKiODfMg0.

Upon seeing the YouTube video about dilator use created by Dr. Robin McGee, one of the women commented that she was given one of these dilators. However, when the doctor found out that she was not sexually active at the time, he took it back and said, "Oh well, you won't need this then." She thanked Robin for the video. She wished she had known all of this two years ago. She had no idea what dilators were for.

Through these posts and others, I realized the depth of outrage and despair of these women matched mine when I found out about the vaginal pain and the possible loss of my healthy sexuality. Through these exchanges, I learned that the external radiation beam goes unforgivingly through the vagina to the rectum, creating scar tissue with nerve pain for most women, yielding painful intercourse, and for some women, permanent bladder damage.i

I met one woman who said that radiation treatments did not affect her sexuality in a significant way. Likewise, two women on the colorectal FB page said they had no pain. I wonder if their tumor's location was farther away from the anus in a way that didn't cause vaginal scar tissue or whether their radiation oncologist knew what dosage to use so scar tissue would not form in the vagina.

Because my radiation oncologist did not provide dilators, a friend suggested we visit a sex shop for help. I explained my situation to the owner. She showed me several possible dildos. I chose a simple, thin silicone dildo called "Your Highness." It cost $30. The owner suggested I use the device daily or as much as possible to maintain the integrity of the vaginal mucosal tissue. She recommended I masturbate and bring myself into orgasm to bring blood flow into the area. She gave me a small vibrating battery-operated attachment to place inside the silicone dilator.

I went home and used the dilator. Penetration hurt. Sliding it past the painful damaged nerves and scar tissue hurt at first, then relaxed as it entered the canal. I did my best to masturbate to make the area more lubricated and for me to feel pleasure. However, motivating myself to use the dilator was difficult because of my aversion to nerve pain.

Several women on the Facebook forums suggested I see a pelvic floor physical therapist (PFPT). The PFPT stretched the vaginal walls and massaged the inside of the vagina, which hurt. She also checked the anal sphincter reflex and the clitoris by tapping on the area gently. The PFPT also stretched the scar tissue she could feel on the left side. She gave me electronic sensors to place in the vagina. She measured the vaginal muscle tone and assigned me a set of Kegel exercises. She had dilators that looked like thick candles; I purchased them from the office. She had six dilators in hard, heavy plastic sticks ranging from extra small to large.

I bought the first five sizes: XS, S, S+, M, and M+. I used coconut oil as a lubricant and could insert the sizes up to medium. M+ was too painful for my vaginal nerves. The instructions were to insert the dilator and hold it in for ten minutes. I should try to use the Kegel muscles to squeeze and release the dilator and to turn it around the vaginal wall. I was to try and scrape the walls where the scar tissue amassed on the left side of the vagina. I stopped the process as soon as I felt considerable pain. I never did the Kegels, which were too painful with the inserted dilator. I continued to use the thinner silicone dilator occasionally to keep up the possibility that I'd be able to have healthy sexual penetration again. I am forty-six today, too young to lose that part of life.

Through the Facebook forums, I learned that some women like silicone dilators from Soul Source as they are easier to insert and more giving than hard plastic. Other women like the plastic Berman and Femani vibrators. I tried the Berman dilator set. The vibrator set includes three sizes. The vibration made insertion easier, as the pain was less pronounced.

I found the medicinal-grade silicone dilators easier on the body. I also liked the aforementioned lightweight plastic vibrators with various sizing. Women need to be consistent about using dilators daily or every other day, especially in the first six months after radiation treatment.ii Women need to lubricate the dilators, insert the size that can go in easily, and keep it in for 10 minutes. These women might want to move the dilator around to stimulate the mucosa. Consider a gradual build-up to minimize rips and vaginal bleeding.

I recently heard from Dr. McGee that in the city of Halifax, information sessions on the impact of radiation on sex lives are offered. All women undergoing pelvic radiation are directed to attend. The information session provides resources for where to get dilators. The groups are led by nurses, some of whom had considerable training to become comfortable teaching this topic. These training sessions occur every month. No referral is required.

In September 2018, I saw the PFPT again. The specialist stretched the vaginal scar tissue again. She showed me a tool called a wand, a glass contraption that is curved on one side, which could perhaps more effectively scrape the walls of the vagina, especially where there was scar tissue. It was painful. I used it once.

In 2023 several women saw my post from 2018 and responded. Some women commented that they were not told anything about the vaginal damage, while others said they were told about it and given dilators. One woman said her radiation oncologist mentioned dilators during the consultation but changed his mind about giving them right before starting radiation. Perhaps awareness and honesty about the sexual damage of radiation treatment is growing, but not yet for all doctors or patients.

SUMMARY AND SUGGESTIONS

1. Radiation treatments to the rectum will most likely create scarring in a concentrated area in the vagina. When the scarring stretches, it may bleed. The scar tissue has damaged nerves from radiation and is hyper-sensitive. Friction or touching this area will create pain sensations.

2. You might call a female rectal cancer patient treated by your radiation oncologist before starting treatments and ask her about vaginal pain afterward.
3. Some institutions discuss the full range of potential side effects. These radiation oncologist offices provide patients with education, dilators, and referrals to a pelvic floor physical therapist and a gynecologist specializing in after-cancer treatments. Consider using their services.
4. Silicone dilators from Soul Source might be gentler on the body than hard plastic. The lightweight Berman and FeMani dilator sets come with vibration, which could make insertion easier as it distracts the pain.
5. Women need to use dilators as many times a week as possible to stretch the vagina. Insert the smallest size, then move to the largest, most comfortable size. Hold it in the vagina for ten minutes, occasionally moving it around the vaginal walls and stretching the vagina. It is recommended to bring oneself to orgasm to bring more blood fluid into the tissue.
6. Most female patients are referred to a pelvic floor physical therapist who may teach a woman how to stretch her vaginal scar tissue and provide exercises for the anal sphincter.
7. I hold you with care, warmth, and tenderness as you navigate your path of finding solutions after radiation treatments.

Chapter Tweleve

WHAT DO FEMALE PATIENTS NEED TO KNOW ABOUT THE SIDE EFFECTS OF RADIATION?

My friend, Colleen Mayne, once came with me to my surgeon's office. She asked him how his office would help me once all treatments were finished. He said his office would follow up and check up on my incisions and answer my questions. She kept pressing him on what his office would do after all the treatments. She asked the same question about five consecutive times. I wondered what Colleen's wisdom was referring to. Now I know. There is an aftermath to the treatments, and patients need help.

Five years after radiation treatment ended, I noticed an unpleasant sensation in my lower abdomen. I went to the ER and had a CT scan. The scan showed fluid trapped in my cervix and soft tissue. My gynecologist referred me to a gynecologist-oncologist, and she did a Dilatation and Curettage procedure. I was sedated, and she opened the cervix and drained the fluid. She biopsied and cleaned the lining of the cervix. She attempted to reach the uterus and do the same, but radiation-induced scar tissue prevented her from entering the uterus.

She mentioned that I would need periodic ultrasounds because my cervix isn't draining due to radiation damage. She said that if I ever had cervical or uterine cancer, I would not know it because the blood wouldn't drain like in non-irradiated women. That was good information to know. The cervical biopsy was benign

When I returned to my radiation oncologist's office, I asked to see the consent to radiation treatment form I had signed. Nothing in the consent form mentioned vaginal damage, vaginal scar tissue, uterine scar tissue, painful intercourse, or bleeding with intercourse. It said that side effects after treatment may include: "rectal bleeding, small bowel obstruction, frequent urination, diarrhea, impotence, ovarian dysfunction (menopause)."

I wondered how can newly diagnosed women be informed of possible side effects and not suffer the same heartache I did. I am not a medical doctor. I am a caring patient who believes we grow from pain; we improve a system when we see a loophole. This chapter, therefore, is directed at patients who want more education. I also hope any medical professionals who read this book will work toward improving a system that will be more patient-friendly and transparent to newly diagnosed patients.

I'd love it if, before a woman receives standard radiation treatment, someone would tell her that:

- Radiation therapy shrinks tumors before surgery, making it easier for some surgeons to remove them.
- Radiation can be used instead of surgery for people who aren't good candidates.
- Radiation can relieve symptoms such as rectal pain and blockage.
- Radiation reduces the risk of local recurrence by about 7 percent.
- Some people have a complete response to chemo-radiation and can be candidates for a watch-and-wait regarding a surgery option.

- As of May 2023, no approved radiation treatment specifically targets the rectum without the surrounding areas. An external beam moves through the whole body as it concentrates on the tumor.
- The vagina (the birth canal) sits directly above the rectum, where it will most likely be damaged after six weeks of radiation to a low-lying tumor in the rectum.
- The ovaries are in the field of radiation. The ovaries make 70 percent of estrogen in the body and 30 percent of a woman's circulating testosterone, which gives a woman her libido.i After six weeks of radiation, a woman will most likely go into menopause. With little estrogen to stimulate the glands of the vagina to produce fluid, penetration will probably feel dry and painful. The sexual drive will lower as testosterone levels decline. Also, estrogen causes increased blood flow to the clitoris and labia so that when they are stimulated, sexual response is enhanced.ii With less estrogen, the sexual response might be diminished.
- A woman may want ovary transposition. It's a separate surgery by which a gynecologist surgeon removes the ovaries from the radiation field. After this surgery and radiation, the ovary glands will function.
- Radiation most likely reaches the uterine lining, making it impossible to carry a fetus.
- Women who want to have a child with their own eggs might consider freezing them and using a surrogate carrier for the pregnancy.
- In rare cases, radiation treatment can create a hole in the tissue between the rectum and the vagina. When that happens, feces can come out of the vagina. This condition is called a rectovaginal fistula and can be fixed surgically.

- Your bladder is in the field of radiation. There is a 15 percent chance of permanent damage to the bladder. Some radiation oncologists tell their patients to have a full bladder when they're receiving radiation to minimize damage.
- Some women have radiation cystitis, an inflammation of the lining of the bladder caused by radiation therapy to the pelvis and typically develops a few months or years after radiation. According to cancer.gov, "symptoms include pain and a burning feeling while urinating, blood in the urine, feeling a need to urinate often or right away, being unable to control the flow of urine, bladder spasms, and pain in the pelvis." iii
- Some radiation damage requires using a sling implant, a thin piece of mesh, or tissue surgically placed under the urethra and helps with urinary incontinence. The sling acts as a hammock to keep your urethra in place and hold it closed when your bladder is full. The urethra is the tube that goes from your bladder to the outside. The sling supports your urethra during physical activity and minimizes urine leakage when a person laughs, coughs, sneezes, exercises, or lifts things.iv The procedure helps close the urethra and bladder neck.
- After six weeks of radiation, there will most likely be some scar tissue in the vagina. It's thick and leathery due to damage from the intense, focused radiation beams. It will be concentrated in a particular area. Radiation also damages nerves in the scar tissue. The nerves become hyper-sensitive. Hypersensitive nerves cause pain anytime the vaginal scar tissue is touched during intercourse or a medical exam. When stretched, the scar tissue may bleed, especially during intercourse.
- Radiation may create scar tissue in the cervix or the uterus, which might prevent fluid or blood from draining properly.

Women might need periodic ultrasounds to assess the health of their uterus or ovaries.

- The clitoris and labia may be in the field of radiation. If the clitoris is in the field of radiation, you might not be able to have a clitoral orgasm. Make sure to ask and to be shown the calculations to confirm that the clitoris and labia have not been included in the radiation field.
- The vagina, bladder, and rectum linings are sensitive to radiation therapy. After radiation, these tissues may atrophy. The glands in the vagina that make the canal wet and pleasurable for sexual intercourse may be damaged and may not be able to produce the fluid that lubricates the vagina during arousal.v Radiation will thin the walls of the uterus. When a woman has sex, she may bleed a little, none, or a lot.
- Radiation-induced menopause may result in a lack of sleep for some months until the body recovers from the initial shock and synthesizes more progesterone through the adrenals.
- For many women, menopausal symptoms include hot flashes. They might experience a sudden feeling of heat and sometimes a red, flushed face and sweating. Hot flashes start when blood vessels near the skin's surface expand to cool off, making a woman break out in a sweat. Some women have a rapid heart rate or chills. When hot flashes happen while sleeping, they're called night sweats. A hot flush is a hot flash plus redness in the face and neck.vi
- Women or men will lose some pubic hair while in radiation treatment, and it may take a few months to grow back.
- Radiation will most likely cause vaginal stenosis: shortening and narrowing of the vaginal canal due to losing the elasticity of the radiated tissue. During sexual intercourse, the vagina

can expand and slightly dilate with sexual activity, which allows sex to be pleasurable for both the patient and her partner. After radiation, the elasticity of the vagina can become impaired as the vagina becomes increasingly rigid.vii

- Women will need to use dilators immediately after completing radiation treatments to stretch the vaginal walls and to ensure that the scar tissue doesn't grow and block the vaginal opening or the vagina.
- Radiation to the pelvis might also affect rectal continence after surgery, as the rectal lining is sensitive to radiation treatment.
- If the tumor grew into the vagina, and the patient received radiation treatment, the vagina or a part of it might be removed during surgery. A patient may not know this before the procedure – and then wake up without a vagina.
- Suppose a patient has a history of osteoporosis in the family. In that case, radiation to the pelvis may induce or increase this condition. Both estrogen and progesterone are necessary for bone building and maintenance, and both hormones diminish after radiation treatment. Likewise, any irradiated bones may become weaker and more sensitive to fractures.

In my imaginary world, women would know that radiation is an effective yet harsh treatment that could help treat cancer and leave lasting damage to the body. Radiation treatment shrinks the tumor and lowers the chances of a local recurrence by 7 percent. A twenty-five-year study involving 13,647 women showed no more than a seven percent ten-year survival advantage for women having radiation treatment.viii

I recently saw an article assessing women's sexual functioning up to 24 months after surgery. Out of 267 women, 52 percent were sexually active before treatment. This figure dropped to 18 percent two years post-treatment. Sixty-two percent of the sexually active women reported either newly developed sexual dysfunctions or aggravation of pre-existing sexual dysfunctions after treatment, with radiation therapy being the only significant risk factor".ix

This article asks doctors to give patients all this information up front, including all the statistics, and let patients decide. In a study by Kunneman et al., the authors discuss prerequisites for shared decision-making based on the individual patients' looking at benefits versus harms caused by radiation therapy for the treatment of rectal cancer. They claim that radiation therapy showed no increase in overall survival rates, and this issue was seldom addressed. On the other hand, the article mentions that increased local control was noted in all consultations. Sexual dysfunction is considered one of the two most prominent side effects of radiation therapy and was only addressed in 65 percent of the consultations with female rectal cancer patients.

The authors conclude that there is considerable variation in information provided to patients before treatment. This variation indicates a need for more clarity on the benefits and harms of radiation therapy that should be discussed before deciding whether to have radiation therapy. The authors advocate for standard-provided information on potential sexual dysfunction, local recurrence rates, and overall survival percentages with or without radiation.

Another article from 2015 states that pelvic external beam radiation therapy (EBRT) has a persistent negative impact on female sexual functioning. The most prevalent problems are vaginal dryness, dyspareunia (painful or difficult intercourse), varying degrees of vaginal shortness / stenosis, lack of sexual desire, and orgasmic problems.x

This paper concludes that doctors must discuss the risks to a woman's sexuality before recommending radiation treatment. "The time has come for openness about sexual matters within the health-care system and for intervention studies to defeat sexual impairment in long-term cancer survivors. Pelvic radiotherapy has a persistent deteriorating effect on the vaginal mucosa impacting negatively on the sexual functioning in female cancer patients...Healthcare professionals are encouraged to address potential sexual dysfunction both before and after radiotherapy and to focus more on quality than on quantity."xi

In addition, a PubMed article supports the shortage of published research papers about women's sexuality after pelvic radiation treatments. "The PubMed search contained specific keywords for applicability to the topic of interventions for sexual difficulties related to radiation therapy. Very few articles were found supporting the fact that not much attention has been given to the sexual difficulties women experience after radiation to the sexual organs".xii

SUMMARY AND SUGGESTIONS

1. Women should be told the survival rates after radiation treatment (overall survival and local recurrences) and the possible side effects so they can decide if they want to undergo that therapy.
2. Articles support the claims of a huge discrepancy between information shared with female rectal cancer patients about vaginal and sexual health after radiation treatments. Authors advocate for a universal sheet of information that presents the likely benefits and potential side effects and lets a woman decide the quality of life she would like to have following rectal cancer treatments.

Chapter Thirteen

WHAT CAN HELP VAGINAL PAIN AFTER RADIATION?

If you're a woman who had radiation to treat rectal cancer, you probably wonder what can be done about vaginal nerve pain during intercourse. You want answers about how to be sexual after radiation treatments.

At age forty-five, I didn't want to be asexual for the rest of my life because penetration was painful. I also wanted answers. I kept asking on the Facebook pages if anyone had found a solution. Finally, one woman replied that after four gynecologists and five long years, she found a gynecologist who knew what to do about this nerve pain. She shared her recipe for being ready at a moment's notice. That person gave me permission to share this information in this book:

- Use a silicone dilator as many times per week as you can. They say to use dilators daily, but this isn't realistic. For most women, three or four times per week is more reasonable, or every other day. This regular intervention keeps the vaginal walls from adhering to each other and brings more blood flow to the area, so the tissue remains supple and active.
- Use LOTS of lubricant on the dilator. YES WB (water-based) lubricant and Good Clean Love (water-based) have organic

ingredients that the body might assimilate without causing a burning sensation. Those products can also be used with silicone and latex condoms. Walnut oil, pomegranate oil, and MCT oil can also be used directly on the body.

- Have your gynecologist create a vaginal cream from a compound pharmacy: Amitriptyline 2 percent and Baclofen 2 percent in a lipoderm base. Apply the cream at the vaginal entrance (vulva) twice daily except on vaginal estrogen cream days. Use just the tip of your finger. The gynecologist said that radiation could lead to vaginitis. The cream is a neurological anti-inflammatory blocker. While the tissue may heal pretty well in some areas, others might be ultra-sensitive.
- Two times a week, suspend the compound cream and insert a dab of a plant-based estrogen cream (Estrace or Estradiol), also applied at the vulva.

I went to a new gynecologist and asked if I could have a prescription for this compound cream. She said Baclofen is a muscle relaxant that would not help my pain. She prescribed 2 percent amitriptyline in a lipoderm base. My gynecologist also prescribed Estradiol cream and said to use it three times a week.

My experience with the 2 percent amitriptyline cream was ambiguous. I wasn't sure where my nerve pain was, and I didn't want to touch the area and experience pain. I didn't use the cream for a while, and it became oily. I was afraid of poking around with my finger to find the pain. I asked the woman from Facebook if, after applying the cream, she had any pain with penetration. She said no. That gave me the motivation to keep trying.

I returned to the compound pharmacy and asked them to make another concoction of 2 percent amitriptyline in a thicker base in a jar, not a tube. I placed a dab on the entrance of the vagina, and for me, the solution stung a bit.

A friend encouraged me to contact Ellen Heed. Ellen teaches sexological bodywork, scar-tissue remediation, anatomy and physiology, pain and orthopedic evaluation, and craniosacral therapy. Ellen suggested I use a finger dipped in castor oil once every three days on the painful scarred area in my vagina and massage the area. She said I should repeat the process three consecutive times every three days. For her doctorate, Ellen studied how warmed castor oil, when applied regularly, dissolves scar tissue in women after Caesarean surgery. She claims she has worked with thousands of women with scar tissue pain and that their pain and scar tissue has diminished dramatically with regular application of the castor oil. I started using it as I was told, but I didn't continue. I moved and fell out of the habit.

Ellen proposed that the next time I get estradiol cream, I should ask the gynecologist for a prescription to take to a compound pharmacy. Ellen said the preservatives in the cream could be toxic to the body. Instead, she suggested I ask for Estradiol in Aloe vera oil and place a drop or two at the entrance of the vagina. I asked the compound pharmacy also to create the amitriptyline in Aloe vera oil. When I went to get pap smears a few years after treatments, I used the oil in the morning before my appointment to have the nerves numbed so I wouldn't feel pain with the insertion of the vaginal speculum. It helped.

SUMMARY AND SUGGESTIONS

1. Have your gynecologist prescribe a 2 percent amitriptyline with or without Baclofen in a lipoderm base in a jar and take it to a compound pharmacy. It will calm the nerve pain

sensations. If you're sexually active, use this cream twice a day at the vulva and vaginal opening or as close to your scar tissue as you can. Apply it on the days you're not taking estrogen.

2. Estrogenize your vulva and the lower third of your vagina with Estradiol cream or Estradiol in Aloe vera oil from a compound pharmacy. Use it two or three times a week.
3. Use dilators with lots of lubricant as often as possible each week.
4. Natural lubricants include organic coconut oil, walnut oil, YES WB (water-based) lubricant, pomegranate oil, and Good Clean Love.
5. Warmed castor oil applied three times every three days at the area of the scar might help dissolve the scar tissue.
6. You may want to use your amitriptyline when you get a pap smear exam so the nerves are calm and the insertion of the vaginal speculum might not hurt.

Chapter Fourteen

BASICS OF HORMONES AND MENOPAUSE

If you're a woman under age 50 who had radiation to the pelvis without removing your ovaries, you are most likely experiencing or will experience radiation-induced menopause. Your estrogen, progesterone, and testosterone production plummeted abruptly, and your body rapidly changed. Are you surprised by hot flashes, vaginal dryness, and a lack of libido? At some point, it will be time to address hormonal health. Should you take vaginal creams and natural supplements? Should you leave your hormones alone? Should you take bioidentical hormones or hormone replacement therapy?

I asked my gynecologist what she thought about my hormonal health. She was against taking hormones except for Estradiol cream to apply at the vulva and in the vagina three times a week. I began applying this cream with the applicator at the top of the vagina for several months. Then I read in Dr. Sara Gottfried's book, *The Hormone Cure: Reclaim Balance, Sleep and Sex Drive, Lose Weight, Feel Focused, Vital, and Energized Naturally with the Gottfried Protocol,* that women have no estrogen receptors at the top of the vagina. So, using the applicator with estrogen cream on top would not be helpful.

Gottfried informs that Estradiol makes the genital skin sensitive and full of innervation and blood supply. With low estrogen, the nerves that densely populate the clitoris, G-spot, and the inner lips of the vulva start to disappear. Gottfried recommends applying one gram of the cream on a finger to the outside of the vagina (the vulva), the inner lips, the clitoris, and the opening to the vagina. Then apply a second gram to the lower third of the vagina, where women have estrogen receptors. That's a total of two grams. She claims two weeks of applying the estrogen cream locally to the vulva and vagina should encourage the nerve endings to come online.i

Some women want to know what to do about hot flashes besides taking estrogen. For me, hot flashes were unpleasant and annoying as my heart raced and my temperature increased momentarily, but they weren't terrible. There are women whose menopausal symptoms are extreme and involve mood swings, depression, and long sweating sessions, especially at night. The local health food store has natural herbal remedies that might lessen the effects. In her book, Dr. Gottfried has diet, supplements, herbal supplements, and lifestyle suggestions to ease the symptoms of hot flashes and menopause, including vitamin E, magnesium, and rhubarb extract. The OB/GYN physician, Christiane Northrop, advocates for a Pueraria mirifica plant extract supplement.

A friend gave me black cohosh supplements to mitigate my hot flashes. The structure seems to mimic estrogen and perhaps could bind to estrogen receptors. Black cohosh is an herb that treats hot flashes, moodiness, vaginal dryness, and excessive sweating.ii My endocrinologist recommended that I use Estroven. I bought two kinds: one with rhubarb extract and another called Menopause and memory support with black cohosh. These products reduced the intensity of my heart rate response, and my hot flashes decreased. I had hot flashes for about three to four years, diminishing in intensity and interval. Consider checking with your doctors and naturopaths about options.

In their book *Tantric Sex and Menopause*, authors Richardson and McGeever report that in menopause, ovary production of progesterone can plummet by about 95 percent. For women who suffer from depression, anxiety, hot flashes, and weight gain, progesterone could be a game changer. Progesterone, they mention, is an antidepressant, promotes sleep, and can soothe edginess, anxiety, and panic. It can also bring surges in libido. Progesterone is imperative for building bone, while estrogen prevents bone breakdown. Progesterone is also made in the adrenal glands. Large meals can deplete progesterone levels, so eating smaller meals and avoiding eating too late can help a woman sleep better.iii

Dr. Gottfried's book has a hormone-balancing program that looks at the adrenals, thyroid, and sex hormones. Likewise, functional medicine doctors, medical doctors who identify the root cause(s) of an illness, including triggers such as poor nutrition, stress, toxins, allergens, genetics, and the microbiome (the bacteria living in and on your body), also look at balancing the hormonal system in much the same way as Dr. Gottfried. Unfortunately, functional medicine doctors, for the most part, do not take insurance. Dr. Afrouz Demeri, a naturopathic doctor, also assists women in learning about their hormonal health in one-on-one and online group sessions.

Authors McGeever and Richardson point out that anxiety or stress can contribute to hot flashes. I noticed it before I read their book. If I had an anxious thought, it brought on a hot flash. So part of the treatment is to use calming techniques, like slow, conscious breathing, yoga, meditation, and learning to disengage from attaching to anxious thinking.

Anxious thinking about anything, fear of the unknown, a lack of worthiness, or doubting your abilities creates anxious feelings. Anxious thinking is a habit people cultivate. Notice when you start having inner palpitations and contractions around the heart that alert you to the thoughts running through you. Did the thinking say you were "less than" and "not enough?" Allow yourself to feel the experience that your thinking created. Completely accept it. Surrender to it. Breathe. Notice the breath. Then let go of giving anxious thinking more attention. Stop listening to the story. Allow your experience and disengage from the story. The thought is already gone. It's in the past.

Sometimes when you're anxious, it feels good to soothe yourself like you would comfort a baby. *Oh, Sweetheart, you got caught up in a frightening daydream. It's all right. Everyone does that. Wouldn't living in a world without buying into fearful thoughts be nice? I love you so much. You're safe, and you're not your fearful thoughts. It's okay to accept your experience. Maybe even enjoy the jolt of hormones that create that experience. You did that. You're so powerful. You're doing so well with your journey. I acknowledge all that you're going through. You're resilient and resourceful. Moreover, you're connected to infinite love, power, and creativity. You are perfect as you are right now. You are more than enough for my love.*

Some women, who don't have hormonally-driven cancer, choose to use bioidentical hormone replacement therapy to balance the new hormonal levels for an increased sex drive, bone building, better sleep, and mood stabilization. Bioidentical hormones are manufactured plant-derived substances that mimic human hormones. Their structure is identical to human hormones made by the ovaries. These hormones restore sleep and keep the vaginal mucosal lining supple. The patient and her doctor tailor the dosage that's right for her through careful monitoring of blood test results. iv There are patches and oral supplements that are FDA-approved. It's not yet conclusive whether these natural hormones cause fewer side effects than their synthetic cousins.v

Other women whose cancer is not hormonally-driven may choose hormone replacement therapy (HRT), in which women take prescribed manufactured synthetic estrogen and progesterone. Synthetic hormones are the most widely studied form of hormone pills. Synthetic hormones are made from chemical sources that approximate the human body's hormones. Systemic estrogen, like the bioidentical hormones, eliminates the flashes and estrogenizes the vagina. Synthetic HRT is similar to what the body makes and helps to relieve symptoms.

There are scientific controversies about the long-term health benefits versus risks of HRT treatment and bioidentical hormone treatments. The benefits include better sleep and increased estrogen and progesterone hormones, which leads to bone building and a moisturized vagina. The risks include increased blood clots, heart attacks, strokes, and endometrial and breast cancer.

Most endocrinologists and gynecologists prefer that patients take plant supplements that mimic estrogen (such as black cohosh, rhubarb, maca root, soy, Pueraria mirifica, magnesium, and vitamin E) and progesterone (Vitex agnus-castus, also called vitex, chaste tree, chastetree or chasteberry) before prescribing hormones. I took these supplements daily.

My gynecologist advocated for FemTouch after radiation-induced menopause to keep the vaginal mucosa moisturized. She said she worked in a clinic where FemTouch was used successfully for women after radiation. However, another gynecologist brought to my attention that the FDA and American College of Gynecology declared that while lasers show some promising short-term results for vaginal health, there can be serious complications. These lasers are not extensively studied in women with radiation. The FDA and ACOG issued a statement warning women that lasers are not approved for vaginal rejuvenation of dry tissue, although they do have some approved gynecology uses.vi

At 48 years old, I discovered that my body had osteoporosis. I made an appointment with a nurse practitioner at a gynecologist's office who believed in bioidentical hormones. I did not want to keep losing bone density at such a young age. I wanted to maintain what I had. The bioidentical hormones immediately created an imbalance in my hormonal system. For the first time in many years, I had a yeast infection. I want to learn how to balance hormones with plants, but until then, I want to maintain my bones.

The nurse practitioner said I must use progesterone to balance the estrogen because I still have my uterus. She prescribed bioidentical progesterone pills and FDA-approved estrogen patches. I used these hormones for two years. One day, the pharmacy refilled my generic bioidentical progesterone pills prescription from a new supplier. My body had a severe reaction, and I needed strong antibiotics to combat a yellow discharge that would otherwise not cease. Our bodies can be sensitive to one brand but not another.

The North American Menopause Society (www.menopause.org) has plenty of resources to read about menopause symptoms, hormonal health, and treatment options.

Authors McGeever, Richardson, and Dr. Gottfried also endorse Chinese medicine to balance hormones. In addition, there are energy medicine exercises designed to bring the body's energies into hormonal harmony. Eden Method has a program called Energy Medicine for a Woman.

As usual, you are the authority in your life. The field of hormones is vast, and options for different comfort levels exist. Check with your doctors, naturopaths, functional medicine doctors, and yourself about what can help you. Some of you prefer plant-based approaches, or energy-based approaches, while others opt for conventional medicine. I know you'll make the right choices for your hormonal well-being. Sometimes it takes trial and error to settle on a program that works for you. You have my love and support as you navigate new territory with your hormonal health.

SUMMARY AND SUGGESTIONS

1. Estrogen makes the genital skin sensitive and full of innervation and blood supply. Without estrogen, the nerves leading to genital sensations atrophy.
2. If using Estradiol cream, rub one gram of cream on the whole vulva, inner labia, and clitoris. Add another gram at the lower third of the vagina.
3. Hot flashes may be mitigated with Estroven natural supplements, which include black cohosh and rhubarb extract.
4. Progesterone is an antidepressant. It helps sleep and soothes edginess, anxiety, and panic. It is imperative in building bone. Estrogen is imperative in preventing bone breakage.
5. Anxiety and stress contribute to hot flashes. Consider incorporating yoga, meditation, and breathing exercises into your daily routine, even if it's fifteen minutes daily in the morning or evening.
6. Most experts suggest trying plant hormonal supplements before adding bioidentical hormones or hormone replacement therapy (HRT).
7. HRT and bioidentical hormone treatments have possible side effects, including increased blood clots, heart attacks, strokes, and endometrial and breast cancer.
8. The North American Menopause Society (www.menopause.org) has plenty of resources to read about menopause symptoms and treatment options.
9. Acupuncture and Chinese herbs might help lower menopausal symptoms such as hot flashes as well as Eden Energy Medicine.

10. Thoughts create your feelings. When you innocently believe a thought that says you're not enough, you'll feel anxiety and contraction. It's your cue to wake up to what thinking is doing. Allow the anxiety expression without changing or fixing it. Relax around it or follow the feeling in the body if you'd like. It's safe to relax. Despite having uncomfortable feelings, you really are okay at this moment. You are so much more than the fleeting feelings. You're doing so well with your journey.
11. You have my love and support as you navigate the waters of your hormonal health. I trust you'll make the right choice, even if it's trying several avenues before you settle on the program that works for you.

Chapter Fifteen

FEMALE SEXUALITY AFTER PELVIC RADIATION

I've been following various threads on Facebook. Sometimes, women vent about sexuality after radiation treatments. They tell their husbands at ages 38, 45, 60, and even 22 that they are done with intercourse because it's too painful and uncomfortable. The women report having no libido with reduced hormonal levels. I understand their pain and frustration.

From other women on the Facebook group who were sexually active, I learned about extremely dry vaginal and vulval linings and painful penetration with thrusting motions. Women wrote about bleeding and pain that comes from small tears of the vaginal lining or the scar tissue during the friction of intercourse. One woman told me that she needs to abstain from sexual intercourse for one week after intercourse to recover her vaginal wellness. I wondered what could be done about sexuality with decreased libido and vaginal damage during intercourse.

I believe sexuality touches women in different ways. There is no one way that is right for all. Sexuality brings women to sense their bodies. Women experience a grounding, a letting go of the mind chatter and the to-do list. They focus on the connection with their bodies and their partners' bodies. They connect with the feelings of love and sharing a beautiful intimacy. They feel pleasure, joy, laughter, intimacy, playfulness, and connection. It's precious, juicy, healthy, and alive.

For some women, sexuality consists of a lively physical connection with another being that brings the body to ultimate states of pleasure and the peak of an orgasm or a series of orgasms. It doesn't matter to them who that partner is as long as there is such a chemistry, skill, and connection that allows a freeing experience of physical rapture and ecstasy. Certainly, these are shared, beautiful, sacred, intimate, and peak experiences.

Other women's sexuality includes an appreciation of consistent time together, safety, trust, and security in the connection or the partners' commitment to each other. Only then do these women appreciate intimate touch and allow themselves to open their hearts and bodies. These women prefer connecting the heart, bodies, and minds. While most sexual encounters are goal-oriented, culminating in orgasm, some women and men prefer a physical connection of pleasuring each other in a way that isn't focused toward a single end.

Communication and Vulnerability

I've participated in both types of sexual encounters, where I know someone deeply or I don't. For me, satisfying sexuality is a shared connection of intimacy, kindness, caring, devotion, physical chemistry, adoration, love, and a depth of knowing each other. In addition, I appreciate the giving and receiving that accompanies a steady connection. For me, intimacy is also vulnerability; it's my ability to share my feelings, preferences, and experiences or share the sensations within me with another as we move through life. My partner creates intimacy by honestly sharing his thoughts, experiences, and preferences.

This kind of conversation can involve words or actions – or both. I find sexual connection satisfying when I'm with a consistent partner. An added layer of connection occurs when I share what is happening with me in relation to my partner. Intimacy for me is when I'm connecting with a partner where we both hold space for each other's life experience, being fully present for what's happening with the other without trying to change, fix, or judge the partner.

When I give and receive honest emotional communication with caring, devotion, and compassion to and from my partner, that's when I want to connect physically. When I am deeply heard, when I can share my good, bad, and ugly with my partner and have him fully present to my experience, I can relax with him. And when he's empathetic and communicates his understanding of my situation without changing my experience, trying to fix it, or having a fit about it, I connect.

This kind of communication arouses my sexuality; it unravels the layers within me. Then I wish to connect sexually. When I am witnessed, accepted, and appreciated by a partner for being exactly as I am, I open my heart and want to connect sexually. Communication and vulnerability open the heart in any partnership orientation.

One aspect of sexuality is a deep intimate verbal, listening connection that arouses my libido. Women who want intimacy this way and don't have it right now have ample opportunities to develop communication skills. I list resources in the back of the book that teach deep listening and sharing without changing another. I imagine that both partners can benefit from those closeness practices.

Another resource to help couples become comfortable with communication about sex is a book called *Woman Cancer Sex* by Anne Katz, RN, Ph.D. This book offers different scenarios of women through different types of cancer treatment and how to explain their changing sexuality and body reactions to their partners.

Acts of Kindness and Appreciation

Another means to sexuality for me is when I witness consistent thoughtfulness and kindness from my partner. When I spent time with my friend Toby, he mirrored an extraordinary level of care. He considered everything I said. And he was willing to help me when I wanted or needed support. He drove to see me when I was two hours away. He spent the night uncomfortably crouched in a hospital recliner chair without one word of complaint. Another time, he drove the whole night so we could be at our campsite in the morning when I wanted to go camping. In addition, it seemed as though Toby had eyes just for me.

Once, I mentioned to Toby that my mom had no photo of me in her house, and I felt sad that she had my siblings' photos but not mine. I said I wished she would ask me for a photo to put in her house. A few months later, he photographed me and, for my birthday, framed pictures in a triptych. He told me to send it to my mother. I cried at his thoughtful gesture. Because I was touched and moved by the deep care and support that Toby offered me and his unfailing devotion, I could connect with him sexually when we spent a long time together, even though I naturally did not want to connect with him physically. When I look for the depth of support and care of the people around me, my heart opens naturally, and if it's an available man I'm spending time with, I'll want to connect sexually with him.

If you are in a partnership with someone, I invite you to focus on how your partner adds value to your life. Does your partner listen to you or do things for you to make your life easier? How does your partner show their caring for you? The more you see how your partner considers you and makes an effort to help you, the more your heart will open, and your sexual libido will increase.

Communication, Listening, and Hormones

I recently listened to Dr. John Gray speak about how communication changes our hormones. He mentioned that when women are in their "doing" mode, their estrogen levels drop, and they begin to feel stressed. When stressed, they're prone to feeling insecure and complaining about everything wrong with their lives and partners. In this state, women will not want to connect sexually with their partner.

Dr. Gray suggests that a female-identified person needs to be heard, even when she's too tired or sick to engage sexually. Empathy and curiosity are what a woman needs in conversation. The moment a partner can open a safe space for the woman and listen and reflect an understanding of what she's saying without taking any of it personally, that's when a woman's estrogen level increases.

As estrogen rises, she can get into a balanced mood, and the complaints melt. There is nothing to change or fix about her. Women need a presence and talking to balance their hormones and increase their mood. Women need to be heard and understood, not fixed. This view is in line with how I open up with Toby. He's masterful at holding space for me and reflecting his understanding of my feelings and experience. And in turn, I want to share myself verbally and physically. I love that Dr. Gray connects this observation with hormones.

For a relationship to work, Dr. Gray suggests that anyone identified as a man needs to be accepted. He/They needs to know that his partner trusts him to make his own improvement. He does not want to be changed. He will be much less open to making changes if he feels rejected. Dr. Gray suggests accepting the partner without trying to change him.

When a person is partnered with a man and has a complaint about him, Dr. Gray suggests noticing the complaint and thinking about what the partner appreciates about him. If that's not accessible, maybe change the environment and focus on a hobby. I understand Dr. Gray's views, as each person has masculine and feminine energies. I love being listened to and understood and appreciate being accepted, not changed, and not complained about. I would want to know if what I did or said felt insensitive or unaware to my partner so I could grow, but not as a complaint or blame.

Gray also suggests that partners continue doing little acts of caring and presence at the same intensity as when they were dating to remind their partners of their care and attention. I suggest continuing to do acts of caring through cancer treatments. Actively courting a woman also raises her estrogen levels, and when her estrogen levels are high enough, she might be willing to connect in amorous, sensual ways.

Sex Therapists and Increasing Libidos

I listened to a CD set by Dr. Laura Berman, a relationship therapist. Her company makes and sells the Berman dilator set I bought. Dr. Berman speaks about sex and connection frankly with humor and ease. She has relationship experts on her show. Her experts talk about topics such as clitoral orgasms, G-spot orgasms, and sexual healing. I enjoyed browsing her website and listening to her podcasts. I noticed that the more I listened, the more aroused I became.

There are also sex therapists who help partners navigate through sexual and communication issues. On Dr. Berman's show, a sex therapist discussed how he was unhappy sexually in his early relationships. He didn't know how to talk about sex. Once he went to a sex therapist, he learned to communicate his needs and hear his partner's sexual needs. That made a huge difference in the quality of his sexual connection.

Some major hospitals have sexual health nurses who function like sex therapists. They can assist partners in becoming close sexually after cancer treatments. Likewise, there are sexologists. One online resource for women's sexual health is ROSY (meetrosy.com). It's an informative and safe space for women who have sexual concerns and want to learn and grow. Doctors and therapists run the site.

I noticed that while researching for this chapter and reading up on sexuality, I became aroused. It was at the forefront of my focus. People say that what we focus on grows. Consider taking time with your partner to explore sexuality by reading a book together about sexuality or listening to a Dr. Laura Berman podcast and seeing how it affects your sexuality. You can schedule a weekly date or however often fits your needs. You could also watch YouTube videos about breast stimulation, clitoral stimulation, slow sex, and other topics.

Tantra Practice for Arousal of the Female Sexual Body

A woman posted a comment on the Facebook page for women with vaginal radiation damage. She mentioned that doctors advised her to have as much sex as possible every other day if she could. She said to keep moving through the pain. If women avoid sex due to pain, she was told, that avoidance will contribute to stenosis, a condition in which the vagina becomes narrower and shorter due to the formation of fibrous tissue. Vaginal stenosis can contribute to sexual dysfunction and dyspareunia, making pelvic exams difficult and painful. To avoid getting worse, this woman said, women must push on. She said women must get to experience orgasm without intercourse so they do not come to associate sex with pain. Eventually, the pain will lessen as penetration becomes more commonplace.

This "push through the pain" attitude was not inviting for me, although I understood the need for regular stretching of the vaginal walls. I searched for a different solution for painful intercourse with possible bleeding and tears.

I knew something was missing from this chapter. I asked universal energy to help me find something to help myself and others. Within a couple of days, I received a thought that reminded me of a Tantra book I had with lovely connection practices for partners. I looked for a Tantra book for women and menopause and found *Tantric Sex and Menopause: Practices for Spiritual and Sexual Renewal* by Diana Richardson and Janet McGeever. Along with the doctor-recommended pain-reducing amitriptyline cream, vaginal hormonal cream, hormone balancing, and moisturizers, I believe these practices could alleviate some of the symptoms associated with vaginal lovemaking after radiation.

Tantra uses awareness in conjunction with the body's energy systems to expand energy and consciousness. It is a practice of being present in every moment, including during sex. In partner work, partners treat each other as expressions of the divine and use words, touch, and energy movements to expand each other's ability to be in the moment and harness the sexual energy that arises for healing.i

The book describes the conventional heterosexual way of lovemaking, but the description can also be used for same-sex couples using dildos or fingers to enter the vagina. The model is described as one that uses foreplay to create excitement by, for example, arousal of the lips and tongue, the breasts, and the male and female genitalia. The foreplay is followed by penetration, repetitive mechanical friction, heightened arousal energy that culminates in a peak experience of an orgasm or ejaculation, and a release of energy. With menopausal symptoms of vaginal dryness plus radiation-induced vaginal damage of a thin lining, scar tissue, and severe nerve pain, this approach may be too harsh on the delicate vaginal lining.

The authors illustrate the masculine and feminine energy polarities within every person and propose that the center of women's sexuality has been mistaken to match a man's center of sexuality. They explain that a woman's vagina and clitoris are sensitive and create intensity and excitement. However, it is not how a woman's body opens deeply and not where her deeper, more subtle sexual energy is raised. "The deeper opening of a woman's body happens via the breasts and nipples, and then, given the time, will be felt as a vibrational resonance or response that opens the vagina and makes the tissues receptive. Engaging a woman's body on this energetic level brings her to a true willingness, where she no longer submits to sex but participates fully."ii Thus, a woman's energy-raising sexual center is in the breast and heart area, while a man's energy-raising sexual center is in his genitals.

The healing chapter of the Tantra book mentions that, with menopause (and for those of us with radiation damage to the vagina), "the fragile walls of the vagina can suffer tears that can be very painful. Some women share that it feels like a knife cutting into them, and they bleed. When pain is anticipated, a woman's body will contract and become tense, even unconsciously. This creates a cycle of fearing intercourse, as mentally, pleasure is mixed with pain. This may lead to women feeling insecure and unworthy about sex."

Moreover, the authors share that pain disturbs the vagina and makes it more contracted and narrow; even the thought of painful intercourse can cause the pelvic muscles to tighten. Therefore, the authors propose a slower and more conscious process of lovemaking, with emphasis for women on the breasts first, which relaxes a woman's body and has a direct impact on the tissues of the vagina. "With relaxation and awareness, the cells of the vaginal wall and the whole pelvic floor have time to soften and expand, readying to invite and receive a penis as a welcomed guest rather than an invader and inflictor of pain."

Richardson and McGeever teach that slower sex, starting in the body's skin and gradually moving to the breasts, creates a relaxed lovemaking environment that gently stimulates the body's energy systems. This relaxation, in turn, stimulates the endocrine glands in the brain that bathe the whole body with soothing hormones that regenerate both partners. Soothing relaxation happens when the partners remain relaxed during sex instead of building and releasing energy through orgasm. It enables the aliveness to expand through the body.

When the vagina is more receptive, the authors explain, "the dynamic energy flow from the penis has a place to move. This action enables the vagina to soften, open, and recalibrate to become the absorbing, receptive organ nature designed it to be." With slow sex, "you will both be more available to the slightest nuance...this slowness and amplification of the senses for a menopausal woman…is tantalizing. She comes alive through slowness; her body naturally and gracefully responds. She can feel more rather than have her senses compressed by friction or mechanical movements. In the same way, man has more time to experience himself on another level. He can begin to open up to a world of sensitivity he may not have felt before with the sexual energy moving gently in waves toward his heart."

By following this way of lovemaking, relaxation in the sex centers can help a woman learn about her receptive energy and thus be empowered in her sexuality as well as transform the male into a loving, centered man who masters his energy.iii This method also creates relaxation for both partners and takes the pressure off the man to perform or attempt to satisfy his partner.

Richardson and McGeever suggest that if a woman feels pain anywhere along the vaginal canal during intercourse, she should try not to jerk away but rather gently speak with the partner and ask him to pull back his penis a tiny bit, as it will take the pressure off and allow for a release and dispersal of the tensions held there.iv

The authors encourage women to moisturize the vagina with coconut oil. In addition, they inform that adequate levels of balanced progesterone and estrogen (for women with a uterus) can solve significant discomfort (for example, with bioidentical hormones). Before intercourse, they suggest lubricating the penis and vagina with raw organic coconut oil, walnut oil, or pomegranate oil, testing it on the skin beforehand to ensure neither person has any allergic response to the oil.

Tantric Sex and Menopause contains numerous meditations and exercises designed to encourage slow sex and good communication skills with a partner. It addresses how to notice the emotional barriers people create to the partner and the sexual experience, work with the energy of feelings that has the potential to close our hearts and our minds, and restore the flow between the partners.

Trying It Out

I tried two of the breast meditations. I warmed coconut oil until it melted and added a few drops of organic frankincense and lavender oils. I followed the guidelines for both meditations; held, stroked, and gently caressed my breasts. I relaxed into the breasts, as suggested. It felt pleasant to relax into my breasts with no agenda, just letting the energy settle while holding the breasts. It's calming. After a while, I noticed my hands wanting to move the energy from my heart toward my genitals. I massaged the body down from my heart to the pubic bone for a while and then intuited that I wanted to use the melted coconut oil on the area of the vulva (inner and outer labia) and clitoris.

I used slow, gentle strokes over the genital area and, in time, noticed that I wanted to see what it would be like to use the dilators. It was a different experience than I'd had before using the dilators. I didn't need to use any vibration to distract the pain. The vagina wanted to have the dilator in it. I first used the thin silicone dildo while continuing to stimulate the area around the labia and clitoris gently. It was still painful but more pleasant than I've tried so far with any of the dilators.

Then I became curious about how a thicker silicone dildo would feel. I used a dildo shaped like a penis. I placed it, like the book suggests, at the entrance of the vagina, and to my surprise, the vagina wanted to take it in, like suction. In the past, this particular dildo had hurt, so I only used it once. It didn't hurt this time. I was surprised at how open the vagina was to receive.

I tried the Berman dilator set. I started with the usual medium-sized one. Again, I noticed that I did not need to use vibration to numb the pain sensation with penetration. I wondered if I could use the large size. Before this, the large dilator felt incredibly painful, and I could only put it in for about an inch before the pain was unbearable. There was also considerable pain this time, but I could insert the dilator about a third up the vagina. I made it a point to relax my breathing and go into the sensations of the pain without resisting them.

I was able to tolerate the dilator inside me for twenty seconds before I had to pull it out. This process was an improvement over my previous attempts to use this size dilator. I did bring myself to an orgasm at the end. I still wanted to experience an orgasm. I hoped that, in time, I would learn to stay with a lower level of sensation for longer times. New habits take time to assimilate.

I repeated the breast meditations a week later using warmed coconut oil and the three dilators. When I used the thin silicone dilator, it entered with light pain as it slid past the damaged nerves inside the vaginal wall. I told myself to relax as I became aware that the vagina tightened in response to the pain sensations. Once the vagina relaxed, I was able to insert the dilator easily. I continued with the thicker silicone penis-shaped dildo, which entered well, with the slightest pain sensations. Again, I didn't need to use any vibration with the medium Berman dilator. There were pain sensations as it slid past the damaged nerves.

Then I used the large-sized Berman dilator. There were pain sensations as it slid past the damaged nerves. Either I became scared of the pain, or the vagina felt the thickness and pain, and I felt the vagina contracting, which caused more pain. This time, I followed the book's suggestions to pull the dilator back a bit, and I focused on continuing to stroke the labia and clitoris gently to soothe and relax the pelvic area. Instead of feeling panic with the pain sensations, I chose to breathe and calm myself down. I could feel my vaginal tightness relax. Once relaxed, I gently stroked the clitoris to produce more sensation while remaining relaxed. I then gently inserted the dilator. This time, there was no constriction. It went the whole way in with no pain.

It's been more than two years since the end of radiation treatment. This session was the first time I could insert a large-sized dilator fully into the vagina, and that's after using this method twice. Before, I experienced the pain of my vagina contracting and the pain of the damaged nerves. I didn't know how to properly relax my vagina's reaction to pain by gently and slowly stroking the breasts and the vulva / clitoral region. I felt grateful that the methods outlined in *Tantric Sex and Menopause* worked for me.

A month after my last dilator experiment, I used the dilator, this time with minimal preparation around the breasts. The dilator penetration hurt. There are no shortcuts for preparation. I have a new normal. Attention to the arousal of the skin, then the breasts, and later the genitals is essential to a sexual connection when intercourse or penetration is desired with a penis, a dildo, or fingers.

Over several years of practice, I noticed that the breasts don't have to be stimulated to get a heightened arousal response. For women who've had breast removals, the area of the skin on the whole body can be caressed gently and patiently to arouse the body. Likewise, gentle stimulation around the entire vulva also awakens the energetic system. The most important thing I found is relaxing and enjoying touch while being together. When you're relaxed, the muscles of the vaginal canal and the entry point can relax and invite a penis or a dildo when ready.

Diana and her husband, Michael, lead a seven-day Tantra meditation retreat in Switzerland for couples called The Making Love Retreat.v Janet also leads a seven-day Tantra meditation retreat in Australia.viTantra is a world of gentle, loving connection on all levels. There are Tantra books and classes in most big cities. I took Tantra classes sporadically about ten years ago. I felt uncomfortable in every class practicing with strangers, but I was there to learn about the energy of sexuality. Another excellent book I read before cancer was *Tantric Secrets for Men: What Every Woman Will Want Her Man to Know about Enhancing Sexual Ecstasy* by Kerry and Diane Riley. This book has beautiful communication and intimacy practices to bring couples closer.

Slow Sex to Minimize Bleeding and Tearing

Diana Richardson's book, *Slow Sex: The Path to Fulfilling and Sustainable Sexuality,* explains how couples can use the slow sex approach to enhance the sexual experience for both people. I enjoyed reading about the slow process of penetration consisting of breathing slow, long breaths in concert with stopping penetration at points along the vaginal canal. It slows the process of penetration considerably, with timed breathing reminiscent of yoga.

Slow sex uses slow movements, and Diana claims it enhances pleasure sensations for both partners. This method does not use strong thrusts. A penis or dildo enters the vaginal canal, and both partners relax and allow whatever wants to arise to do so. They wait to see how they want to move. Perhaps there will be gentle movements. Maybe the couple will stay together in an embrace. This method outlines sex as being in the moment and seeing what arises for both partners without thrusting or expectations.

Overcoming Anger, Fear, and Shame

After discovering the associated pain with sexuality, it took me over a year to overcome my anger and grief at having my sexuality compromised by pain. It was the straw that broke the camel's back, one more thing I'd need to deal with and find solutions to. I felt exhausted from treatments and their aftermath. I mourned the loss of my sexual life at a young age. I blamed radiation and doctors for the vaginal damage and for withholding this information.

As a result, I experienced anger, rage, bitterness, depression, and shame. At the time, I had no solution to the vaginal damage. I was given no answer when I asked doctors. I also dreaded disclosing to a potential partner that pain would be associated with intercourse. I had fears that a potential partner might not want to be with me because of it. I felt embarrassed disclosing to a potential partner that after my second surgery, my underwear was soiled often and that I needed to shower before engaging in sex. I saw myself as physically damaged. It was a mentally challenging time for me until I found solutions.

Three and a half months after my reconnection surgery (2nd surgery), I went to a community retreat called Sahale's Human Relations Lab. I came intending to open myself to dating. This retreat helped me remember that I was a lovable and valuable person with love to share. I cried and grieved for what I wasn't and accepted what my body is today.

Two years after cancer treatments, I still wasn't dating much and had lost interest in sexuality. Then I signed up for the Oregon Tantra Festival online, where I took classes about connecting with myself, being my own lover, and touching my body with love and tenderness. I learned to take the pressure off anyone else needing to satisfy my touch needs. I could be my own lover.

The Live Practice...

More than three and a half years after my encounter with Toby, I met a sweet and handsome man who pursued me for a relationship. I wasn't sure we'd be life partners, so I hesitated. But we both felt the physical chemistry and were hungry for a physical connection.

I agreed to go out with him. After a while, he asked me about sex.

I shared with him how radiation affected my sexuality. I explained there was pain with penetration and that I was afraid of penetration. I told him of my multiple bathroom trips due to the surgeries, that I often shower multiple times daily, and that I felt embarrassed. For a while, we enjoyed each other's bodies, kissing, touching the bodies, and enjoying relaxing together.

After a couple of months, he suggested that we try intercourse. I asked him to read this chapter so he might understand more in-depth what I needed. I felt scared and apprehensive. We used lots of lubricant, starting with coconut oil. Then we tried slow penetration. We looked into each other's eyes and took a breath, then he entered his penis into my vagina on my time, with our eyes communicating silently. I felt pain and asked him to stop and for us to breathe together. We breathed while I relaxed the vagina and my whole body. When I was ready again, we inhaled together, and with the exhale, he entered my vagina deeper until I asked him to stop to allow me to relax. Then we took another breath, and he entered my vagina fully in the next exhale. I asked him to stop and wait, and he did. I breathed until my vagina relaxed. It had been three and a half years since engaging in intercourse.

Once the penis was entirely in, we engaged in intercourse. In subsequent trials, we used walnut oil, which I liked more for its viscosity. It took a while before we found a small dispenser with a push-down mechanism where the oil didn't spill on the sheets. Our first few trials were more common, regular intercourse with friction. With each penetration, we practiced breathing and inserting the penis slowly. This partner had a normal-sized penis, making it easier to insert and make love. I didn't have to use the pain-reducing amitriptyline cream with him.

Then, one day, we practiced slow sex, just keeping the penis in and seeing what wanted to move and when. I enjoyed this practice much more than the usual friction. It was relaxing. It also allowed natural lubrication to build in a juicy way. I loved connecting in the slow sex method. I always felt pain with penetration when I didn't use amitriptyline, but it was doable with breathing and slow penetration. When we engaged in consistent intercourse practice, the pain with penetration reduced. I never had bleeding. I'm grateful to be able and willing to connect in this way.

A year after I left this relationship, I met another handsome man to practice with. We had beautiful physical chemistry, and he was interested. He read this chapter and ordered a tantra book, which he read thoroughly. He was open to feedback about slowing down. We practiced extended foreplay with slow sex and penetration. Without amitriptyline, penetration was somewhat painful but was lessened with slow penetration. After penetration, intercourse felt amazingly satisfying and pleasurable. Our lifestyles didn't fit, and we both moved on, blessing each other with a more fitting partner.

More Resources

I've been listening to some experts about Tantra and sexuality. I listened to Dr. Nancy Moonstar's series called *A Man's Guide to Intimacy: Open Her Up to Tell You What She Wants*. One of the interviewees, Susan Bratton, mentioned that a woman's erectile tissue is not just in the external clitoris. The erectile tissue, she said, is also in the vulval and labial areas. She and her husband make it a habit for him to gently massage her entire erectile tissue before lovemaking.

I received the 2 percent amitriptyline in an Aloe oil solution to assess if it would sting. It didn't. The method is to place a few drops of the solution at the entrance of the vagina and let the substance travel up on its own into the nerves.

If a female rectal patient undergoing cancer treatment wants to maintain a sexual connection with her partner and doesn't know how to broach the subject, I would encourage her to be brave, authentic, and honest. You are dealing with a body that has been altered medically. You are not flawed; you are not less than you were before. You are a beautiful being with a lot of love to share. Celebrate yourself. And be courageous and slow in your experimentation, vulnerability, and honesty. Ask for what you need. Ask for slow sex.

I recommend another book, *Sex and Cancer, Intimacy, Romance, and Love After Diagnosis and Treatment*, by Guntupalli, MD, and Karinch. In chapter seven of this book, the authors suggest sexual healing practices that are not goal oriented. The exercises are designed to reconnect gradually after the trauma of cancer treatments. Of course, sexuality does not require penetration. There are many ways two bodies can enjoy each other without penetration. Books, websites, classes, therapists, and intuition can help if you need more information or suggestions.

Sexual Healing in a Group

For people who want to heal sexually within a group, there is a movement called New Culture. "New Culture people are dedicated to examining every aspect of our existing cultures and experimenting to find out how to create a world based on love and freedom, rather than fear and violence. In our explorations, we have looked at everything from inner aspects of one's self-experience to global consequences of our societal choices. Some areas we have focused on include: methods of dealing with painful emotional reactions, developing healthy boundaries, conflict resolution skills; alternative models of family, community and "tribe"; improving communication across gender, ethnic, and racial line; acceptance of neurodiversity and diverse mental experiences; freedom in sexual and loving connections; freedom from shame around our sexuality; reducing consumption and global impact of our lifestyles; living in healthy relationship to children; making sustainable choices around food and diet; organizing to create local, regional, and global change. Our Hawai'i camps offer a unique depth and quality of experience."

Before cancer, I'd taken some classes with Amara Karuna, one of the New Culture practitioners, in Los Angeles, as part of sexual growth classes. I have appreciated the practices. Amara was also one of the organizers of the Oregon Tantra Festivals I attended.

Another way to heal sexually in a group is through the Orgasmic Meditation movement. I heard about it from several friends who had attended their groups. They gained value and sexual healing. They had experiences of "normalizing" sex, acquiring authentic communication skills about sexuality, speaking their truth, de-personalizing sex, not shaming anything that is a natural human reaction, and the experience of being honest with boundaries and self-expression. I recently read a fascinating account of a man living in such a community. If people are interested in exploring this option for sexual healing after cancer within a sexually accepting community, you might be interested in this article.vii The practice of slowly stimulating the clitoris for fifteen minutes very gently seems to cause heightened states of awareness, the same as Tantra practices.

I know sexuality after radiation treatments is a delicate, sensitive area to navigate. You might have a full or partial vagina after your surgery. If you have a partial vagina or a reconstructed vagina (from the small intestines or otherwise), penetration might be painful and can only go as far as it does. You might not have sensations in a reconstructed vagina and need to research more resources. You might have a partial vaginal blockage from scar tissue. I'm certain there are more options than what I presented in this book. Check with your doctors whether urologists, gynecologists, sexual health providers, tantra teachers, or other patients on the Colorectal Facebook pages.

Please be as tender, compassionate, and loving with yourself as you can. You and your partner will need to navigate these new waters. I honor your courage in initiating a conversation about a new way to be sexual and sensual with your partner. I believe in your ability to find your way with your new body. You are beautiful, loving, and powerful. You have my love and tenderness as you explore your new sexuality.

SUMMARY AND SUGGESTIONS

1. To raise a woman's libido, her partner should deeply listen to her. If a partner can deeply hear a woman and reflect the essence of what she's saying without fixing, changing, or blaming her, the woman's estrogen will rise. When estrogen increases, her mood returns to balance; as she's listened to, she'll want to connect sexually, that is, if she's not actively undergoing cancer treatment, pain, and fatigue.
1. To increase libido, a woman or a couple can listen to podcasts about sexuality, for example, Dr. Laura Berman's podcast.
1. To learn how to talk about sexuality, a couple can go to a sex therapist or a sexual health nurse, read a book, or start by sharing honestly and courageously.
1. A woman's body opens via the skin, breasts, and nipples. Given time, the vibration will open the vagina and make the tissues receptive to a penis. Authors Richardson and McGeever recommended that couples spend ample time relaxing a woman's skin and stroking or kissing the breasts (not the nipples).
1. Thoughts of anticipated pain close a woman's body, and the vagina will contract and tense. The sensation of pain

contracts and narrows the vagina, which creates more pain. This fear can affect a woman's confidence, and she might feel insecure or unworthy about her sexuality.

6. Relaxation of the body is the preparation for satisfying intercourse. Start by stimulating the skin (excluding the genitalia), then stimulate the breasts (excluding the nipples). This way, instead of arousing the woman too quickly, the endocrine system will make soothing hormones that bathe and relax a woman's body. When a woman's body is bathed in hormones and relaxed, the vagina gets ready to receive a penis as a welcomed guest.
7. If a woman feels pain during lovemaking, she needs to speak gently with her partner and ask her partner to pull his penis or the dildo back a bit.
8. Consider using a method of slow sex, super slow penetration that accompanies breathing, and having a no-goal lovemaking session to explore slow sensations. Slow sex might minimize vaginal tears, bleeding, and pain and heighten both partners' sensations.
9. There are online Tantra teachers and Tantra festivals.
10. You can learn to be your own lover, share pleasure with yourself, and take your partner off the hook from needing to please you.
11. For healing sexually within a group, there is a New Culture Group in Hawaii and Orgasmic Meditation centers all over the world.

Chapter Sixteen

MALE SEXUALITY AFTER PELVIC RADIATION

Just like for women, sexuality for men is vital and health-promoting. Sexuality is a celebratory and beautiful part of living in a body. It's also about sharing love and pleasure with a partner and connecting physically, emotionally, mentally, and spiritually. Sexuality brings aliveness and can relax both partners.

Engaging in sexuality is also a way to focus on the body and the present moment sensations. The process of inviting, creating a sacred space, welcoming the beloved, touching, looking, caressing, slowing down the process, enjoying, engaging, pleasuring, connecting, giving, receiving, feeling, sensing, and climaxing takes men out of their heads and to-do lists and brings them present to the joy and aliveness of life. It's like pressing a reset button.

In addition, men informed me that they derive much joy and purpose from being able to pleasure their partner and to see their partner enjoy themselves. They love to provide, to help the partner unravel, relax, and claim pleasure. They love to see their partner orgasm. Couples bond through their sexuality, physicality, verbal communication, fun, play, playfulness, sexual healing, the released hormones, and the ensuing relaxation. Many men view sexuality with their partner as sacred.

Men can also benefit from slowing down sexuality. They can connect with their partner's energy center, breathe together, and set an intention for their time together. They can focus on appreciation and on seeing the beauty and divinity in the other. They can caress the energy body first, then the skin very lightly, then gently touching, hugging, kissing, holding, massaging, and checking in with their partner about how it feels. Even slow penetration, feeling the sensations, stopping, breathing, focusing on the sensations, entering further, then keeping the penis in without trying to climax, being in the unknown, can be more satisfying than the usual mechanical thrusting and climaxing. Some men enjoy creativity, games, monogamy, or polyamory.

I wondered how rectal cancer treatments affect the physicality of male sexuality. I asked for feedback on this topic on the colorectal Facebook pages, asked friends, and researched the internet to learn that there could be various outcomes from treatment, from dry orgasms to impotence. Let's look at the technicalities.

Dry Orgasm

I asked one of my friends who underwent rectal cancer treatments how treatment affected his sexuality. He said sex felt the same to him. He enjoys sex and can have an erection. He can experience an orgasm, though the ejaculate is dry, without semen. According to oncolink.org, "radiation therapy damages the prostate gland and seminal vesicles, which are responsible for creating the fluid that makes up ejaculate. In turn, ejaculate after radiation therapy for prostate cancer is diminished or absent (called dry ejaculation). This is not harmful and does not affect the ability to achieve orgasm."[i]

My.clevelandclinic.org mentions that the prostate gland resides below the bladder and in front of the rectum in people assigned male at birth. The prostate gland adds fluid to the semen, and the prostate muscles help push semen through the urethra. The semen the body produces will either stay in the testicles or be pushed into the bladder.

Painful Orgasm During Radiation Treatment

Some men wrote that while they were going through radiation treatment, orgasm was painful. According to the charity Cancer Research UK website, "Having a sharp pain when you ejaculate can be a side effect of radiotherapy to the abdomen or pelvis. This is because the radiotherapy can irritate the tube that goes through the penis from the bladder (the urethra). The pain should ease off a few weeks after the treatment ends".ii A woman shared with me that her husband had sensitivity during ejaculation while receiving radiation treatment. It went away a few weeks after radiation was over as the area healed.

One man wrote that a year after cancer treatments, he's still experiencing painful ejaculations. Another man suggested he take Cialis, which helps regulate the prostate. He said it took a couple of weeks, and his pain weaned. A different man said he had pain after urination and received alpha-blockers. Speak with your urologist about possible solutions

Testosterone Count Reduction

One man wrote that his testosterone count decreased after treatments, and he couldn't have strong erections. Many men have lower testosterone levels after rectal cancer treatments. In the prostate gland, testosterone is transformed into a biologically active form, dihydrotestosterone (DHT).iii The man who wrote manages his erections with weekly testosterone injections and Viagra. He says that although it was a shot to his male ego, using Viagra was one of his best decisions ever.

Another guy reported that he felt very stressed during treatments. His testosterone count went down. He, too, is taking weekly testosterone injections. Unfortunately, this man also reported having scar tissue buildup in his penis from radiation treatments. Scar tissue can cause fibrosis which can build up for several years after radiation treatment has finished. Fibrosis can prevent strong erections.iv The worst part for this man is that his erection doesn't last as long as it did before treatment.

Another fellow shared with me that he has a low libido, and when he does get excited sexually, he has an immediate orgasm and ejaculation. It's incredibly frustrating to him and his partner as they're just starting, and it's over for him. Because testosterone gives people libido, some men with low testosterone counts report not wanting to engage in sexual activity often. One gentleman told me that he is just not as interested in sex as he was before.

Impotence

One person told me he has the desire but no erection. I learned that this could be due to surgery or radiation. Surgery can damage the parasympathetic and sympathetic nerves responsible for erection and ejaculation. At the same time, radiation therapy may cause nerve damage to the nerves and blood vessels involved in erections and scar tissue buildup.v

Another man wrote that his male parts shut down permanently, and now he has severe back problems, which might be caused by radiation therapy damage.

The treatment process can be so physically and emotionally stressful and demoralizing to some men that they won't engage in intercourse. One woman told me that her husband wouldn't even try to engage in intercourse for two years as the process was upsetting and traumatic for him.

Urination Issues

For most men, the urinary system will recover after radiation. Yet, for a few men, their urinary system will be damaged with radiation treatment. A gentleman wrote that years after having radiation, he experienced problems with his ureters, the tubes that connect the excreted fluid from the kidneys to the bladder. At one point, he had both a colostomy and a nephrostomy bag strapped to his legs to collect urine. Luckily, he had reconstructive surgery, which fabricated ureters from his intestines. His new ureters are functioning well, and he is elated. Although radiation "fried" his ureters, he appreciates being alive.

Erectile Dysfunction

The Mayo Clinic reports erectile dysfunction (ED) is "the most common sexual side effect of cancer treatment for men." These side effects include the "inability to achieve or maintain an erection, difficulty climaxing, orgasm without discharge of semen, weaker or less satisfying orgasms, loss of interest in sex, pain during sex, less energy for sexual activity, and feeling less attractive. Surgery, radiation therapy, hormone therapy, chemotherapy, and other medications can all cause sexual side effects."

Surgeons do their best to spare the nerves involved with creating an erection; however, at times, the tumor's location is such that the nerves must be cut. Sometimes the side effects appear right after surgery; at other times, they start slowly six months to a year after treatment. Men with a history of heart disease, high blood pressure, or diabetes may be at a higher risk of ED after radiation therapy as those conditions cause artery damage that may be made worse by radiation.

The Mayo Clinic article notes that some chemotherapy drugs also reduce the amount of testosterone produced in the body. This reduction could mean a loss of libido and difficulty achieving an erection after chemotherapy. The effects of chemotherapy drugs typically wear off within a few weeks after treatment.vi

Sexually active men who can get their partner pregnant should wear a condom if having sexual intercourse while having treatment and for several months after treatment. The effects of radiation and chemotherapy may damage sperm for some time, and chemotherapy could transfer to the partner through fluid exchange.

The Mental-Emotional Effects

Sexual issues can bring low moods for some men. Low libido and no or super-fast ejaculation can lead to thoughts of insecurity, frustration, lack of worthiness, anxiety, fear, anger, or depression. A man may feel defeated and not want to connect with his partner. He could withdraw emotionally from the connection, affecting his health and mood even further.

If you're a man who lost sexual function due to cancer treatments, I can imagine you might feel devastated and want a solution. You might be angry, bitter, or grieving a beautiful part of your relationship that is gone. I so get it. I hold you with tenderness and compassion. I was angry for nearly two years until I found solutions to my sexual damage. Consider being kind and gentle with yourself right now. Consider having empathy and compassion for your healing path. You chose life and did what had to be done. I encourage you to accept yourself, your choices, and what is occurring in your life. Give yourself time for your mind to settle into your new reality.

In addition, I gently remind you that believing your thinking is causing your feelings and how you're interpreting what happened to you. If you live in past comparisons to how you were, you might believe your current sexuality has left you damaged and unworthy of love. Notice how contracted and distant from the flow of life that thinking feels. Give yourself time to settle that kind of thinking. Love yourself as a beautiful, giving, creative, loving, and unique expression of life. That has stayed the same.

Consider doing activities that bring you joy and engagement in life. They will help balance you and relax your attachment to painful thinking. When your thinking settles, you'll feel more balanced and open to new perspectives.

Perhaps you'd realize that as much as you'd like to bring the past back, you cannot. The past is in the past and is truly gone. You only live in this moment. At this moment, you are a handsome, vibrant man with much love to share in the world, including with yourself. Accept yourself and love yourself as you are right now; the only moment there ever is. Right now, you are gorgeous. You are breathing, lying on a couch, or sitting on a chair; your back and body are supported, and the wind moves the leaves on a tree. Without a thought that goes against this moment, life is quiet. I invite you to accept life as it is, including your body. Consider speaking with your partner, a therapist, or a support group to help you accept yourself and your new body.

If you're in an intimate relationship, I suggest you speak with your partner about what you're experiencing. That communication alone might bring the partners a sense of connection and vulnerability. Your partner might feel rejected if you withhold your concerns and thoughts. In addition, it's also helpful to notice what action or fantasy still pleases you right now. Let your partner know what works for you so you can share the experience together. Maybe your partner might have ideas to help you regain sexual function. In addition, you may consider speaking with a sex therapist. You can always use the colorectal cancer Facebook pages to ask other men how they deal with their sexual issues after cancer treatments.

The spiritual teacher Byron Katie reminds me that things happen for us, not to us. If treatments compromised your sexuality, how can it benefit you, and why is it a good thing in your life? Do you want to take the time and learn how to connect with your partner on more levels of pleasure that may not include the same kind of sexual ritual you had before?

What are your thoughts about learning to pleasure yourself and your partner more subtly, giving massages, connecting with the energy systems and breathing, slowing things down, communicating more openly, and opening your heart to your partner and yourself? Would you and your partner like to read tantra books or other love-making guides for couples? Would you be more communicative and open with your partner? There are books devoted to pleasuring a penis (often called a lingam). Did you know that you can have a full-body orgasm without ejaculation? Did you know that you can experience an orgasm without an erection?

What occurred could be an incentive to grow as a lover. How can you be a better lover to yourself and your partner regardless of any sexual issue you face? How can you drop into a deeper level of love and acceptance for yourself and your partner as you are? How can you be in the present moment without habitual comparisons to a past that doesn't exist except as a thought in your mind? How can you find even more joy and fun in life and love-making?

More Treatment Options for ED

According to the Mayo Clinic, if the sexual side effects of cancer treatments do not resolve fully, but you can still get erections, pay attention to what helps. Does more extended foreplay help with erections? Is it self-stimulation or sexual fantasies?

Please check in with your urologist about your testosterone levels and whether it would be helpful to take Viagra, Cialis, or Levitra orally. It could be a valuable addition to your sexual life.

If those drugs don't work well for you, there is also a therapy called the Muse System (Medicated Urethral System for Erection). This system uses prostaglandin E1 (the drug is alprostadil) as either an injection directly into the penis or a suppository placed into the urethra (the opening in the penis where urine and semen exit) using an applicator. Alprostadil makes the blood vessels expand, thus bringing blood flow to the penis. It is more effective as an injection (works for 80 percent of men) than a suppository (works for 30-40 percent of men).vii

If alprostadil alone doesn't work, there are specialty compounded medications you can inject directly into the base of the penis with a needle to create an erection. Your urologist might know of such compounds and whether they would work for you. Follow the instructions carefully. One medication is Trimix-11 Injectable Compound (0.3- 0.4 ml per injection). This compound is made with alprostadil 30 MCG/ ML, papaverine 30 MG/ML, and phentolamine MES, 2MG/ML. This compound expands blood vessels and increased blood flow engorges the penis. After fifteen minutes, a man experiences an erection lasting a couple of hours. This approach is not pain-free. I have heard that when the blood recedes into the body, a man can experience pain, and injecting oneself with a small needle could create momentary pain.

Another option is the penile implant system. Some implants have malleable rods that are surgically placed in the penis. The rods are connected to an inflator/deflator bulb placed inside the scrotum. A fluid reservoir is surgically placed in the pelvic area, and all systems are connected. Fluid from the reservoir is pumped to the rods in the penis, erecting the penis. To make this happen, a man repeatedly pushes on the bulb at the scrotum to pump the fluid into the penis. Most men who underwent this procedure I have spoken to have been elated to have this option. They can have an erection at will and sustain it for as long as they'd like. For men who have no erection at all, a penile implant operation is a viable option.viii

For many men undergoing treatments, dry orgasm is the only side effect they'll have. If you're in the other categories, you have options. Check with your urologists as new treatments are available. I recently heard of a new Botox therapy for ED. Remember to be compassionate with yourself as you navigate your new sexuality. You chose life, and you did whatever you could to be here. Own your depth of love for yourself and your family. You have true grit and fortitude. Your sexuality may not be what it used to be, but you can still enjoy sex. It might even be better. You could become an even more sensitive, caring, more aware lover. You have my love and support as you navigate your new sexuality.

SUMMARY AND SUGGESTIONS

1. If you've had rectal cancer treatments, your sexuality may be compromised. There is a considerable variation in outcome based on surgery, radiation, tumor location, tumor size, and pre-existing conditions.
2. If you're experiencing a low libido or soft erections, have your doctor check your testosterone levels.
3. If your erections are soft, consider talking with your urologist about taking Viagra, Cialis, or Levitra. If these don't work for you, there are injectable compounds that a compound pharmacy can make for you. Find a urologist who knows which combinations could help. There is also the Muse suppository system. Consider consulting with your urologist about all options.
4. Consider talking with your partner about your experience. Are there times when you can be stimulated and have some erection? Does it happen through self-pleasuring or fantasizing? Consider speaking with your partner about what you are going through so that your partner does not feel rejected.
5. Sex therapists are available to speak with you. There are also sexual health nurses who specialize in the side effects of cancer treatment.

6. If none of the above treatments work for you, you may consider a penile implant. Please speak with your urologist about it. I've heard from at least four men how grateful and happy they are for their implant and the return of their sex lives. They reported that healing from the surgery was painful but well worth it.
7. If cancer treatments have compromised your sexuality, I can imagine the devastation and mourning you may be experiencing. Please remember that you are not alone. Reach out to other patients on Facebook support groups.
8. I wonder how your new sexuality could be good for you. Do you want to take the opportunity and grow as a lover to your partner and yourself? Do you want to open your heart to yourself even more, love and accept yourself at every time and condition you go through?
9. Remember that your feelings are a product of your thinking. You are not your thinking or your feelings. You can't be something that comes and goes many times a day. You are the vast, intelligent space beyond the fluctuations of the mind. Relax. Let the thinking settle. Come back to your center of well-being. From there, decide what you'd like to try and experiment with next. Be curious about the next steps. Your body has changed, and you're in the process of experimenting. Be kind to yourself as you do your research. You have my love and support.

Chapter Seventeen

WHAT'S NEW AND OLD WITH THE STANDARD OF CARE FOR RECTAL CANCER — FOR NERDS

When I asked stage II/III rectal cancer survivors on the Facebook forums if they had advice for a new patient, several said they wished they had known how much havoc radiation would cause. They weren't told how harmful the vaginal effects would be. Other survivors said they would have skipped radiation because the long-term side effects were too much to bear.

One person described how radiation relieved his pain from the tumor before having surgery and chemo. Years later, he experienced trouble with his ureters not draining urine from his kidneys to the bladder. He dealt with stents, nephrostomy bags, and reconstructive surgery. He now has stage III-b kidney disease. The targeted radiation affected his ureters. Another woman wrote about the aftermath of radiation and, being a young woman, dealing with the pain with sex, diarrhea, constipation, and gas.

Another survivor said her doctors downplayed the side effects of radiation. She had significant pain and incontinence issues that she was not expecting. She is disappointed that the medical profession doesn't tell patients how to deal with these side effects. She would have loved to have had a simple chart outlining what to try for side effects instead of playing telephone tag with nurses and doctors.

Dr. McGee, who's been doing advocacy work on behalf of women for several years after her cancer journey, told me that radiation keeps working in the body for years after surgery. She's spoken to women who began having bladder damage four to five years after radiation and whose vaginas continue to deteriorate following radiation treatments. She said the ionizing energy that radiation creates in the body continues to work for up to twenty years after the end of radiation treatment.

One article states, "The accumulated radiation dose to the pelvic organs is important for acute bowel, bladder, and genital toxicity. Radiation effects are progressive and may become symptomatic after a latent period, but there may be a continuous progression from the acute oedema, mucosal and sub-mucosal inflammation, and persistent ulceration and necrosis to fibrosis...On the longer term, vaginal wall thinning, adhesions, atrophy, and fibrosis may occur often followed by decreased vaginal elasticity, narrowing, shortening and ultimately total vaginal stenosis... Further, ischaemia from radiation... may give rise to a fragile neovasculature that tends to bleed. The end result may include vaginal and vaginal entrance stenosis and fragility. Similar effects are observed in the bladder and rectum, resulting in late effects as urgency, hemorrhagic cystitis, tenesmi, and fecal incontinence."I This article acknowledges that radiation treatment impairs sexual function, and its effects last beyond the treatment time.

I wondered if radiation was necessary for rectal cancer stage II/ III. I understood radiation therapy shrinks the tumor and decreases the likelihood of a local recurrence by seven percent. I wondered if there could be selective radiation use or a lower dose. Are there options? Should there be a discussion about choosing whether to use radiation treatment or not depending on the Carcinoembryonic

Antigen (CEA) marker, how spread the tumor is in the pelvis, how advanced and aggressive the cancer is when diagnosed, and a family history of osteoporosis?

The National Institute of Health (NIH) conducted clinical trials with a PROSPECT study evaluating whether using only chemotherapy and surgery is an appropriate choice for most patients. The study compares patients not receiving radiation treatment with a control group, which gets the standard treatment of chemoradiation followed by surgery and chemotherapy. The experimental group receives a higher dose of heavy-duty chemotherapy for six cycles. Afterward, the patient has an MRI or an endoscopic ultrasound to evaluate the tumor size. If the tumor has shrunk by 20 percent, the patients proceed to surgery, then follow up with four to eight cycles of the same chemotherapy. The patient will receive chemoradiation if the tumor borders are abnormal after excision. Suppose the tumor does not decrease by 20 percent. In that case, the patients will receive Xeloda and radiation.ii The chemotherapy agent has side effects of long-term neuropathy, short-term nausea, and heat-cold sensitivity.

Doctors have administered low-dose radiation therapy in Europe for the past twenty years. The treatment consists of a lower radiation dose five times a day for five days (about half the daily dosage used in the United States per day). An analysis of several studies "demonstrated that preoperative short-term radiation is as effective as long-term radiation treatment for the treatment of rectal cancer in terms of overall survival and disease-free survival."iii I researched articles to find whether this lower dose gave a better outcome for women's sexual health. Still, I did not find any article addressing this issue.

How have rectal cancer treatments changed over the years until chemoradiation surgery became the standard of care? In the 1970s and '80s, rectal cancer recurrence rates were 50 percent at five years.

iv Several studies looked at patients treated with chemoradiation and surgery and found significantly lower recurrence rates than those who only received chemo, radiation, or surgery alone.v

From studies like this, researchers learned that the chemotherapy agent 5-FU acts as a radiation sensitizer by improving the effectiveness of radiation therapy. In 1990 the NIH declared chemo, radiation, and surgery as the standard of treatment for rectal cancer stage II/III.vi Further studies in 2004 determined that chemo and radiation before surgery (called neoadjuvant) were more effective at reducing local recurrences.vii

Surgical standards for rectal cancer have also improved and contributed to higher survival rates. In 1979, a British surgeon, Bill Heald, published the surgical excision technique for rectal cancer. He excised the entire rectum with its surrounding perirectal lymphatic tissue contained within a thin fascial layer. This surgery is called Total Mesorectal Excision (TME).ix In 1986, Heald published a paper reporting his first series of statistics for 112 rectal cancer patients who underwent surgical TME. His results show a remarkable five-year local recurrence rate of 2.7 percent, with the probability of survival at five years at 87 percent. The tumor-free survival by stage is 94 percent, 87 percent, and 58 percent.x After more experiments validating Heald's numbers, Heald's publication helped introduce TME as a standard surgical technique for this operation.

A study in Norway between 1993-1997 with 3,319 patients with rectal cancer studied the local recurrence, survival, and postoperative mortality and morbidity difference between standard rectal excision (not excising the whole rectum) and TME. They found that local recurrence rates for patients up to stage III was 6 percent in the group treated by TME and 12 percent in the conventional surgery group. Four-year survival rate was 73 percent after TME and 60 percent after conventional surgery. Radiotherapy was given to 5 percent and chemotherapy to 3 percent of the patients in the curative resection group. The article concludes that the technique of TME can be widely distributed, and surgery alone can give good results.xi

TME has produced excellent local control of cancer. Because of this dramatic improvement in local control reported by earlier studies, some have questioned whether chemoradiation therapy is necessary to achieve acceptable local recurrence rates.

The Dutch Colorectal Cancer Group undertook a study investigating the efficacy of preoperative radiotherapy in combination with TME for rectal cancer and its impact on overall survival. The researchers divided patients into two groups: short-term preoperative radiotherapy (5 Gy on each of five days) followed by TME (924 patients) or TME surgery alone (937 patients).

After two years, the overall survival rate in the radiation group was 82 percent. In the surgery alone group, it was 81.8 percent, essentially the same. The local recurrence rate at two years was 2.4 percent in the radiotherapy-plus-surgery group and 8.2 percent in the surgery-only group, which is a significant difference. The rate of distant disease was 14.8 percent in the radiation group and 16.8 percent in the surgery alone group, which is also a significant difference.

The Dutch study concluded that short-term preoperative radiotherapy reduces the risk of local recurrence in patients with rectal cancer who undergo a standardized TME. They showed that preoperative radiotherapy combined with TME is beneficial for local disease control but does not affect overall survival despite a higher incidence of distant disease in patients not receiving neoadjuvant radiotherapy.xii

At present, for stage II/III, with the protocol of neoadjuvant radiation therapy (RT), chemo, TME surgery, followed by operative chemotherapy treatments, local recurrence is at 5 to 6 percent. In comparison, metastases remain at 25 percent recurrence within a five-year after-surgery interval.xiii

In addition, some people who received chemoradiation show no cancer cells in the rectal tissue sample examined after surgical removal like me. How does the percentage survival rate change when patients have a total response to early treatment of six weeks of radiation and Xeloda pre-surgery?

Several papers report slightly different findings. In one pooled analysis, the authors say that 15 to 27 percent of patients achieve a complete response.xiv The analysis demonstrated that the five-year survival rate of patients who achieved a complete response and then had surgery was 83 percent compared with 66 percent. Additionally, the five-year distal metastases-free survival rate was 89 percent in the complete response group and 75 percent in the non-complete response group. This analysis concluded that patients who achieved complete response had better long-term outcomes with organ preservation, decreased likelihood of developing both local and distant recurrence, and improved disease-free survival.xv

There may also be patients with a complete response who may be candidates for a "watch-and-wait" approach—thus avoiding surgery. In a study done in the UK, patients who achieved a complete response had a 34 percent recurrence.xvi

Another Dutch group wanted to compare the overall quality of life for patients with radiation treatments with patients who underwent TME alone. A study assessed the presence and magnitude of long-term side effects of preoperative radiotherapy and TME. They studied 597 patients, with a median follow-up period of 5 years. Stoma function, urinary function, and hospital treatment rates did not differ significantly between the treatment protocols. However, irradiated patients, compared with nonirradiated patients, reported increased rates of fecal incontinence (62 percent v 38 percent), pad wearing as a result of incontinence (56 percent v 33 percent, respectively), anal blood loss (11 percent v 3 percent), and mucus loss (27 percent v 15 percent).

Satisfaction with bowel function was significantly lower, and the impact of bowel dysfunction on daily activities was greater in irradiated patients than in patients who underwent TME alone. The study concludes that "although short-term preoperative radiotherapy for rectal cancer results in increased local control, there is more long-term bowel dysfunction in irradiated patients than in patients who undergo TME alone. Rectal cancer patients should be informed of the late morbidity of both radiotherapy and TME. Future strategies should be aimed at selecting patients for radiotherapy who are at high risk for local failure." xvii

Radiotherapy decreases people's quality of life while reducing the likelihood of local recurrence. These papers suggest that radiotherapy can improve local recurrence by about 6 to 7 percent. For those who achieve a complete or downgraded response, the percent survival is even higher. But radiotherapy significantly impacts sexual health, bowel control, and urinary health. Should patients be informed of all possible side effects? Should patients be aware of and included in a discussion?

Because of the extensive damage from radiation, Memorial Sloan Kettering Cancer Center, in 2010, evaluated the concept of selective use of chemoradiation for patients. They enrolled stage II/III rectal cancer patients with tumors 5 to 12 cm from the anal verge. Patients received strong chemotherapy for six cycles, followed by re-staging. Those with a clinical response from the induction regimen received no further preoperative treatment (no radiation) and proceeded to TME surgery. Patients who did not respond adequately received additional chemoradiation therapy before surgery.

Of the 32 patients enrolled, 30 patients achieved a marked response with chemotherapy alone. The remaining two patients who could not tolerate chemotherapy received CRT instead. This pilot study demonstrated that chemotherapy alone is sufficient for local and distant disease control in carefully selected patients and provided the background to support the currently ongoing prospect study available across the United States.xviii

Likewise, in 2015, a Chinese study enrolled stage II / III rectal cancer patients and divided them into three groups. One group received the standard 5FU with RT (control arm, the standard of treatment today), another group received mFOLFOX6 (strong chemotherapy) with RT, and the third group got four to six cycles of mFOLFOX6 alone.

Preliminary results demonstrated that the resection rates were 90.1 percent (control arm), 88.2 percent (FOLFOX-RT arm), and 91.2 percent (FOLFOX arm). The PCR (complete response) rate was significantly higher in the FOLFOX RT arm (31.3 percent) compared with the control arm (12.5 percent) and FOLFOX arm (7.4 percent). The overall down-staging was similar across all arms.

As expected, doctors found greater toxicity and postoperative complications in patients who received RT. Based on these preliminary data, it appears that mFOLFOX6 concurrent with RT resulted in a higher pCR rate and that neoadjuvant mFOLFOX6 alone achieved similar down-staging with less toxicity and postoperative complications compared with preoperative 5FU with RT.

Recently, I read an article on Chris Wark's website written by Jodi Ledley, whose husband, Casey, was diagnosed with stage III rectal cancer in 2017. Casey's tumor was surgically removed, and he decided not to use chemo or radiation. He instead followed Chris' Square One protocol for clean living. Casey is cancer free.xix Jodi Ledley is a researcher. She found that people with colorectal cancer have too little protective bacteria called Lachnospiraceae (LS) and an increase in cancer-promoting bacteria called Fusobacterium. Jodi discovered that LS feeds on plant matter and produces a short-chain fatty acid called butyrate, which has antitumorigenic properties. She found which foods feed the good bacteria. If you're interested in her research, check her website, adventureswithjodi.com, and read about Casey's story.

Chris Wark was also diagnosed in his twenties with stage III colon cancer. He made the tough decision to have surgery but no chemotherapy. Instead, he used food and detoxification of his body, environment, and emotions. He's been cancer free for many years. He markets his Square One program, and I wonder what the statistics are for people who use his program. I'd love to see a study with his program for selective patients.

Management of rectal cancer is complex. My surgeon also explained to me that cancer grows in finger-like projections. Perhaps radiation can kill those projections, thus lowering local recurrences by 6 to 7 percent with TME and chemo-radiotherapy.

I see younger people being diagnosed with rectal cancer. To put numbers in perspective, cancer.org predicts that in 2023, an estimated 46,050 new cases of rectal cancer will be diagnosed. Statistics show that from 2012 through 2016, rectal cancer statistics increased yearly by 2 percent in people younger than 50 and 1 percent in people 50 to 64. When colorectal cancer is discovered early, it can often be cured.xx

I learned from my research that the current trimodal model has been much more effective for survival than the approach used thirty years ago. I realized there could be choices about trying shorter-term radiation therapy, like in Europe, or choosing a more potent chemotherapy than Xeloda and seeing whether it reduced enough of the tumor before deciding on radiation treatments. But there will also be longer-term chemotherapy issues, such as long-term neuropathy. Depending on the cancer staging, the CEA number, and family history of osteoporosis, patients might have choices about whether radiation should be administered.

A couple of years after I finished my rectal cancer treatment, I started feeling my low back cracking more and some heaviness around my hips. I wondered if radiation and the abrupt lack of estrogen and progesterone were causing osteoporosis in my hip bones and lower lumbar. I went for a DEXA scan, and the results were that my lower lumbar spine and hips had osteoporosis. I then researched articles to see whether this is a documented phenomenon.

One study reported that abdominal irradiation, as in the adjuvant treatment of gastric cancer, decreases bone mineral density. It can cause insufficiency and stress fractures from regular weight-bearing on weakened bone. The study concluded that the insufficiency fracture risk in the radiation-exposed vertebral bones increased significantly between patients who had radiation and those who didn't.xxi

Another study reports that radiation treatment for malignancies in the prostate, rectum, anus, or cervix may increase the risk of insufficiency fractures in the pelvic region by damaging osteoblasts essential to bone formation.xxii In yet another article, researchers studied fractures of the sacrum after chemoradiation for rectal carcinoma. They concluded that sacral insufficiency fractures after adjuvant radiation for rectal carcinoma could present similarly to recurrent disease. Patients should be aware that this is a complication associated with pelvic radiation.xxiiiThese papers suggest that radiation may not be the best treatment option for people with familial osteoporosis.

When I decided to do radiation, eighteen months had elapsed after my diagnosis. The tumor had grown around the rectum, possibly in the lymph nodes, and spread beyond the rectum. No one presented the full range of radiation statistics and possible lifelong damage to me, including vaginal and osteoporotic damage. Had I researched and known all these numbers beforehand, I might not have chosen radiation or asked for a course in short-term low-dose radiation. I possibly would have taken high dose Xeloda for six weeks, had the surgery, and another four months of the higher dose

Xeloda. I'm not sure. I would have liked to have known all possible damages and statistics. I would have made a more informed choice.

It was important for me to research and present my findings. It took a long time to look for papers and extract information. I didn't have that time when I was ready to do conventional treatments. I was scared and rushed and had no patience to read technical papers. I'm not a medical doctor. I'm a person who went through rectal cancer treatment and realized that I needed to know more about the disease and its treatment. I hope you find this information useful as you think about your quality of life after radiation, including your sexuality, hormonal health, rectal health, bone health, bladder health, neuropathy, and survival statistics. I know you'll make the right choice for yourself.

SUMMARY AND SUGGESTIONS

1. Radiation can affect blood vessels in the vagina, and there may be bleeding during intercourse.
2. Radiation can result in fecal incontinence, pad wearing, mucous loss, and long-term bowel dysfunction.
3. Radiation may affect osteoporosis and insufficiency hip breaks and vertebrae breaks. A patient's familial history of osteoporosis must be considered before treatment and discussed with the patient during the consultation.
4. Several studies show that for most people, a higher dose of chemotherapy at the onset of treatment followed by TME surgery has similar outcomes as with radiation therapy and low-dose chemo followed by TME surgery.
5. A prospect study is underway to evaluate the effectiveness of chemotherapy followed by TME compared with the standard of treatment.

6. Cancer grows in finger-like projections, and radiation can kill those projections from spreading.
7. TME surgery on its own is a highly effective treatment.
8. Some people respond completely to chemo and radiation, meaning no tumor cells can be felt by the surgeon's hand or seen in the tissue sample after radiation and low-dose chemo. These people can be candidates for the "watch and wait" approach and not elect to do TME surgery. Cancer will recur in about 1/3 of the people in the "watch and wait" category. Also, suppose people have a complete response to chemoradiation. In that case, their overall survival statistics increase when they do have TME.
9. Cumulative radiation effects can affect sexual and bladder health years after the end of radiation treatments.
10. In Europe, low-dose radiation is used five times daily at about half the dosage of daily treatment in the United States. I could not find one article addressing women's vaginal health with this lower-dose treatment.
11. I believe patients need to have all the information before choosing their treatment options.
12. If you want to read more about the prospect study, you can find it in clinical trials.xxiv
13. You have choices once you are informed. I know you'll make the right choice for yourself. Talk with your team and support people. You have my love and support.

Section III

THE MIND-BODY CONNECTION, PART I

Chapter Eighteen

FORGIVING YOURSELF, ADDRESSING GUILT

Engaging with and indulging in painful emotions about the past could contribute to dis-ease. In *The Truth About Cancer* docuseries by Ty Bollinger, I heard an interview by Jordan Rubin, the founder of the herbal supplement company Garden of Life. He said he healed from aggressive prostate cancer by doing everything holistic he could to treat cancer. In addition, Jordan addressed and released every past emotional wound, no matter how small. He said holding onto past emotional wounds is an energetic separation from God. His cancer disappeared after six weeks.

The author Anita Moorjani ran habitual fear loops about disease prevention until lymphoma appeared in her body. After four years of holistic treatments and progressing cancer, her body shut down her organs. During her near-death experience, Anita saw she was connected to divine power and a part of it; in fact, she WAS that power. She understood that her obsessive fear of disease created her cancer. Anita's father told her that if she chose to return to her body, she'd need to live her life fearlessly. Because Anita's vibration and understanding expanded, she knew her tumors would dissolve if she returned to her body, and they did.

In addition, the cell biologist Dr. Bruce Lipton reports in his books and speeches that beliefs directly influence the cells of the body. When people repeatedly run angry, fearful, guilt-ridden thought circuits about the past or a future that isn't here, those thoughts and emotions can turn genes on and off and lead to disease.

But you already know that. You know you prefer calm over agitated. You know your nature is peaceful, quiet, calm, and loving. When you have nothing on your mind, you are relaxed and clear. You have ease when you're not overthinking life, not trying to keep yourself safe constantly, not comparing yourself to anyone, including your past self, and not trying to figure out the future. You are present. Without attaching to thoughts that attempt to micromanage or control life, you are well. You are okay with the unknown. You trust your ability to handle everything because you've done it your whole life. You are guided to respond effectively when you show up to life with nothing on your mind.

But somehow, in life, you've developed thought habits of fear, anxiety, worry, insecurity, guilt, and shame. They accompany you when you drive, meet new people, work, or create something new. They're those voices of "You don't have enough time. You have to hurry. You need to know right now. You're not good enough; you're not enough. There's something wrong with you, you can't, and you'll fail if you try; you're alone in this. You're not worthy. You did it wrong. You should have known better; you should know it by now." Notice how contracted those sentences feel in the body.

Yet the truth is that you are not thought limitations. You are light. You are a tremendously creative energy. You are a loving being. You are gifted in your area. You are part of a whole, and you contribute your gift to the tapestry of humanity, the same as everyone else. You are important. You matter enormously. You are not supposed to be anyone else. You're supposed to be yourself and grow in directions that feel joyous to you.

When you focus on the joy of being you, your innate gifts, the activities you enjoy, gratitude, and the people you love to hang out with, you are feeding the Orchard of Life. It's a life-giving energy. And it's the truth of who you are.

When I was in my alternative phase of healing, a friend of mine who is a channeler gifted me a session. The channeled entity mentioned I might benefit from seeing where I held on to guilt and release it. The entity suggested that I list everything I felt guilty about. Then the entity suggested that I make amends for my wrongdoings.

But does it make sense to look at guilt? The past is in the past; no matter what occurred, you and I cannot change it. It is gone. Looking at guilt takes us back to our traumas and brings back guilty feelings. We relive the past with its pain. But the past is gone. You live here now. Now it is a new moment. Your hands are touching something, your back is feeling something, and you're looking at something. That's all there is. Now. And what do you want to create now? Guilt feelings or joy?

In the past, you did what you did because you believed in thoughts that told you to behave in a certain way. You probably heard the inner guidance not to do what you did but overrode it because you listened to thoughts versus your knowing. Then you felt guilty, wrong, or bad. Do you learn from it and move on, or do you continually bring the past into the present and feel guilty? Everyone has done things they're not proud of.

Guilt is a feeling that tells me I did something wrong. It's a clear and beneficial messenger. It feels contracted in my body to grab my attention so that I won't do it again. It reminds me that I might have been insensitive toward another being or myself. It may nudge me to reflect and apologize for my momentary lack of awareness or conditioned reaction. It may direct me to think about other ways to engage in the world. However, guilt can also become a conditioned response. If people were repeatedly punished or told they were wrong, they could cultivate an overdeveloped sense of guilt.

When I was young, I was asked to keep secrets by my dad. Secrets were uncomfortable to hold and felt out of integrity. I often thought I had done something wrong by witnessing, participating with, or keeping the secrets mostly from his wives. In addition, my stepparents often told me I was wrong. I got a good dose of parental guilt-tripping if my wishes differed from theirs. I was often dismissed when I voiced what I saw and felt.

I adopted thoughts of insecurity, guilt, hyper-vigilance about how I acted with others, and over-responsibility for how others felt if my actions contradicted their desires. I walked around the world small, contracted, hiding. That's unhealthy guilt, not being okay with being myself and disappointing others. But it was my conditioning. Doing my best to address emotional cancers, I wanted to transform my habit of guilt into a healthier version, where it's okay to disappoint others when I am in integrity with my inner guidance.

I looked at approaches to forgiving myself and releasing guilt. One way, through the teaching of Sydney Banks, says painful memories resurface because I haven't come to peace with what was. I haven't accepted what happened or myself. The memories return for me to accept myself as having done my best from the state of awareness that I had.

Guilt tells me that I did something out of integrity. But given everything I believed then, I had done my best. I couldn't do anything else. It's the difference between intellectual knowledge that I should have done differently in the past versus a clear KNOWING and DOING something different. When we KNOW, we DO, and we stay with our integrity. When we're still on the learning curve, we do something out of integrity even when we have an inner nudge that it's not an optimum choice.

The way to make peace with guilt is to accept the past because it happened. Nothing that you can do today will change the past. It's easier to accept yourself and your human frailties. It's saner to admit that you're on a learning curve. The past is over. The thoughts are an illusion, just a passing memory. The past is truly gone. There's nothing to do. It's over. I cannot change it. I did the best I could from my level of understanding at the time. If I knew what to do differently, I would have done it. I did my best. As I realize this truth more deeply, I could engage less with a painful memory when it comes up. Gradually, it will lose its force field. Engaging with guilt feelings won't make sense because the past has gone, I can't change anything about it, and I don't want to focus on it at present for too long.

In this approach, if thoughts of guilt come up, I notice and accept the feeling and the memory without analyzing it or going into an internal discussion about it. I allow the sensations. I breathe. I accept the experience without fixing or changing it. I follow the sensations in the body. I enable the experience of feelings in the body. I remind myself that my feelings are my alarm bells to disengage from habitual painful thinking, taking me away from my peaceful and loving nature. The more I see that I cannot change the past, the less I engage in guilty thinking. Then the force field of guilt diminishes, and I spend more time in my place of inner peace.

It's beneficial not to judge yourself for having a painful or guilt-ridden memory come up or for how long it takes for the memory's energy field to not have a hold on you. The experience will subside when you stop engaging with its alluring nature.

Guilt can also point to perfectionistic tendencies and harsh self-judgments when falling short of an ideal version of yourself. Be easy with yourself. You're always on some learning curve, and it's okay to falter and retry. You'll learn to listen to your guidance when you see more deeply. Life has a way of teaching you, as the consequences will be more significant until you learn.

When you let go of buying into wrong-doing, your personal mind quiets, and your innate wisdom might say to do nothing; let the memory pass because it will disappear. Your wisdom might say to apologize to that person (make amends) if you sense you did something that hurt another, to accept yourself for your human frailties and your learning curve, or to contribute something positive to life. Then you would follow your inner guidance.

When you apologize to another, you may wish to express your regret for what you've done (name them clearly). You may ask the person if she wishes to tell you how your actions impacted them so that you may understand. She may or might not. If she wants to share, listen. Notice the tendency to become defensive, explain yourself, or have self-deprecating commentary and let that go. Just be there. Just listen to the impact your actions had. You may choose to reflect your understanding. Ask them how you can make amends.

Then let the past go. Forgive yourself. It's done. You might notice the furniture around you, the colors, the sounds, your breathing, and where your feet and buttocks are. You'd remember that you live in this moment, and now, the flowers, the blanket, and the table are still. You'd notice how pleasurable it is to relax your shoulders. You're grateful that sensing the world, just seeing, feeling, smelling, and touching, is so pleasant. You'd be thankful for the present moment and being alive.

Likewise, you might remember who you are beyond form, your inner light unaffected by thoughts, feelings, or your past. You connect with your purity of spirit. You recall the essence of a newborn baby. That essence was and is you. You remember goodness, kindness, joy, and playfulness that is your nature. You get in touch with the health inside of you. You look at your innate well-being more often. You feel your light more strongly. You feel good more of the time. You accept yourself unconditionally and are soft with yourself. Can you imagine how wonderful you'd feel if you remembered your inner light more often?

Some guilty thoughts and feelings seem seductive and real, and your ego might be firmly attached to them. In these cases, other approaches might help you to release your attachment to guilt. A method to complete the past could be by revisiting it.

For revisiting the past, I love Byron Katie's method of inquiry. You'd put your sentences on her Judge-Your-Neighbor Worksheet. *I feel guilty about leaving that relationship*. Then you'd question it. Is it true that you feel guilty about leaving that relationship? Can you absolutely know that it's true? How do you react when you believe you feel guilty about leaving a relationship? What's the effect of believing that thought on you and them? Who would you be if you couldn't believe that thought? And turn it around: *I don't feel guilty about leaving that relationship*. Is that truer or as true? Which thought do you want to attach to? This method is powerful. I once did The Work with Katie in a workshop. I read my first sentence full of emotion. When she asked me, "Is it true?" I looked inside and saw that it wasn't. It was just a story my ego told me. Then it disintegrated—Katie is a powerful mirror.

Another approach is to go into a younger version of yourself and give yourself empathy and understanding for where you were when you did what you did. Once your young self understands that she was curious, shocked, felt alone, stuck, ashamed, or guarded, but that you're with her, and that's how she learns on planet Earth, she can start to relax. Sarah Peyton is a neuroscience educator and author who helps people heal trauma and cultivate self-compassion with resonant language. She teaches people to time travel back and give the younger versions compassion, warmth, understanding, naming what is, speaking to it, and bringing it back to the present with you.

My intuition told me to contact a man I was in a relationship with in my twenties. I left the relationship, and he was devastated. I wrote to him about my cancer journey and shared that I still felt guilty because he was reluctant to let go. (I felt over-responsible for his feelings and caretaking of his feelings). He assured me that he had recovered and left the past in the past. I felt relieved. But even if he hadn't, it would be vital for me to let go of any guilt. My responsibility is to be in integrity with myself, and my guidance told me that I had to leave the relationship. The other person's responsibility is to free himself from his painful interpretation of you being in integrity with yourself. Stick with your knowing about what's right for you, no matter how much they want you to do otherwise.

In some situations, your wisdom tells you not to connect with the person even though you feel guilty about the past. Instead, allow everything. You really did do your best. Those thoughts will pass the less you interact with them.

In those cases, maybe ask your right brain to soothe you. *There there, you're all right. You're safe. I got you. You did your best with what you believed and understood then. If you KNEW otherwise, you would have DONE differently. I know you can't speak with that person. Instead, drop into me. I'm here for you. I'm holding you. Release the energy into me. That's right, just like that. Release some more and more. Breathe. Let go even more. I got you. It's safe to release. I love you so much. I understand you want to make things right inside of you and in the world. The way to make it right is to release those feelings. Just allow yourself to release the energy into me. There, there. Breathe and release some more.*

If the people you've impacted are deceased and you want to connect with them, you can write a letter to them with your dominant hand, expressing your remorse and regret. Then center yourself in your quiet and intend to connect with the departed's soul. I encourage you to write a letter to yourself with your non-dominant hand from them as if this being is writing to you through your body. Start it with Dear (Your name). Allow yourself to write whatever comes to you, uncensored.

A few years before my diagnosis, I had guilt about not doing enough for someone who had already departed. I intended to connect with this person's soul and wrote a letter to him. Then I switched to my non-dominant hand and wrote from his soul to me. I received perspective about what happened and how much he appreciated that I didn't do more than I did. All was in order, and he was happy with my actions.

My guilt also plagued me about an abortion I had two years before my cancer diagnosis. I got pregnant with my lover Joe a couple of months shy of my forty-first birthday on the day of a breakup. I knew I would not be with Joe long term. Due to my upbringing, I felt I could not have this child as a single parent. My mother was in Israel, and I couldn't see anyone who could help me. And Joe and I were not in a good financial space.

In addition, thoughts of this child being abducted at twelve years old and moving to another country without my knowledge took hold of me. I could not shake them off. Those thoughts felt so real to me like it was already happening—a child gone. I couldn't bear it. I also could not imagine the challenging women Joe might bring into this being's life and what they might need to deal with. I transposed my past onto this pregnancy. I was overthinking everything and wanted to ensure this child did not have a childhood like mine. I did not share my pregnancy with Joe nor what was occurring in my thoughts.

I still felt guilt and regret for not sharing my pregnancy or abortion with Joe, even though I did tell him a couple of weeks after the abortion. For my healing, I contacted Joe, and we had several heartfelt conversations about our feelings about my secret pregnancy and abortion. Although he was disappointed about my choice and my keeping this process to myself, he knew that the past was in the past, and he had forgiven me. Then I had to come to terms with my choice.

I sat on my bed and intended to connect with this unborn child's soul. I spoke to it from my heart. I told it how sorry I was for being unable to accept the challenge of being a single parent. I apologized deeply for transferring my past onto my present. I asked it to forgive me, and I asked that we meet in Spirit when I'm out of the body. I shed many tears. Then I moved my body to another part of the bed and asked for the spirit of this being to speak through me. I spoke from this unborn soul to me. This process was profoundly moving for me. The unborn soul forgave me. It asked that I accept myself and my actions. It asked me to forgive myself. It assured me that we would meet again in a space where I could love and support it. I cried with gratitude. Gradually, I came to accept that the past was in the past and that I could not change it. It was done. I had done my best. I forgave myself.

When thoughts about "could have, should have, would have" about this pregnancy come to mind occasionally, I notice them and choose whether I want to go into a place of gratitude for having been pregnant or leave the thoughts alone, not engage with them. I don't need to be dragged into habitual guilt any longer. The past is truly gone, and I do not need to relive or retraumatize myself by listening to painful, guilty thoughts about a past that I cannot change.

Yet my strongest attachment to guilt occurred when I was a child. When I was ten, my mom's fiancé moved in and influenced my mom's parenting. I was not too fond of the change and moved to my father's custody. Little did I know that within a few months, my father would tell me he was leaving for the United States first and would leave us children in Israel with a stepmom until he had enough money to bring us over. He told me to keep that a secret from Mom.

Boom. Shock.

I was in a difficult position of choice. I felt I couldn't go and live with my mother and her new family. I felt trapped by my father's request. I could not find a solution that worked for all. I hated lying to Mom, but I chose to obey my custodial parent's request. I felt stressed for nine months living with my stepmom and family while my dad was in the United States. My stepmom eavesdropped on my phone calls and read the letters that I sent. It didn't help that she had a reign of terror. I was a nervous wreck holding my anxious thoughts without a healthy outlet. My grades plummeted, and I was nearly failing a few classes. When we arrived in the United States, my dad had me inform Mom of my whereabouts through a letter.

When I was 22 and living back in Israel, I asked Mom how our leaving affected her, but it was too painful for her. She wouldn't tell me. I asked my stepfather about it, and he said they believed that at twelve, I knew what I was doing and should have done otherwise. And because I lived with my mom until I was ten and a half, I was to blame for withholding the information from her. Until that moment, I saw myself as placed in an unfortunate life circumstance. But after speaking with my stepdad, I became firmly attached to guilt; another thing put on me that I was "wrong."

On this journey of healing from cancerous energies, I asked Joe, "How do I forgive an act of an eleven-year-old that caused my mother such pain that she can't forgive me?" He said, "You just do. You let it go. You choose to let it go. It's a choice. It's up to you to release your guilt. And did you apologize to your mother? Have you told her you're sorry?"

I had many conversations with my mom over the years, but this time, I called my mother to acknowledge the pain of separation she experienced due to my choice. I apologized deeply. I told her I wished she had never had to experience the pain of separating from her children in this way. I acknowledged that I had played a role in that life-shattering event that I did not fully understand at eleven.

I shared with Mom my struggle with guilt and that I needed to release it. I wouldn't carry self-punishment in my body any longer. It was a painful conversation, and we both shed tears. But Mom still did not see my innocence and said she would not forgive me for the choice that separated us across continents.

I went back and forth between punishing myself and accepting myself for a few weeks. I spoke with a few coaches. One coach asked me to find a photo of myself at that age. I found a photo taken when my father left at the airport. I looked so sweet, so young, so innocent. I felt compassion for this beautiful child that carried this burden of a lie. She made the best choice she knew to survive.

Life is full of challenging examples, join the gang or else, take these drugs or else, shoot that person or else, steal that or else, turn the friend in or else, cheat on a test or else, have sex with me or else, sell your child or else, work abroad and leave your children or else, lie in your job or else, have a child and give it up for adoption or else.

At eleven years old, I couldn't even understand my choices deeply. Saying no to my father was not even an option in my mind. To risk losing his love and support after I had already left my mother's new family would have been devastating at that age. I couldn't risk saying no to him and carrying his blame, shame, or contempt. I looked out for my survival as best I could at eleven years old. I finally accepted that little girl who did her best when placed in a terrible position. I chose to let go of attaching to guilt.

Coach Mavis Karn pointed out that my parents' choices were about them. One asked me to lie to the other without understanding the consequences for me and the other parent. My other parent believed I had purposely betrayed her without understanding my position as a child, then blamed me for her pain. Something about what Mavis said clicked. I realized we live in separate realities, each seeing what we're able to see.

And I got caught in the middle of their thinking. I understood it was my job to free myself from pain. It wasn't up to my parents to see my innocence. Their job was to be themselves and create the situation I would learn from. I learned to separate myself from them and my past.

Moreover, I saw everyone's innocence. Everyone was attached to what they were thinking and believing as if it were true in their reality. Thoughts hypnotized all of us, and we acted from our best understanding.

Looking back with more mature eyes, I have compassion for all involved. It was a sincerely impactful choice to make. However, I no longer need to attach to painful thinking about myself about the past. I'm a caring, loving human who does her best. My humanity is not perfect. My familial and cultural conditioning can be insensitive at times. I don't expect perfection from myself anymore; just learning, apologizing, and growing. I can't change the past. I can create a loving and healthy future for myself.

I let go of believing wrongness about myself and everyone else. That was the gift of looking at guilt. Today, I'm grateful for my parents, exactly as they are. I don't need them to change. I've changed. I've seen my innocence and the situation I was in. My parents created the perfect scenario for me to get muddled up so I could look more deeply. And my parents love me very much. Mom and I had gotten much closer over the years. It was a windy road to regain trust, but with open communication, we are now close and loving.

Self-forgiveness is when you return to innocence. For your health, consider accepting what was and having done your best. If you were a child and others were involved and asked you to do something for them that didn't feel good, and you did it, accept yourself. You did your best with the thinking that was available to you at the time.

As a child (or an adult), you were in a situation, and you believed your thoughts of fear, lack, separation, pain, hurt, or insecurity. Understand that you innocently believed fearful thoughts as if they were true, then you acted on them. Accept yourself. You forgot your light. You forgot that your well-being was with you while that happened. You misplaced your attention outward when your health and well-being were inside you all along. You focused on judgments and believing in thoughts rather than the light. Let the past go. Focus on now. The bigger It that is always with you has held you and never left you. It's with you now.

Consider giving yourself permission to start a new phase of loving and accepting yourself as you are, your light, and your humanity. Allow yourself to be a work in progress. Each person is challenged and is on a learning curve her whole life. You get "do-overs" constantly. You learn from your mistakes at some point. You apologize. Then you earn your KNOWING. That's the difference between learning and earning. Accept that mistakes are a normal part of life and have an impact on another. Life isn't a fairy tale where everyone acts perfectly. Life's pain and challenges exist until you wake up to who you are now: a beautiful, free being of light beyond any past conditioning who is learning how to live on planet Earth with the human machinery of thoughts and feelings.

You decide if you want to go into the past or if you want to focus on the now. You are now and only now. Now is a new moment. Now is you lying on the bed holding a book and reading, birds chirping in the background, your muscles tense or relaxed, and you're breathing. It's hot, or it's cold. Now, without attaching to concepts, you are peaceful.

Be grateful for life and its challenges for awakening you to your inner beauty. You have well-being inside of you. It's been there all this time. Look in that direction rather than the past. Look in the direction of creativity, goodness, and contribution. Own your innocence of buying into thinking, acting from that, then waking up, apologizing, and starting over. Feel your wholeness that is beyond conditioning. Sense that beautiful, magnificent, expansive Feeling inside of you.

Go there often. Notice the magic of life, how green, resilient, and silent the tree is outside your window, like you. Allow yourself to feel vibrant about the goodness of life and the possibility of creation. You are learning. You are loving. You are whole. You have well-being. Forgive yourself and become free right now without concepts. I acknowledge your strength of heart, beauty, and light. Focus on that. Do what you love and what makes you come alive. Live in that beautiful Feeling and move forward more and more. You have my love and support.

SUMMARY AND SUGGESTIONS

1. Excessive fear, anger, or depression thinking can turn genes on and off.
2. If there's lingering guilt about the past, check in with your wisdom if you want to have a heartfelt conversation with anyone and express to them your regret. You might ask them how your behavior affected them. Please listen with a compassionate heart. Consider setting an intention not to have any excuses or defensiveness. Hear and hold space for another person's experience. Don't run away. I know you have the heart and the courage to listen. Kindly ask them how you can make amends to them. Then do it.
3. If you cannot access these people, animals, or other beings, you may choose to write a letter to them with your domi-

nant hand expressing your remorse. Then set an intention to connect with their soul and write a letter to yourself from them using your non-dominant hand. It should start Dear So-and-So (your name). Then write anything that comes to you, uncensored. Please thank their souls for their willingness to convey their message through you. Please thank yourself for your strength of heart and willingness to make things right. If you have a specific direction for making amends, do it.

4. You may ask your right brain to soothe yourself if you can't speak with others. Consider releasing any feeling of remorse into it. It will take them with love. If you believe in a notion of God, consider releasing feeling of guilt into it, and it will take them with love.
5. Please remember that your essence is that of well-being. When you're not caught up in thinking of wrongness, or thoughts of the past, you are well in the right here, right now.
6. You might remember your commitment to your health and well-being as your priority. When thoughts of past wrongdoings come up, you may choose to stop engaging with them. Remind yourself that the past is in the past, and you did what you did from your best level of understanding at the time. No, you couldn't have done otherwise because you didn't. Acknowledge the experience but stop engaging with it. In time and repetition, it will lose its force field on you.
7. Sometimes, you've apologized and asked to make amends, and the other party refuses to forgive. In those instances, it is advisable to forgive yourself. Remember

that forgiveness is a choice to release the attachment to a painful illusion that tells you you can change the past somehow. No, you can't. The past does not exist. You learn by making mistakes. Have compassion for your humanity and learning curve. Chuck the notion of idealized perfection and accept yourself with gentleness as you are.

8. You can focus on the light, your pure essence. Notice how calm it is. Notice the goodness, aliveness, joy, loving, giving, helping, and creating. You have innate well-being inside of you. Look in that direction. Spend more time there. Feel your wholeness. Sense that beautiful, magnificent, expansive Feeling inside of you. Go there often, and you'll realize it's where you want to be. You have my love and support.

Chapter Nineteen

FORGIVING OTHERS, RELEASING RESENTMENTS

Louise Hay gave up resenting those who sexually and physically abused her. For her healing, Louise sought to understand why they acted the way they did. She saw a therapist several times a week until she found forgiveness. She also cultivated compassion for these people's childhood and the state of their mind that would lead them to abuse a child. In addition, Louise healed her relationship with her sister. Along with forgiveness, Louise primarily ate fruits and vegetables and did reflexology several times a week. Her cancer disappeared within six months. She believes resentment drove her cancer.

Resentment occurs when you take your pure potential healthy Canvas of Life, and focus your awareness on thoughts of wrongness about something that happened to you in the past. You judge someone as having behaved in a wrong manner in a past you cannot change. The thoughts you focus on blame the other person for your own created pain from your judgments. When you believe the thoughts to be true, you suffer. Then you blame the person for your pain when the cause is you used your awareness to focus on thoughts of wrongdoing. You take your beautiful, positive life force energy and focus it on pain. And it's done innocently over and over.

Of course, you have discernment. There are things that need to evolve in this world, and you want to do your part to raise awareness. I felt resentment toward the doctors for withholding the information that pelvic radiation therapy creates vaginal scar tissue that will hurt with intercourse. I created pain for myself for two years with that thinking until I found solutions. I judged something in the past that I could not change and created emotional pain for myself. I took my positive life force energy and channeled it into hurt. I also looked for solutions. However, it is a much more efficient use of your life force energy to let go of resentments. You'll feel calmer and more relaxed. And from that neutral space of living in now and creating a new future (rather than a repeat of the painful past in your head), you can create something to elevate consciousness. For me, it was writing this book to inform people of the sexual side effects of radiation therapy.

Constant forgiveness for yourself and others is a sane way to live because everyone errs in judgment. People forget they are an immortal light and have everything they need inside of them. Often people are greedy and use others for their own gains because they don't know they are who they are looking for. The love and attention they seek are already inside of them. People also behave automatically in ways they were treated or in the pattern they bought into from their past. They lead a conditioned life living from their limited level of understanding. You and everyone else are a work in progress, and often you have no awareness of how your action impacted another person. When healing from cancer, it's crucial to let go of resentments from the past, especially with your nuclear family

How was or is your relationship with your parents? A thirty-five-year study at Harvard showed that a person's relationship with their parents might affect health in later life. Study participants described their relationship with each parent using the following scale: "very close," "warm and friendly," "tolerant," or "strained and cold." Ninety-one percent of participants whose relationship with their mother was tolerant or strained were diagnosed with a significant health issue (such as cancer, coronary artery disease, hypertension, etc.) in midlife, compared with forty-five percent of participants who reported that their relationship with their mothers was warm or close.

The study reported that eighty-two percent of the participants who reported tolerant or strained relationships with their fathers had significant health issues in midlife, compared with fifty percent of those who had warm or close relationships with their fathers.

"If participants had a strained relationship with both parents, 100 percent had significant health issues, versus 47 percent of those who described their relationships with their parents as warm and close. Another study, conducted at Johns Hopkins University, followed 1,100 male medical students for fifty years and found that cancer rates correlated closely with the degree of distance a participant felt toward a parent."i

About ten years before my cancer diagnosis, I had strained relationships with both parents. They say it takes rectal cancer about ten years to show itself. If you haven't fully cleared out your childhood or present wounds with your parents and other close family members, consider cleaning it up now.

Current Resentments

Are you resentful that certain people aren't doing more for you as you heal from cancer or care for someone with cancer? Would you like to be more supported by your loved ones but are not asking, and instead, you find yourself making them wrong?

I was upset with some family members for not checking in more with me. I wanted more connection, more help with food preparation at times, and more people visiting and telling me about their lives. At the same time, I felt anxious when others projected fear about my diagnosis, and then I didn't want them around. I also didn't want to repeat the story of how I was feeling. I only sometimes asked for what I wanted. When I did ask for specific, positive, actionable tasks, like, can someone come and cook for me once a week when my thyroid was enlarged, my family responded.

If you want help, consider asking for concrete, positive action. For example, "I'd love more human connection. It's hard for me sometimes to be by myself so much. What are your thoughts about coming once a week to walk with me in the afternoon? I would love the support." If I were to say, "I don't want to walk alone anymore. Why isn't anyone coming to visit me more?" Notice that I'm focusing on what I don't want. This statement will likely bring defensiveness or resentment in another as I play the victim.

Realistic Expectations

Sometimes, you have unrealistic expectations for your loved ones. Each person has their strength. If you want someone to listen to your feelings, but their gift is to support you financially, notice what a realistic expectation from your loved one is. You may need to ask someone else to listen to you. Or, ask and see how your relationship changes. It is your time to ask for what you need and want from your loved ones. It takes courage to get out of a habitual way of playing small. It will be worth it. I honor your power and courage in asking for what you want. Your loved ones cannot read your mind and want to support you. Ask for what you need.

I heard the panic in my mom's voice after I was diagnosed. I asked her to speak to me from a calm place. I explained to her that her panic and anxiety provoked anxiety in me, which was hard for me to deal with. I asked her to be supportive of my choices. Mom heard me and changed how she spoke with me. I invite you to ask for what you need. Your loved ones can't know how to support you on your journey unless you tell them.

People Who Say No to Your Requests

Sometimes, you might ask for support and receive a "No." The person who says no could be someone close to you. Do you accept their no easily, or do you personalize their no and make it about you? Do you tell yourself, if this person loved or cared for me enough, he would do what I ask? Or can you see that it's not about you and let it go? Can you ask someone else for the same support and accept it without resenting the first person you asked? If you have a negative feeling about someone's "no," you have work to do to free yourself from your interpretations of what it means when they say "no."

During my cancer journey, I asked my mom, who lived in Israel, if she wanted to come with me to Mexico to the clinic. She said, "No." I later asked her twice if she wanted to visit the suburban home where I lived with housemates. She said, "No." I had difficulty dealing with my issue of personalizing her response. Every time, my mind would make her response about me: *she doesn't care about me, she doesn't love me, if she cared about me, she would come.*

But in truth, Mom called daily for the first year and a half of my journey. She listened and asked pertinent questions. She helped me catch medical errors with her keen mind. She supported me. She does love me, but not in the way that my controlling mind said that I needed to be loved. My inner child wanted face-to-face physical care of "a mommy," and I had a child-like reaction. I could think of several valid reasons why she refused to come. It was still hard for me to accept her choice with an open heart.

Doing my best to heal from emotional cancers, I wanted to stop buying into hurtful thinking. I wanted to leave behind the pattern of personalizing Mom's actions and reactions. The spiritual teacher Byron Katie says that victims are violent people. And I could see how righteous and violent my mind became when

Mom refused to come and be with me.

I did several Byron Katie Judge-Your-Neighbor Worksheets to help me understand my judgments of Mom. When I believed thoughts like, *She doesn't care about me; she only cares about my sister's family*, pain and anger followed. "Is it true that my mom doesn't care about me and only cares about my sister's family?" is the first question. My answer was: no. "Who would you be if you couldn't believe these thoughts?" asks Katie. I closed my eyes and asked myself, who would I be if I couldn't attach to these thoughts in the same situation?

After a few moments, I saw that without believing the painful thinking, I was happy and loving. I realized that my state of being had nothing to do with what Mom said or did. It was about whether I was attached to a painful interpretation of Mom's actions. I understood that Mom didn't need to be or do anything differently for me to love her. When I didn't believe the thought that *she should be with me,* I was happy and loving towards her. I didn't love her when I didn't respect her no. My belief in thoughts was causing my hurt, not Mom's refusal to come.

What is Occurring is the Best Thing for Me

In the past years, I softened to Katie's idea that what is occurring is best for me. Why? Because it's happening. Any resistance to what is occurring in the form of a thought causes me pain, pain I could not afford to maintain while healing from cancer.

I asked myself, *If I know she loves me and refuses to come, why is it good that she's not here?* And the answers came. *She's anxious. She doesn't deal well with diseases. I would need to calm her down. She hates flying, especially long distances, and will be a nervous wreck. She doesn't drive here, and she'd hate to be stuck at home with me in a country she doesn't know. She'd be anxious to be with my sister's family and sup-*

port her. I wouldn't enjoy adding her anxiety to mine. And when she's anxious, she can have physical issues, especially during flights. Having Mom stay in Israel was best for everyone. I was learning to respect my mom's choice and not personalize it. I was learning resilience and well-being independent of my mom's actions.

I let go of the fantasy that I'm supposed to have a different outcome than what I have. Whenever my mind told me Mom should be here with me, I devoted time to questioning that thought and getting to a place of openness and loving with myself and Mom. Mom wasn't rejecting me. I was rejecting myself by believing in painful thinking. I stopped that self-destructive separating mechanism. Seeing Mom's commitment to herself taught me that every person has a right to honest yeses and nos. She taught me that loving is who I am and has nothing to do with what anyone says or does.

You might want to watch Byron Katie on YouTube guiding others doing the work. Watch how she questions her guests. The questions are written at the bottom of the sheet. You can ask yourself a question, close your eyes, and answer. On her website, you can also go to the helpline and have a facilitator guide you through one of the questions for free. There are also registered facilitators on the website that you can hire to help you do a worksheet. In addition, Katie teaches this method of inquiry at her 9-day School for the Work. She also does The Work on Zoom weekly

People Who Shut You Out

Is there a person in your life who is shutting you out because of something you did in the past? Are you feeling frustrated that you are trying to heal old wounds and bridge the gap with that person while on a cancer journey, yet the person is not open to speaking with you? It can be painful when you're trying to heal from your judgments of someone close and come back to connection, and they won't participate.

I propose using Katie's Judge-Your-Neighbor Worksheet. Write your judgments: *she doesn't care about me, she doesn't love me, I need connection.* Ask the four questions and the turnarounds. And see what you get.

I have a sister who shut me out. I'm sure she believed her unquestioned thinking about me. She and I have had our share of misunderstandings and unfulfilled expectations without helpful communication about the misconceptions over the years. But when I questioned my judgments of her not wanting connection with me, I felt loving, open-hearted, and in my joy toward her. She taught me the same lesson as my mom: Loving is an inside job and has nothing to do with what anyone does or says. The only thing that stands in the way of loving her is my unquestioned thinking (story) about her.

With deep gratitude for what my sister taught me, I could surrender any need to connect or have anything different from what I have in my life. Once I surrendered any attachment to having her in my life, she opened up a bit.

My work is about staying in my loving. I'm clear today that the only things that matter are: am I loving me, am I loving her, and am I in integrity with my inner wisdom? My discernment might say to love someone and not connect with them. My common sense might say no to their requests and stay in the loving. I am the only person that can separate me from loving anyone, including myself. I am, likewise, the only person that can choose to be loving to others and myself.

The Hardest Person to Forgive

Do you have a person in your life that you can't forgive? Maybe you made headway in therapy, but still, there are remnants of "it's not fair, he shouldn't have done this to me" or "he shouldn't treat me this way." Is there a person with an addiction in your life that you're having difficulty separating yourself from and wish they acted differently? Sometimes, people feel over-responsible for their loved one's feelings when in reality, they can only heal themselves. Did you experience an "offense" that you refuse to let go of, like abuse or unexpected violence? Perhaps this offense involved politics, war, rape, an accident, a natural disaster, being used in an experiment, murder, addiction, or social injustice. Are you the kind of person with a strong sense of justice, and you can't let THAT go?

Notice what happens when you fuel that thinking about the person or what happened. You seethe with anger and rage. That energy covers your natural state of joy, love, creativity, and empowerment, which is you underneath that thinking. You're bringing the past to the present and reliving the experience. Each time you think of the person or see them, a memory resurfaces, and you feel the pressure, contraction, separation, resistance, and anger around your heart, abdomen, or face.

Notice that you've personalized what they did. You made it be about you, when in reality, they're doing the best they know given their conditioning. The painful energy can dysregulate your nervous system and signal to your body that you are unsafe, ultimately leading to discomfort or dis-ease.

Consider finding out what story is bothering you: *it shouldn't have happened to me, they should treat me with more respect, I should have had a different life/parent/circumstance, I should be treated differently; if they loved me, they would treat me another way. I don't matter to them; I don't belong. I need inclusion from them. It wasn't safe.*

Notice your story. It's made of thoughts about the past. You're creating and recreating it by retelling the story in your mind. The past is truly gone. It should have happened because it did. They really couldn't do more or different than what they did, given their conditioning. It's done. It's over. You've learned and grown from it.

The other person was or is doing his best from his state of understanding. If he knew better, he'd do better. He didn't or doesn't. He's living out of his conditioning. It's not about you. Let it go. Surrender your thinking. Are you ready to prioritize your health?

I had a hard time forgiving my resentments toward my dad. Of course, I love my dad deeply. Dad was free-spirited, fun, warm, loving, creative, outgoing, charming, magnetic, and adventurous. He could fix anything. Dad taught me to cook, clean, sew, write legibly, do well in school, ride a bicycle, drive, and enjoy life, abundance, food, and cultures. He ensured that I had a motorcycle license because his daughter should know how to ride a motorcycle in case of an emergency. Dad provided; we always had shelter, food, and a car at sixteen. And he loved me and took me to doctors for medical care. He never raised his voice at me, never hit me, and was there when I needed advice.

And yet, after the divorce, Dad chose women to marry who scared me. One woman hit with a belt, yelled, and said hurtful things. A second drank alcohol daily and picked verbal and physical fights—while a third controlled Dad's every move. Dad's tolerance and affinity for negativity and injustice confused me. As a child, I hoped for more safety and protection. Instead, I walked on eggshells, constantly trying to dodge the verbal and physical bullets. My nervous system was always on alert.

In addition, Dad was a "ladies' man." He had affairs and a mistress and sometimes took me on a date with one of them. I felt awkward. Then he'd ask me to keep secrets from his wives. I felt insecure, wondering, what if they found out I knew his secrets? How would they treat me? I felt terribly guilty from a very young age.

By the time I was eighteen, Dad had married and divorced four times and had had several girlfriends in-between. I had lived with stepparents, a stepsister, my brother, and a younger sister. I saw fighting.

My interpretation of the tumultuous home relationships brought me to a place of depression, despair, powerlessness, hopelessness, insecurity, and anxiety. I felt heavy. I had no tools to deal with my young thoughts and feelings except overeating. I didn't feel like I belonged with any family. I did my best to avoid the women and the fighting, stay quiet, play small, and be out of the way as much as possible.

At 23, I asked Dad how he could justify taking his children away from their mother. "I did the best I knew. I have no regrets," was the response he offered. It was true. He did his best, but I thought it wasn't ethical and began blaming him for Mom's pain.

At 45, I asked my dad again, "Could you tell me why we left Israel?" This time he shared multiple factors that drove him from Israel. He was vulnerable and couldn't find a solution to his thinking and feelings. His best strategy to deal with his bad feelings was to start over in a new country away from the issues in Israel. He loved his kids so much that he had to take them with him. He rationalized why our leaving would be better for Mom and her new family. Once I understood what Dad had been thinking and believing, I stopped judging his actions.

When I was 28, my dad dated a woman he was excited about. She eventually became "Mommy #5." With a new partner and a new religion that he adopted, he changed his rules towards his kids and began voicing complaints to his kids about the past.

Then Dad stopped seeing his kids alone. His partner did not allow it. When I called Dad, his partner picked up his cell phone. She spoke for him. She made decisions for him. He had no friends aside from her. She kept repeating that they were one. I was livid that he accepted her dictums. I could not understand how to accept Dad's behavior and choice. Where had my decisive dad gone? I continually worked on releasing my judgments of the two of them.

During my cancer journey, Dad called every three weeks to ask how

I was doing. I knew Dad had his own health issues to contend with, but his calling frequency would drive me nuts. I thought he should call me more often. Again, I made that assumption: *He doesn't love me; he doesn't care about me. If he did, he'd make more effort to connect with me.*

I am gaining familiarity with my pattern. When people I love don't treat me as I believe they "should," I tell myself that they don't care about me and I'm unimportant to them. I tell myself that I don't matter to them nor belong in their lives. I reject myself over and over with that thinking.

I've made my close family responsible for my feelings and sense of worth. I've been looking outward for those I love to feel good about myself. It's been an unconscious way of being lazy about taking responsibility for connecting with my inner loving.

When Dad said, at the end of every phone call, "I love you," I felt angry. In my mind, he'd have to "show me" he loves me by behaving according to my standards. I had a controlling ego. I had too much pride and anger at Dad's choices to ask him to call me every three days or call him every three days to get my needs met for care and connection. It was easier to play the victim.

I felt livid about my dad's relationship with his wife. If anger could drive cancer, my attitude toward my dad did. My anger would flare up when Dad would spend time with his wife's kids and grandkids but not with his. His wife would say her children were meeting with him for Father's Day so I could come another day. She wouldn't let my father visit his family in the hospital and instead was okay with him celebrating her daughter's graduation. This lack of balance drove me mad. No therapist could make me understand how he had abdicated his power, and all was under his wife's approval. I did my best to release my judgments. Time after time, I hoped I had released all judgments about my dad and stepmom. At that moment, the next "offense" would pop up. Judgments of him consumed me. It was an addiction. I couldn't let him off the hook.

At some point after my first surgery, I connected with Dad. He admitted he had developed an addiction in his first marriage. His admittance validated what I felt and sensed, bringing me some measure of peace. I understood why Dad wasn't present and watching out for my safety. In addition, I learned Dad's current wife knew about his addiction and the lies that can accompany it. She wasn't afraid of it. Instead, she became his guardian, not allowing him to do anything alone or see anyone without her. Dad had chosen this lifestyle. With this information, I let go of my judgments.

In addition, I've come to appreciate Mommy #5 with her meticulous care of my father's health. I can absolutely see her loving essence and how well she cares for herself and my father. She's been a teacher of mine to learn to grow out of judgments, hear and respect others, and connect with the love that's beyond any judgment. I am grateful for all my teachers.

Dad did his best, given all circumstances in his life and his conditioning, and it had nothing to do with me. I was finally able to for-give my own loving back to myself. I stopped believing those judgments. I for-gave me life. I for-gave myself my life force back. I made my health and well-being more important than righteousness. I learned separate realities. He's his own person responsible for his life. I'm my own person accountable for my life and well-being. Forgiveness was for forgiving my judgments.

The Collective Traumas and Choosing to Let Go

My story resembles life in most families with the shared themes of trauma, miscommunication, misunderstandings, withholding, secrets, ego cravings, fear, addictions, wars, righteousness, abuse of power, power-over youngsters, resentments, and victimhood.

Everyone has family trauma; memories that weigh them down; family secrets they don't understand that bring judgment, pain, and confusion. When secrets are hidden within the family, they can cause confusion and unconscious patterns for the next generations.

Life is not what I think it should be. Instead, life is what it is. Fighting against how people are brings me pain. People deal with life challenges by people-pleasing, anger, criticism, blaming, seeking approval or love, numbing painful feelings by addiction to substances and behaviors, addictions to thoughts and anxieties, addictions to being a "me," to getting what "I" "need," addiction to religion, or addiction to the consuming anger of resentment or hurt. Yet everyone is doing their best given their level of awareness (what they're thinking and believing) and the circumstances they were born into.

I wonder if it was necessary to understand my dad's choices. If I truly understood the mechanism of forgiveness, I'd know that forgiveness is a choice to let go of any painful "story" about anyone, including myself. I'd know that only my thinking about anyone is causing me pain. And I would leave it alone.

I'd realize that underneath a painful story, there is love, and people act from their best understanding. I might have compassion for them and myself. They're trying to meet a human need with their best strategy. Forgiveness becomes a process of accepting them in their separate reality while letting go of the resistance to my own loving. It is returning home to the loving and powerful It, the Third Orchard, a quiet space inside of everyone. The inner loving is there regardless of what anyone says or does, including myself.

The Ultimate Gift

My family gave me the ultimate gift of growth and acceptance in this forgiveness journey. They helped me find my own loving beyond judgments of their behaviors. I couldn't have learned this lesson without them. They had to be consistent in their behavior for me to wake up from the pain I had created for myself. Cancer was the impetus to clean up what my ego was doing. I learned, after forty-five years, to stop hurting myself with my thinking.

I've come to appreciate my parents. The level of commitment and service of parents is tremendous. It takes exquisite love and energy to raise children. My parents have done a marvelous job with what they had. They even loved me when I had judgments and pain toward them. They are still committed to loving me. I'm so humbled. It is incredibly challenging to parent children, given people's patterns and cultural conditioning. My very young single parents had to raise themselves, make mistakes, and raise me too. They gave me so much. I have compassion and gratitude for all they've done to raise me. They're still teaching me how to be a better human. I am still growing, and so are they. I still stumble, and so do they.

Because of my family, I learned to direct myself beyond thinking into my loving essence. I let go of the past. I set myself free. If I can do it, so can you. Choose to free yourself from cancerous emotional energies. Forgive and come back to yourself. Stay in that space of loving beyond resentment. Stay in the purity of loving. Then go and enjoy your life. Create a joyful life for yourself. Go after what you want and what you love. You are an enormous wellspring of love. Live from your beautiful feeling. You have my love and support.

SUMMARY AND SUGGESTIONS

1. Consider asking what you want from your loved ones using positive, actionable, specific requests that inform the person how this will affect you. If they can't, find someone else who can.

2. Consider telling your support system how to support you.
3. When a loved one says "no" to your request, remember it's not about you. Please do not personalize her "no." A "no" to you is a yes to her life. Trust her to know herself. It's better to receive an honest "no" than a resentful "yes."
4. When your loved ones do not want to connect with you, they believe a thought about the past. You don't have to personalize it.
5. You can fill out a Judge-Your-Neighbor Worksheet. You can search Byron Katie on YouTube, "How to fill a Judge-Your-Neighbor Worksheet." Fill it out and ask yourself: Who would I be if I didn't believe this thought in this situation? Consider closing your eyes and looking; if you couldn't attach to the thinking causing you pain in this situation, who would you be? Byron Katie's website, thework.com, has a helpline where people can help you move through this sheet for free. You can also attend her nine-day School for the Work or find a certified practitioner through the site.
6. If you have unanswered questions for a loved one with whom you're having issues, consider asking them directly. You might gain insight into their lives and thinking, making it easier to have compassion for their journey.
7. The mechanism of forgiveness is simple. The past is in the past. It does not exist. Whatever you think happened, you've personalized it. Determine what the painful story is: They don't love me, they don't care about me, they should include me, I don't matter to them, I need respect and consideration. Then see how you feel when you believe these thoughts.

You feel pain. Who would you be if you didn't believe these thoughts about this situation? Go inward and see. Do you wish to hold on to the punishing judge about a past that does not exist anymore, or do you commit to living in your health, present, and loving? You get to choose. You have free will and the dignity of your process.

8. Everyone is doing their best from the level of understanding they have and the level of thinking they believe. They are probably perpetuating behavior that was done to them or their parents or grandparents.
9. You and I sometimes need to be more active about owning our power and loving from the inside. Some of us erroneously make other people responsible for how we feel. Feeling peaceful and loving is an inside job once we let go of attaching to painful thoughts.
10. It's okay to have painful thoughts. It's okay to get hooked on them and feel pain. It's okay to choose to see how you're personalizing the other person's actions. It's okay to stay addicted to painful thoughts and behaviors. It's okay to allow yourself to get hooked for a day, a month, or even years. It's okay to choose to stop attaching to painful thinking. It's all okay. You get to choose how much you want to stay in pain or not.
11. You are not your thoughts. You are the loving energy underneath your painful thinking. You have my blessing to free yourself. I know you can do it when you set your intention to free yourself from attaching painful thinking. I trust your wisdom about how to navigate your journey with forgiveness. You have my love and support.

Section IV

THE SECOND PART OF THE MEDICAL JOURNEY

Chapter Twenty

LOW ANTERIOR RESECTION SURGERY AND A NEW STOMA

"I don't know if my surgeon will be able to resect the rectum and reconnect my very low-lying tumor tomorrow." I shared my concerns with my friend Dina as we lounged on our bellies on a towel at the beach a day before surgery. "I hope he can clear the tumor margins by two centimeters and still have some rectal muscle to sew the colon into." I felt nervous. I had never had surgery and was concerned about the possible outcome, pain, infection, and healing process.

The Technical Details

Low Anterior Resection (LAR) surgery is a complex procedure that involves removing the rectum and sigmoid colon along with the adjoining lymph nodes, reconnecting blood vessels and nerves, cutting the splenic attachment of the colon, and pulling the colon straight down. The freed colon is then sewn or stapled to the remaining cut rectal muscle. Removing the sigmoid colon allows the surgeon to remove more lymph nodes that could be cancerous.

There are variables in this surgery. If the surgeon cannot sew the remaining rectal muscle, he'll need to remove the anus, the rectum, and the lymph nodes. He'll sew the muscle inside of your perineum and close the anal opening. You'll wake up with a permanent colostomy or ileostomy. This surgery is called an Abdominal Perineal Resection (APR).

In addition, while the pelvic region heals from this surgery, patients usually get an ileostomy or colostomy, depending on the tumor location, your body, and how the rest of the surgery goes. The ileum is the end portion of the small intestine. The surgeon will make an incision through the abdomen and pull the ileum tube outside the body. Then they turn the ileum inside out and suture it to the abdomen to create a stoma. Waste coming through the stoma is deposited into an external pouch. A colostomy is when the surgeon pulls a part of the colon out of the body to create an opening called a stoma.

A surgeon might create a stoma so the cut rectal area can heal without stool passing through it. A person can dispose of feces easily into the stoma bag. I spoke with one woman who adamantly refused an ileostomy or a colostomy. She stood her ground, and her surgeon operated on her without creating an ostomy. She said it was painful to eliminate during the first weeks when everything was inflamed around the cut and newly stapled rectum. But, she healed. Regarding bowel habits, she goes two days without eliminating waste, followed by one day where she's eliminating feces most of the day.

Thinking

Where does your mind go when you read or think about your upcoming surgery? Do you stay in the wonder and curiosity of the process you are about to have, or do you dip into negative "what if" fantasies and believe the scary possibilities that might but haven't happened? This surgery will indeed change your body forever. It will be a considerable change.

However, I remind you that you are brilliant and resilient. You are an innate problem solver and have been your whole life; that's how you've made it so far. And although there will be both pain and a learning curve to the next phase of your life, you will be able to heal and master the learning curve and move on to the next phase. Look at how much you've learned: to walk, talk, dance, hike, cook, work, make art, play music, parent, heal from radiation and chemotherapy, and work in your field. Whatever you needed to learn, you did it, and this is no different.

When the habitual scary thoughts and feelings arrive, notice them. Allow fear sensations to be there. Surrender to it, maybe even enjoy the ability to create feelings and feel them. Yes, your consciousness created them. Allow the feelings in their coming and going. They're just thoughts of insecurity felt in the body; there's no reason to fear them. All thoughts and feelings are welcomed; they show us where our consciousness attaches to fear. Allow yourself to experience everything, knowing that it comes and goes. Notice the fast mind that wants to distract you from feeling uncomfortable, the mind that runs forward before you have even experienced your feelings. Allow it also. Let it be with love. Consider letting go of trying to figure things out right now. Let it all be, and let it all go. You are resilient. You will move through the next phase with grace.

You could also shift your awareness to questions of curiosity. *Hmmm, I wonder what healing from surgery would require of me. I wonder what I'll learn about the next phase.* Alternatively, you might want to question your fear. Is it true that you're afraid of your upcoming surgery? Can you absolutely be sure that you're scared of your upcoming surgery? Look inside. Byron Katie teaches this brilliant and effective way of inquiring into the validity of the thinking. Who would you be if you couldn't attach to the thought that you're afraid of surgery? Close your eyes and look for the answer.

In addition, you may allow yourself to relax when fear comes up. Give yourself permission to be a human experiencing fear created by your thinking. Accept everything. It's all okay. All feelings are welcomed as messengers to wake up from the dream of thought and stop. You come present, and notice that you got caught up. You inhale, then exhale and relax your shoulders. It's all okay. Inhale, then exhale some more. Let yourself slow down. Allow yourself to soften around all thoughts and feelings.

Notice your breath coming in through the nostril and out of the nostril. And some more. Notice sounds. Notice smells. Notice where your feet are and where your back is. Relax into your body. And some more. Notice the space between the end of your nose and your upper lip. Can you feel the air there as you exhale? Relax into the present moment. Feel your feet. Feel your arms. Relax into Now. And some more. Allow yourself to melt into now. Nothing to do, no one to be. Permit yourself to be.

Picking a Surgeon

The most important action to take about this upcoming surgery is to pick the best surgeon you can. I interviewed two surgeons at two teaching hospitals. They both had impeccable records. The colorectal surgeon I consulted with was a "by the books" kind of doctor. He wanted me to follow the healing protocol precisely.

On the other hand, the surgical oncologist felt more open. He introduced himself as Shawn and was open to examining my options. He affirmed my previous efforts and commended me on my healing diet. He acknowledged my questions thoughtfully. He welcomed my hesitations about using radiation or chemotherapy. He understood and respected me, while the colorectal surgeon felt intimidating. The colorectal surgeon said he didn't believe a surgical oncologist could sew my resected rectum by hand for a successful surgery, as it was very complex. His statement brought upon thoughts of fear and insecurity.

I asked Dr. Shawn Steen, the surgical oncologist at Ventura County Medical Center, if he felt comfortable operating. He said he was and even introduced me to a patient he had worked on two years prior. I adore Dr. Steen and have felt comfortable connecting with him before, during, and after my surgery. In addition to his humane and medical attributes, he saved my life. My advice to you is to find the best surgeon that you can and that you also feel comfortable with. You have choices. You can speak with three or four surgeons. Use your power. Then, trust their abilities and their minds. They are great surgeons with impeccable records for a reason.

Preparing for Surgery

For the best possible outcome, it's helpful if your body is in good shape before surgery. Consider eating clean foods and exercising daily a few weeks before your surgery.

Where will you be recuperating after the surgery? If at home, you may need someone to food shop for you when you get home. You won't be allowed to lift over 15 lbs after surgery. If you recuperate elsewhere, bring your bag and toiletries to the home before surgery.

My uncle and aunt offered for me to recover at their home. Uncle Yacov offered to drive me to the hospital and stay there during my surgery and beyond. What a caring mensch! I felt incredibly grateful and relieved to have my family's loving support. Aunt Susi suggested I arrive there a day early with my clothes and necessities and set up for comfort after the surgery.

The Procedure

My surgeon and the team worked on this complex and delicate procedure for five hours and forty-five minutes. Some institutions use robots for this surgery, while in other institutions, the surgeon will operate by hand. The surgery will be performed laparoscopically, meaning your surgeon or the robot will access the abdominal cavity through the belly button. He may create one additional incision to pull out the rectum. In my case, that was unnecessary. You'll receive IV antibiotics during surgery to stave off infection.

In addition, the surgeon will send the rectum with the lymph nodes to a pathology laboratory to determine the presence of cancerous cells after chemoradiation. If your cancer spread to other organs, your surgery will be extended. Some surgeons look carefully at the entire body cavity to ensure that cancer hasn't spread, which could prolong the surgery time.

After surgery, I awoke feeling disoriented initially, then slowly began recognizing the world. I felt happy, grateful, calm, and loving. I felt loving towards my surgeon, the nurses, the nurse's aides, and everyone involved in my healing. Those happy drugs are the best. In addition, waking up from surgery feels vulnerable. I saw how precious and valuable my medical team and family are. I wouldn't be here without them. I felt humble and infinitely grateful. My uncle, brother, and sister-in-law were in the room. I felt loving and appreciative towards everyone who accompanied and was with me. Perhaps you'll feel that way too.

Recovering in the Hospital

After surgery, your nurse will ask you to walk. Within an hour of my arrival in my hospital room, a nurse encouraged me to walk. I couldn't believe she wanted me to walk so soon. "Not yet," I replied. I was gentle with myself, but perhaps you'll be up to the challenge. I trust your discernment to know what's right for you.

Either way, you cannot delay walking for long. The day following my surgery, the certified nurse assistant (CNA) and my uncle helped me to stand up. I did not anticipate such pain! Any movement caused intense pain. Even with pain medications, I could feel intense pressure in my body's bloated lower portion.

I did my best to walk three rounds in the room slowly, then gently sat on my bed. The CNA helped bring my legs up to the bed. Her fast movement brought such intense pain I almost cried. I learned to ask for help to slowly and gently bring my legs up to the bed. Consider remembering this tip and asking your nurse or a loved one to help you bring your legs up to bed very slowly and gently the first few times you try walking after surgery.

Most people will feel considerable pain right after the surgery as blood vessels, nerves, and organs have been cut, removed, and manipulated. The healing process of inflammation also adds to that discomfort. Of course, people have different tolerance levels for pain. While in the hospital, your pain will most likely be managed with pain medication.

When you wake up from surgery, you will probably have a urinary catheter for a few days, and urine will flow into a collection bag. When you have general anesthesia, the doctors place a catheter to empty the bladder during surgery. However, some patients get a urinary tract infection from the catheter, even though it's placed using sterile techniques. You'll also have a draining tube from your abdomen into a bag. As your body is healing from surgery, fluid will be created in the abdomen, which needs to drain.

After this surgery, you will have a liquid diet for a day. Then, you'll graduate into eating a low-residue diet of easily digested foods. The surgeon will want to see that food material is draining into your stoma bag.

At some point, you will get the pathology report on the rectum and the lymph nodes sent to the laboratory. You might be told that the tissue sample looked at had no cancerous cells or that your tumor shrank. It depends on the size, the location of your tumor, how advanced it was before treatment, and how your body responded to chemoradiation. My surgeon visited me a couple of days after surgery. He informed me and the family that the tissue he sent to pathology came out completely clear, displaying a complete response to the radiation and low-dose chemo. No cancerous cells appeared in the rectum or lymph nodes in the sample areas examined. I welcomed this news.

Who Will Stay with You?

Who will be staying with you at the hospital? Will you want one person or more? Will people take shifts? Do you feel comfortable staying by yourself? I believe that you know what's suitable for you with your healing. I wanted people with me, but I also needed to rest. Consider having a few close people with you with ample time for your rest. You will be dealing with pain, and your body will need to sleep with help from your pain medication.

I had an intuition that my healing would not go smoothly. I felt afraid of staying in the hospital alone after surgery and voiced it to my sister Hanna. Although my uncle offered to stay with me in the hospital, I did not want to place such a burden on him. Hanna thoughtfully offered to create a schedule for the first five days so that someone would always be with me if I needed support or assistance. It was a lot of work to coordinate such a schedule with family and my friends. What support from all! Hanna's efforts were a blessing to me. I was too nervous to coordinate such a schedule.

I experienced complications. My fever went up slowly after surgery, and by the end of the third day, it was 103.6 degrees Fahrenheit (39.8 C), and I was afraid I might die. Luckily, my brother and sister-in-law visited me that evening and asked the doctors for more immediate attention, especially to connect with my surgeon, who was off duty. It took persistent efforts, and the on-call doctor finally agreed to communicate with my surgeon. My surgeon saw my fever spiking on an app and arrived at eleven at night to take me to a possible surgery to see where the infection was coming from.

When we arrived at the operating room, the nurse noticed that my urine bag was cloudy. It was inferred that was the source of my infection, and now the surgeon would know what kind of antibiotics to prescribe. I still went under anesthetics for Dr. Steen to check the newly stitched rectal area. All was fine. I felt grateful to have my loved ones' assistance and my surgeon's help in my healing journey.

A Stoma

When you wake up from the surgery, you'll most likely have a stoma: an ileostomy or a colostomy, depending on your body. Your pulled-out and cut red-colored intestines will protrude outside your body, and a bag will cover the stoma. There will also be some temporary "toothpicks" that keep the stoma elevated out of the body for the first few days.

You probably already met the kind stoma nurse a few days before surgery. She might have marked your body as to where the stoma should go. This nurse will come to your room a few days after surgery. She will show you how to measure the stoma, cut the stoma bags to the right size, and apply a leak-proof adhesive around the stomal opening in the abdomen. You might practice putting the bag on your knee. I was curious and apprehensive as I gained the necessary information.

If you follow your surgeon's dietary suggestions, you'll have secretions from the stoma into the bag. After the first liquid day, you'll eat solid, low-residue food. The output will miraculously collect in your stoma bag. If that happens, you'll most likely go home after five days in the hospital. The next phase of your healing will begin.

What Not to Eat with A New Stoma and Why

I had secretions from the stoma into the bag for the first few days. I asked for fruit from my brother's garden. I looked forward to sweet organic fruit as soon as I could eat solid food. On the third day, I ate figs, grapes, mango, and family-prepared food. The hospital food tasted terrible and I asked my family to prepare food for me. My cousin made a natural gelatin dish, and the family brought yams, potatoes, carrots, and applesauce. I ate these delicious soft foods for two days.

Then secretions stopped. When I drank or ate, I threw up. I stopped eating and drinking. The pain began in earnest when the stoma got blocked. Within a few days, Dr. Steen prescribed IV nutrition. Walking was painful with a blocked stoma, and I felt feverishly miserable. Dr. Steen investigated where the blockage was with a dye and an X-ray. Once the surgeon saw the location of the backup, he put a larger catheter inside the stoma to drain the intestinal blockage. A day later, he flushed the stoma from the outside with a saline solution. The doctor's technique proved successful. Material came out, and the stoma began functioning again.

I realized later that a new stoma is inflamed after surgery. Eating peels, seeds, or fibrous material can block the stoma. Please make sure to eat low-residue food after surgery with no raw vegetables or fruit, peels, or seeds. Stick with low-fiber foods to prevent stoma blockage.

The Gushing Slime

Ten days after surgery, feeling more energized with a clear stoma, I walked in the hospital garden with my family. A massive gush of slime came pouring down my legs. Apparently, the colon's mucous gets discarded a few days after surgery. I was surprised. I hurried back to the room, and another gush of slimy liquid released onto my legs and floor. Feeling incredibly embarrassed and helpless, I called the clean-up crew, apologized for the mess, and asked for diapers to put on after showering. This event will most likely happen to you. Be prepared and consider using pull-up adult diapers starting a week to ten days after surgery.

Going Home

Once my stoma worked well, I got the okay to go home. My hospital stay lasted eleven days. I cried with gratitude when I left the hospital, realizing the care and love that goes into every patient for their healing when they're most vulnerable, raw, and dependent. I deeply appreciated the nursing staff, CNAs, support professionals, and doctors.

I was concerned about going home, wondering if I could manage my symptoms at my uncle and aunt's home without immediate medical support. Notice my habit of negative "what if" thinking. Instead of owning my and my body's resilience, healing abilities, common sense, and natural problem-solving abilities, I innocently bought into fearful thinking. To allay my fears, my surgeon assured me that a home health nurse would visit me, attend to my wounds, and help me with bag changes. Your surgeon will also request a nurse who will come to your home.

Then begins the next adventure: recovering from the surgery and living with a new stoma.

SUMMARY AND SUGGESTIONS

1. Depending on your tumor and its spread, there can be variables in this type of surgery. The surgeon may or may not be able to clear enough margins to reconnect the colon with a bit of rectal muscle. You might wake up from a LAR surgery with a stoma or an APR surgery with a permanent colostomy. If your tumor went through to the vagina, uterus, bladder, or prostate, the surgeon will address that, and you might have a portion of your vagina removed or a hysterectomy performed.
2. Notice if you're over-attaching to thoughts of insecurity about the upcoming surgery and your healing or whether you are trusting yourself and your medical team. Your feelings tell you what you are attached to. Remember that you are resilient. You've made it so far and are capable of handling your journey. Although you will have pain and a new body after surgery, you will find solutions to live your best life.
3. Consider allowing the feelings, accepting them, and giving them space. Consider giving yourself space to feel your feelings. Follow them. They'll change as life summons your focus to change.
4. Most people feel considerable pain right after the surgery as blood vessels, nerves, and organs have been cut, removed, and manipulated. The healing process of inflammation also adds to that discomfort.
5. As you sit on the hospital bed after your first walk, have the CNA or your family member help bring your legs up slowly to minimize jarring pain.

6. A hospital stoma nurse will come by a few days after the surgery and teach you to change the stoma bag.
7. Slime will come from your anus a few days after the surgery and may gush onto your legs. It might be a good idea to wear an adult pull-up seven days after surgery and keep it for a couple of weeks as the colon will continue to expel mucous.
8. If you'll recuperate somewhere other than your residence, consider bringing a bag with clothing and toiletries to this home before surgery.
9. Consider having visitors or someone you trust at the hospital. However, you may need downtime to rest and sleep during the day, especially after taking the pain medication. Your body will need to sleep.
10. When you leave the hospital, you will likely feel so grateful to your medical team for their excellent care. You can do this. Your body will heal.

PHOTOS

September 2015, at my sister's wedding, ten days before seeing the red smear.

September 2016, after the Optimum Health Institute raw food regime in my alternative healing phase.

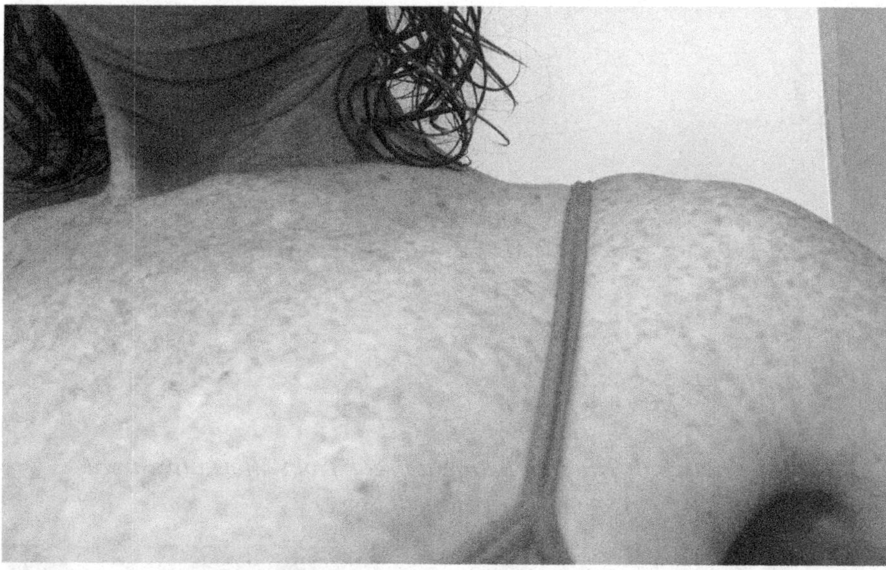

The port under the skin.

This is what my port looked like after it was taken out at the end of 2018

Getting ready to take my port out.

On the Beach in Tijuana, taking a break from alternative treatments at Hope4Cancer

This man kept walking into the photo, so my friend invited him to join the photo. At Hope4Cancer check-ups a few months after I left, still on a strict anti-cancer diet.

With my assigned nurses, Miguel Vasquez (L) and Fernando Durazo Camacho (R) at the Hope4Cancer Clinic in Tijuana, Mexico.

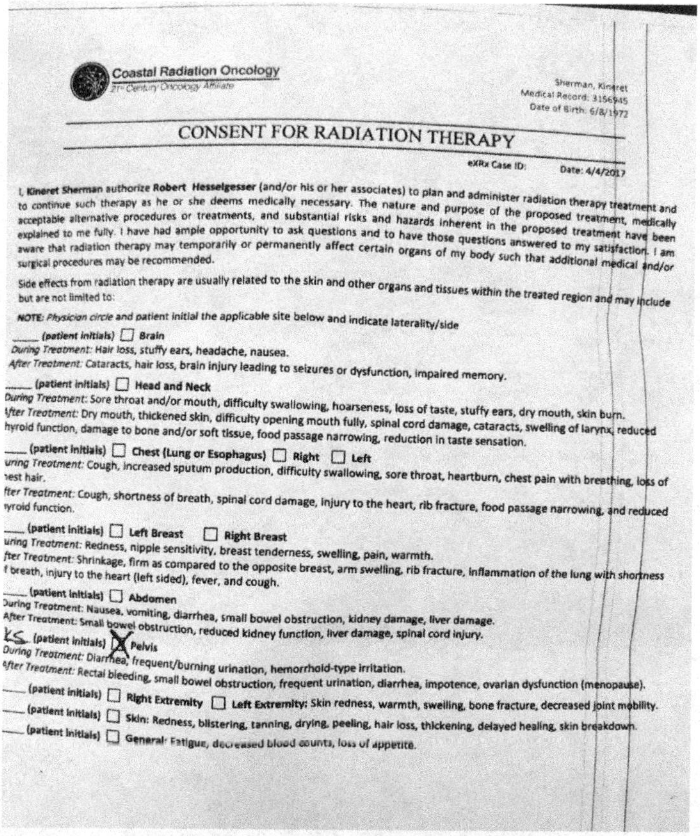

Coastal Radiation Oncology
21st Century Oncology Affiliate

Sherman, Kineret
Medical Record: 3156945
Date of Birth: 6/8/1972

CONSENT FOR RADIATION THERAPY

eXRx Case ID: Date: 4/4/2017

I, **Kineret Sherman** authorize **Robert Hesselgesser** (and/or his or her associates) to plan and administer radiation therapy treatment and to continue such therapy as he or she deems medically necessary. The nature and purpose of the proposed treatment, medically acceptable alternative procedures or treatments, and substantial risks and hazards inherent in the proposed treatment have been explained to me fully. I have had ample opportunity to ask questions and to have those questions answered to my satisfaction. I am aware that radiation therapy may temporarily or permanently affect certain organs of my body such that additional medical and/or surgical procedures may be recommended.

Side effects from radiation therapy are usually related to the skin and other organs and tissues within the treated region and may include but are not limited to:

NOTE: *Physician circle* and patient initial the applicable site below and indicate laterality/side

____ **(patient initials)** ☐ **Brain**
During Treatment: Hair loss, stuffy ears, headache, nausea.
After Treatment: Cataracts, hair loss, brain injury leading to seizures or dysfunction, impaired memory.

____ **(patient initials)** ☐ **Head and Neck**
During Treatment: Sore throat and/or mouth, difficulty swallowing, hoarseness, loss of taste, stuffy ears, dry mouth, skin burn.
After Treatment: Dry mouth, thickened skin, difficulty opening mouth fully, spinal cord damage, cataracts, swelling of larynx, reduced thyroid function, damage to bone and/or soft tissue, food passage narrowing, reduction in taste sensation.

____ **(patient initials)** ☐ **Chest (Lung or Esophagus)** ☐ **Right** ☐ **Left**
During Treatment: Cough, increased sputum production, difficulty swallowing, sore throat, heartburn, chest pain with breathing, loss of chest hair.
After Treatment: Cough, shortness of breath, spinal cord damage, injury to the heart, rib fracture, food passage narrowing, and reduced thyroid function.

____ **(patient initials)** ☐ **Left Breast** ☐ **Right Breast**
During Treatment: Redness, nipple sensitivity, breast tenderness, swelling, pain, warmth.
After Treatment: Shrinkage, firm as compared to the opposite breast, arm swelling, rib fracture, inflammation of the lung with shortness of breath, injury to the heart (left sided), fever, and cough.

____ **(patient initials)** ☐ **Abdomen**
During Treatment: Nausea, vomiting, diarrhea, small bowel obstruction, kidney damage, liver damage.
After Treatment: Small bowel obstruction, reduced kidney function, liver damage, spinal cord injury.

KS **(patient initials)** ☒ **Pelvis**
During Treatment: Diarrhea, frequent/burning urination, hemorrhoid-type irritation.
After Treatment: Rectal bleeding, small bowel obstruction, frequent urination, diarrhea, impotence, ovarian dysfunction (menopause).

____ **(patient initials)** ☐ **Right Extremity** ☐ **Left Extremity:** Skin redness, warmth, swelling, bone fracture, decreased joint mobility.

____ **(patient initials)** ☐ **Skin:** Redness, blistering, tanning, drying, peeling, hair loss, thickening, delayed healing, skin breakdown.

____ **(patient initials)** ☐ **General:** Fatigue, decreased blood counts, loss of appetite.

Consent to Radiation Treatment Sheet.

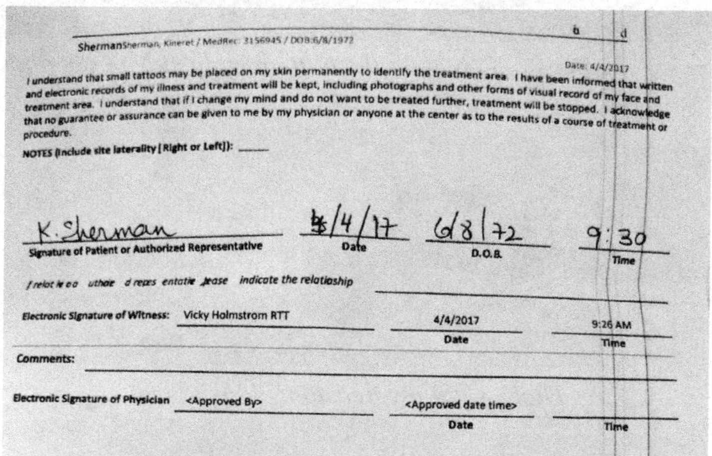

ShermanSherman, Kineret / MedRec: 3156945 / DOB:6/8/1972

Date: 4/4/2017

I understand that small tattoos may be placed on my skin permanently to identify the treatment area. I have been informed that written and electronic records of my illness and treatment will be kept, including photographs and other forms of visual record of my face and treatment area. I understand that if I change my mind and do not want to be treated further, treatment will be stopped. I acknowledge that no guarantee or assurance can be given to me by my physician or anyone at the center as to the results of a course of treatment or procedure.

NOTES (Include site laterality [Right or Left]): ____

K. Sherman — 4/4/17 — 6/8/72 — 9:30
Signature of Patient or Authorized Representative — **Date** — **D.O.B.** — **Time**

If relative or authorized representative, please indicate the relationship ____

Electronic Signature of Witness: Vicky Holmstrom RTT — 4/4/2017 — 9:26 AM
Date — **Time**

Comments: ____

Electronic Signature of Physician <Approved By> — <Approved date time>
Date — **Time**

Consent to radiation treatment, tattoo

Can you see the ileostomy bag on the bottom right side of the abdomen?

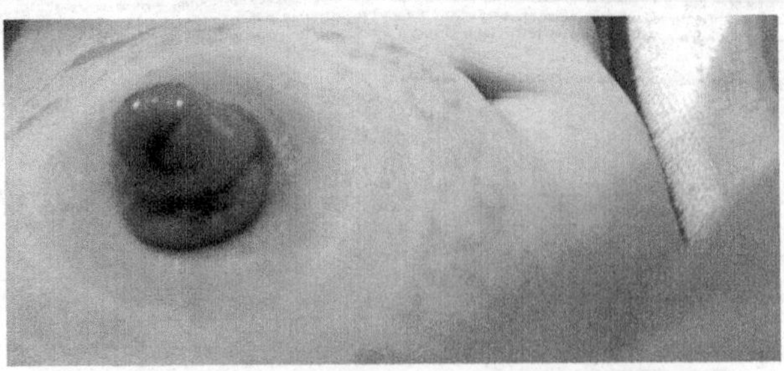

That's what my ileostomy looked like.

Chapter Twenty One

HEALING FROM SURGERY

Aunt Susi looked into my eyes behind the kitchen counter and said, "It's good you're out of the hospital. Now your body will be able to heal faster." I looked incredulously at her caring brown eyes. I could not imagine feeling healthy again. I wondered if she realized how much pain, despair, and vulnerability I felt. I lost seven pounds during the hospital stay with my blocked stoma. My face lacked color. My spirit lacked zest.

Aunt Susi took it upon herself to feed me with scrumptious food, and in a few days, I regained color in my face. It was helpful to be pampered and nourished by Susi. But a friend of mine went home and began cooking for his family. You'll see what's right for you, given your family situation.

Some of you might feel like I did. You might feel vulnerable and shocked after your body goes through this physical trauma. You feel physical pain. You have no experience caring for a new stoma and recovering from this surgery, and you feel apprehensive. You're wondering how to sleep through the night and how to get up and lie back on the bed while minimizing the pain. You might wonder if the pain will ever go away.

LAR is a major surgery, and you are dealing with pain with every little movement. Everything inside of you feels inflamed, and you might be feeling depressed. Please have patience with your healing process. See if you can relax during your rest time. Life forced you to slow down. Maybe watch those shows and read those books you've meant to read. Perhaps look for why the situation is good for you. Perhaps you needed to slow down. Some people might even cook and clean for you. Dealing with your new stoma will be a thrilling experience that, at times, will make you laugh. But laughing hurts at first. Please remember to be tender, soft, and loving with yourself as you move through this phase.

I encourage you to walk daily, even when it hurts. It will get better. I promise. I could barely hold my back erect for the first two weeks after surgery. However, as days progressed, I improved. Every few days, my body could walk more. I did my best to recover by going on walks two times a day, even if they were short. By the beginning of the third week, I could hold my body upright. I remember that delight.

After three weeks, the pain will ease. In four weeks, you will walk two to three miles. In six weeks, you will walk as you did before surgery. I hope it's not scorchingly hot or bone-chilling cold where you reside after surgery. I trust your knowing where and how much to walk.

When I got home, I called the home health agency and asked for a stoma nurse. She visited a day or two after I returned from the hospital. The nurse tended to the incisions and taught me how to change the stoma bag with scissors, powder, adhesive removal pads, skin protective barrier pads, a measuring template, and a pen to mark the diameter of the stoma opening. She told me the stoma would reduce in diameter after a few weeks as the inflammation reduced. I measured the stoma at least once a week and learned to have pre-cut stoma bags ready with the correct sizing. I was supposed to change the bag with its adhesive every three or four days.

Sleeping After Surgery

Any movement to get into and out of bed was painful. I felt concerned about sleeping on my sides with this new bowel protrusion. When I wanted to lie on my right side, I'd place the pillow under my right torso and swing my body over the pillow. It's helpful to be on a bed where you can get up easily from it. A bed that is too high will be painful to climb onto in the middle of the night, and a bed that is too low will make it painful to get up from. You might need to add a foam or eggshell mat to your bed or remove it. I trust in your ability to find a way for you to sleep.

To get a good night's sleep, I took Jetty Extracts' cannabis oil, Indica preparation 1:1 or 3:1 THC:CBD, which I placed under the tongue. Cannabis put me soundly to sleep and kept me asleep after I woke up at night to urinate or deal with the stoma. Just like my need for respite from the pelvic itching and burning of radiation, I now needed respite from the pain, at least at night, so that the body could relax and heal. If sleeping is an issue for you after surgery, consider a cannabis preparation, melatonin, or any other sleeping aid you choose. You might need to experiment with the quantities that work with your body.

Getting Cleared to Drive and Cooking

Within a week or two of your hospital discharge, someone will drive you to an appointment with your surgeon to check on stitches, rectal healing, and be cleared to drive. After a couple of weeks at my uncle and aunt's place, I went home.

Cooking was challenging. It was painful to hold my upper body up. I'd sit by the counter and chop vegetables, then get up to cook. It was fatiguing, and I wish I had asked people to cook for me. I knew cooking was a way to regain strength, but I felt exhausted. Because I was scared of the stoma clogging, I laboriously peeled every fruit and vegetable and deseeded them before cooking. Perhaps you'll ask for support when you need it. I know people are eager to support you. Consider asking.

Returning to Exercise

After four weeks, you're eager to exercise and move your body. I bet you want to lift heavier items and be more independent. But I caution you. Consider waiting eight weeks before exercising and lifting more weight.

Five weeks after surgery, I attended a gentle yoga class at the cancer support community. The teacher called for twists. I was uncomfortable with the movement and left after a half hour. The following day I picked up a small watermelon, believing I could lift up to fifteen pounds. That night, I felt a sharp pain around the stoma. I saw a protrusion as if a hernia was forming. Great, now I have a hernia too, I thought as I grimaced from pain. I freaked out. Luckily, I rested, and this pain and hardening around the stoma eased after a week. It did not develop into a hernia, but it does for some people. Be careful and have patience with your healing.

Your Mood After Surgery

How is your mood after this surgery? Are you taking everything in stride, or are you feeling cranky? Are you easily irritable and overly sensitive, possibly snapping at your loved ones? Are you feeling depressed or bitter? Please know you're in a tender and vulnerable time, physically and emotionally. Your body has been through major physical trauma, and you are sensitive to pain. Please be extra patient with your healing process.

The physical pain was getting to me. Everything hurt. Sometimes I'd be curt and unpleasant as pain responded to the smallest perceived slight. My uncle and aunt forgave me every time without comment, realizing that the crankiness sprang from pain. They also endured my depressed, hopeless, and bitter sides. I felt helpless that I needed assistance with lifting and driving. I could not imagine feeling well. Perhaps my foul and depressed mood was due to pain, momentary loss of independence, hospital pain medication withdrawals, or a combination. I credit my aunt and uncle for enduring my most vulnerable, sensitive, and hurting sides.

Even after I came home, my spirit sank further. Thoughts of dealing with the pain of unknown duration, a new stoma with which to deal, and not trusting that anyone around me could understand what I was going through created depression. Moreover, I began researching what dilators were for and realized they prevent vaginal stenosis after radiation. It was the last straw that broke me, and I felt angry and discouraged that none of my healthcare workers had mentioned this terrible side effect and how to remedy it.

Unfortunately, my bitterness spread to people around me. I did my best to isolate myself, so my energy wouldn't hurt others. I called the cancer support center in the hospital nearby and asked to see the social worker for support.

If you're feeling dark moods, I assure you that you're in good company and that those moods will pass. They will. I promise. You'll be in a low mood if you think about your pain or lack of support. It's okay to have low moods, especially after surgery. Just know it doesn't mean anything about you or others if you're experiencing a low mood. You are not your moods. Moods come and go depending on your reaction to what you're experiencing. And you're experiencing a lot of painful sensations.

If you're an ultra-sensitive person like me, every physical and situational pain feels enormous. I'm here to remind you that it will pass. In time, you will feel hopeful again. Your body will heal. And your thinking will change and become lighter. You'll probably be engaged in many aspects of life and not even have time to think about pain and stomas. So, while your mood is there, give it space to be. Accept it wholeheartedly. Give yourself a break. Surrender to what is. Your mind is having a hard time with the changes and the pain. There is one way to go with this when you're ready - up.

If you like to express your feelings, there are community resources for support. Support groups in every major cancer center at hospitals or a local Cancer Support Community can be helpful and also be accessed online. Many hospitals have a social worker who is connected with the cancer center. You may see a therapist for extra support.

I continued to be angry for another month until my body felt better, and I regained independence. It was a trying time for me. Eventually, the foul thinking subsided, and I returned to a more balanced state.

SUMMARY AND SUGGESTIONS

1. Consider placing pillows on both sides of your body when you want to sleep on your side after surgery. Pick a bed from which you can get up and sit down easily. You might need to add or subtract an eggshell mattress.
2. I encourage you to walk daily. Two walks if you can swing it. It doesn't matter how long you walk. Walking will help your body heal.

3. If you experience emotional/mental distress after this surgery, consider asking for help from a support group, commenting on Facebook groups, or contacting an ostomy group, a social worker at the nearest cancer center, a therapist, or a trusted friend. I know it may feel lonely as others are not going through what you're going through. Alternatively, you can rest knowing you don't need to do anything. You'll feel better physically with time, and this dark mood will pass.
4. Wait to exercise and lift weights for six to eight weeks after surgery to minimize the risk of a hernia.
5. Remember that your mood reflects the quality of your thinking about your life experience, not the experience. If you're feeling heavy, depressed, and irritable, you may choose to notice what you're thinking and believing. You don't need to manipulate your mood. Your mood will change as you focus on other aspects of your life. Your wisdom will direct you. Consider engaging in fun and relaxing activities, whether watching TV, calling friends, reading a book, or listening to music. You will move through this mentally and physically challenging part of your life.
6. Be extra patient with yourself during this time.
7. Consider using a sleep aid after surgery. If you have a prescription for pain medication, it may help you sleep at night. If you don't want to take narcotics after coming home, use whatever sleep aid might help you. I appreciated cannabis oil, Indica preparation 1:1 or 3:1 THC:CBD. If you take it, place the oil under your tongue. It takes

effect within an hour or an hour and a half. You will need to determine the dosage through trial and error. Start with the directions and add or subtract the quantity.

8. You have my support to accept yourself as you are, unravel, appreciate, be patient, be accepting, go dark, or have humor. Just be yourself, and love yourself with everything that comes and goes, as it's a love message to yourself to accept what is and wake up from what your thinking is saying about your situation.

Chapter Twenty Two

LIVING WITH AN ILEOSTOMY

Can I shower with a stoma? I wondered when I got home. The stoma nurses told me that I could shower without the bag. I was terrified of more pain. Two weeks later, I bravely took the bag off and showered. My fear melted during that wonderful shower. I felt free. There was no pain associated with the intestines outside of the body. I delighted in cleaning the skin around the stoma with glorious, warm water.

Eating and a New Stoma

How is your culinary adventure going after surgery? I was too adventurous initially and found it painful to eat food that the body could not yet digest (tortilla, hummus, melon). After I ate a tortilla for the first time, I sat frozen on the couch for an hour; stabs from any movement, including breathing, shot through my upper torso. My uncle and aunt observed me carefully. After an hour, finally able to move enough to get up, I called the home health agency to see if my experience was typical. They asked me to track my diet and determine what my body couldn't digest. They also said I should go to the emergency room if the symptoms worsened.

After that experience, I read online that an inflamed stoma

cannot digest many foods. Some forbidden foods inevitably clog new stomas: seeds, nuts, peels of any kind, raw fruit and vegetables (except for bananas, avocados, and possibly papayas), tortillas, corn, mushrooms, whole grains, mangoes (fibrous), beans, lentils, and quinoa (they have a seed coat and are harder to digest). Trust me; you don't want to experience the agony I did from eating foods that the body can't digest yet. Please watch the list above for forbidden foods and spare yourself the experimentation for six to eight weeks after surgery while your stoma is healing.

Easy-to-digest food includes cooked applesauce, white rice, cooked potatoes and yams, banana, avocado, blended soups, pasta, meat, fish, poultry, bread, cooked peaches, and cereals. Susi created tasty bananas, almond butter, and coconut water shakes that I adored.

Are you craving salads and raw fruit and vegetables? I was! Two months after the surgery, I slowly added small salad portions and raw fruit. I added small quantities of nuts, seeds, tortillas, and beans. Often, if I introduced a new food, I'd have digestion pain. Sometimes, if reintroduced in a week or two, my body would manage to digest the food. After eight and a half months, I comfortably ate everything I wanted. I never tried popcorn or corn.

Fluid Intake

It's vital to drink more water. Your large intestines' job is to absorb water from the waste that goes through the colon. But your colon is now asleep, and waste is coming out of the ileum if you have an ileostomy. To prevent dehydration, you need to be vigilant about drinking more water than ever before. Drink between meals, and drink water with your meals. Drink water all the time.

In addition, you'll notice that when you eat heavy starch food like yams and potatoes, the digested food in the bag is thick. This material can cause "pancaking," a phenomenon where the thick, digested material collects at the top of the bag and stays stuck there. It doesn't move down the bag. The pressure from this entrapped food and gas can lift the glue, and the digested material can leak out of the top or sides of the bag. To mitigate this effect, drink water with your heavy starch meals, to dilute the output. You'll want to adopt the practice of drinking fluids with your starchy, rich meals to reduce "pancaking effects."

Changing the Stoma Bag

Is there a good time to change your bag? I watched several YouTube videos to see how others managed their stomas. Some people said their stoma "rested" at the same time every day. Notice how your stoma operates. My stoma remained active when I woke up each morning, but after an hour, it stopped producing output for two hours. This interlude became my window to change the bag. Some days my efforts worked.

You'll learn to have all your supplies ready before a bag change. Don't worry, you'll become a pro in a bit, but there is a learning curve that everyone has to go through. Keep at it. Practice makes perfect. I learned to pull off the soiled bag, clean the adhesive around the stoma, put powder on the areas of the skin that were mildly digested by the acid that came out of the stoma when I didn't have a tight seal around it, clean the skin with a protective skin barrier pad, measure the stoma size, have the cut stoma bag prepared, and put on the new bag.

Sometimes, in the middle of this multi-part routine, the stoma spewed a fountain of digested matter on the sink, the cabinets, the rug under my feet, my body, and my clothes. It was a source of great amusement, dark humor, and at times, frustration.

Emptying the Bag's Contents

When you are ready to empty the bag's contents from the bottom of your bag into the toilet, place a bunch of toilet paper in the water before you open the bag. Then as you empty your bag, aim it at the toilet paper. It will prevent the content from dropping into the water and splashing onto your clothes, face, and hair. I learned this the hard way.

Stoma Support Groups

It was helpful for me to attend a stoma support group. I found one through the United Ostomy Association website. Once when I experienced a "leak week," I asked the group members for support. Even though I didn't find a solution through the group to my issue, the fact that others experienced the same thing brought spaciousness and relief, and I could accept my challenges better.

Also, at the group meetings, I met a stoma supply company representative who brought different types of bags and products, such as waist wraps with a pocket that I could wear and insert the stoma bag into. The representative mentioned ostomy underwear. She said I could call them if I ever had problems with the stoma. I called them many times after her offer. You can also connect with people on Facebook pages and ask questions and receive support.

Stoma Leaks

One of the first times I went outside the home alone, I had a stoma leak from the top of the bag. I had no stoma supplies, and my skin was burned from the acidic juices. I realized I must always have an ostomy kit in the car and purse in case of a leak.

When you leave the hospital, call a stoma supply company and ask for a kit. It's free of charge. The first time I called Convatec, Hollister, or Coloplast stoma supply companies, they sent me a small kit that included stoma measurement paper, bags, adhesive remover, scissors, skin barrier, powder, and dark tinted throw-away bags. I added lots of paper towels to the kit.

You will have leaks as you learn about your stoma. And it would help if you changed your bag as soon as possible to avoid acidic skin burn. The digested food from the ileum is acidic, and when spilled on your skin, it will digest your skin and hurt.

Many nights I'd wake from wetness from a stoma leak from the top into my pajamas and the sheets. I'd force myself to get up and change my clothes and sheets, working as quickly as possible. A leak often caused me to clean the floor, carpet, and cabinets. The adhesive that glues the bag to the skin is strong, so frequently pulling the bags would make my skin sensitive. I got itchy rashes when I was allergic to some bag adhesives.

Some days I had two or three leaks. I'd need to change the bags as soon as the leak occurred in the day or at night. The stoma changes; it is a living entity, sometimes protruding an inch above the skin, and other times, when leaks occur, contracting inward and lying flush with the skin. When I would have a "leak week," I'd call the companies to have new bag samples sent to me. I'd try the different bags until one worked satisfactorily.

I also noticed that the stoma leaked if I was emotionally or mentally stressed or disturbed. If you're bothered by anything in your life, address it. Tell the people involved what you need to say and let it go. It will help reduce leaks.

Four months after my surgery, I was walking in the street in Israel when I suddenly felt warm wetness in my legs, culminating on my socks and shoes. Luckily, I was with my mom, with no other people around. My bag opened from the bottom. How surprising! I hurried home to wash and get changed. A friend with an ileostomy for life suggested that I use a binder clip to clip the bottom of the bag to avoid future bottom leaks. It worked. I've not had a leak from the bottom since adding the clip.

Sleeping with a Stoma Bag

You'll wake up periodically to empty your bag to avoid stomal bag explosions from gas or too much output at night. I would wake up two times a night to empty the bag. After seven months, I figured I should stop eating by four PM. That gave me seven hours of food digestion before bedtime to empty the bag. Then I could sleep through the night. There are also two-piece bags, one that stays on your body near the stoma, and the other piece gets hooked to the first part. There are larger night bags that you can attach to the flat piece that's around your stoma. Those bags are large enough for you to sleep through the night.

Ostomy Wraps

I used an ostomy wrap when I exercised. The wrap, a wide elastic band around the waist with a pocket that I could slide the stoma bag into, flattened the bag and kept it close to my body. I could move and bounce and feel secure. However, I continually checked the amount within the bag with my hand (and you will do this also). I constantly went to bathrooms to check the fullness of the bag or open it so gas would escape and flatten it. On occasion, I'd go dancing and smell food. After a few seconds, I'd realize the smell emanated from me. The stoma leaked from the top, meaning I had to go home to change. Ileostomy-digested material does not smell like poop; it smells like lightly digested food.

You will have your ups and downs with your stoma. Every few weeks, I'd have three to five leaks per day that sometimes lasted three or four days. Those were challenging times, as my skin would get irritated from pulling the bags off with the strong adhesive. I continued to call the ostomy product companies for help. I learned to figure out what was bothering me emotionally and attend to it.

As I tried this tactic several times with some success, calm gradually replaced panic and frustration. Eventually, I accepted nights when I'd wake up to clean my clothing, body, bedding, bedroom floor, and bathroom floors and cabinets as my new normal. The real issue of fear of leaks eventually subsided. I accepted that leaks would continue and that I could handle them. I did not panic even in close public contact. I had gotten used to the situation to the point where I could shrug off and even laugh at and enjoy the effects of having to poop through a hole in my side.

Four months after my surgery, I flew to Israel. On my return flight, I experienced leakage from the stoma. I calmly took my kit and waited in line for the bathroom. When I noticed the person taking her time in the bathroom, I gently knocked on the door, asking the current occupant to come out. Then I efficiently changed my bag in the bathroom.

After eight and a half months of living with a stoma, I felt comfortable. I was hiking, dancing, and flying with my stoma. Except for occasional challenging leak weeks and raw skin around the stoma, my quality of life was excellent.

Here are comments from other people who had a stoma and wanted to connect with you, the readers of this book:

- One person said that although she is stage IV, had she known the reversal would have been so difficult, she would have kept the stoma. She could go out to places and enjoy herself, but now it's difficult for her. She advises you to consult with your surgeon.
- A man wrote that he wished he knew life with a stoma would not be complicated. He worried too much for no reason. He would have instead pushed that mental energy into healing.
- Another woman said she has a permanent ostomy that she had gotten to love.

- One patient said her surgeon told her he wouldn't try to reconnect her bowels because she'll have a better quality of life living with a permanent stoma.
- Another patient wrote that he thought the products they gave in the hospital for the stoma were all he could use. He had no idea there were so many products out there to try. Knowing there were options would have been helpful to him.

I hope this chapter helps you to begin your journey with your stoma. As usual, you are the authority in your life. Your story is your own. I trust you will learn to care for yourself through this phase. You have an innate capacity to learn and problem-solve. You've done it your entire life. Most people have a good quality of life with their stomas. You have my love and support.

SUMMARY AND SUGGESTIONS

1. You can shower luxuriously without your stoma bag and clean the skin around the stoma.
2. Please refer to the forbidden foods in this chapter and refrain from eating them for the first six weeks.
3. When changing your stoma bag, you'll need to roll your pants down and place a washcloth and lots of folded paper towels on top of it. Consider watching YouTube tutorials.
4. When you empty the bag's contents into the toilet, water will splash on the toilet seat, floor, clothes, legs, and even face. The way to prevent it is to place bunched toilet paper in the water and aim the bag's content at the toilet paper.
5. My stoma shrunk three times over eight and a half months: after eight weeks, then after four months, then

after six months. Keep measuring your stoma size for a tight fit with your bag to reduce raw skin issues.

6. The stoma retracts inward at different times of the day and night. When it retracts, it can leak. Consider calling ostomy supply companies: Convatec, Coloplast, or Hollister to speak with their knowledgeable and empathic customer care representatives.
7. You may wake up once or twice per night to empty the bag to prevent nighttime explosions from trapped gas and material. There are bags that people can pull off (two pieces). You can buy a large bag and hook it to the base at night to catch more output. Also, if you stop eating by four in the afternoon, you will have emptied the bag a couple of times before going to bed, and you could enjoy a whole night's sleep.
8. It's helpful to figure out when your stoma is inactive to change bags.
9. The United Ostomy Association website (UOAA), ostomy.org, lists ostomy support groups.
10. To prevent stoma leaks from the bottom (so unpleasant when it happens in public), use a binder clip to clip the bottom of the stoma bag.
11. When exercising, ostomy wraps or stealth belts are helpful. They can be found online.
12. When you leave the hospital, call the various stoma supply companies and ask them for a free stoma kit. You'll need one in your car and another in your purse when the bag leaks.
13. Sometimes, the stoma bag inflates because of gas. You'll soon realize how to open the bag from the bottom to release the gas.

14. M9 Odor Eliminator Drops in an ostomy bag are magic for eliminating odor (tip shared by another patient).
15. Consider attending to your emotional stresses. When I didn't address emotional issues, my stoma leaked.
16. You will find solutions and learn how to live with your stoma. You have my love and support as you navigate the new territory of living with your new friend.

Chapter Twenty Three

ADDING CHEMOTHERAPY

9/27/17: Six weeks after surgery, I began taking higher-dose Xeloda chemo pills. I refused IV Oxaliplatin. It's constant decisions; do I need to take this medicine or not? How do I know? One of the psychics I spoke with and other channelers said yes, I need chemo, and there is room for negotiation if the science can back it up.

10/18/17: I looked forward to dance class all day but have a chemo headache. It comes on every few days, usually in the afternoons. I am reminded to drink and drink. I drank more than four cups of water mixed with coconut water, but still, there is a headache. Today is the last day of the second cycle of chemo—two weeks on, one week off. Maybe tomorrow I'll feel better.

For stage III rectal cancer, my protocol called for six rounds of stronger chemotherapy after the LAR surgery. Suppose your medical team decides you need the second round of chemotherapy. In that case, the protocol calls for a higher dose of Xeloda than you took with radiation, either pills or IV, depending on your doctor's recommendation. I took Xeloda for two weeks, then had one week off. In addition, depending on your CEA number and other statistics, the protocol might call for Oxaliplatin or FOLFOX chemotherapy infusion into your port on the first day of every Xeloda cycle.

I started chemotherapy for six cycles. The protocol was Xeloda pills, taken twice a day with food, a larger amount than before. In addition, I was supposed to have an Oxaliplatin chemotherapy infusion through my port. Because the tumor was stage III, in the lymph nodes, I had no idea whether cancerous cells went around the body and implanted themselves elsewhere.

I asked my oncologist, "What is the difference in recurrence rates between taking or not taking Oxaliplatin?" He told me that five percent of patients who forego this treatment suffer a recurrence. From speaking with other patients, I learned that Oxaliplatin creates neuropathy in the hands and feet and damages the tender lining of the digestive tract.i Several patients I previously spoke with had neuropathy two years after treatment in either the hands or feet, and could not handle dairy, fried food, cooked tomatoes, or other common foods.

My CEA number was normal throughout my cancer journey, and chemoradiation eliminated all cancer tested in the rectal tissue. I deliberated for days, not knowing what to do. I even called a few trusted psychics to weigh in. Finally, I chose to forego Oxaliplatin and take my chances by eating cleanly. Sometimes, the hardest thing in this journey is choosing and making peace with one's choice.

I don't know what side effects you will have from taking high-dose Xeloda, Oxaliplatin, or FOLFOX. Each person is different due to different body chemistry. The dosage you get is based on your body weight. One woman told me she was allergic to Oxaliplatin and went into the hospital for weeks.

During the second cycle of Xeloda, I experienced a headache every few days and general fatigue, especially toward the end of the two weeks. Chemo created patches of redness of lit-up pre-cancerous cells on my face, and my knees felt stiff and arthritic. As the cycles progressed and more chemotherapy accumulated in the body, I noticed a tenderness at the bottom of my feet, so I couldn't wear wool socks as I had in previous winters. A friend of mine going through the same treatment couldn't hold anything cold and had more severe irritation to the bottom of her hands and feet from the beginning.

When I was on chemo, I experienced allergies that I hadn't had before. If I introduced a new supplement, my body was often allergic to it. I even had an allergic reaction to supplements I had taken before. I had a similar response to certain foods. The allergies went away after I finished chemotherapy treatments.

Xeloda is generic, and my side effects were often attributed to the non-active pill ingredients and their interaction with my body. Because my insurance changed a few times during treatment, I was prescribed different brands of Xeloda (Capecitabine) pills. Each brand created different side effects. I even flew to Israel with my chemo pills, and when they ran out, I bought Teva-made Xeloda pills. Those pills created increasingly worse headaches that progressed to migraines and throwing up. I stopped taking the tablets immediately and waited until I returned to the United States to finish my last chemo cycle.

My stoma function was not affected by chemotherapy. But chemotherapy is poisonous. When you discard fecal material into the toilet from your bag, consider cleaning the toilet seat and flushing the water twice to protect others using the toilet. It would be best to have a designated toilet when you receive chemotherapy. Chemotherapy can be excreted through feces, urine, and other body fluids, so be cautious if others are using the same bathroom, and consider using a condom if sexually active.

While on chemotherapy, you will probably visit your oncologist's office every three weeks. The nurses will check your blood work before administering the infusion and before you see the doctor for your next Xeloda cycle. The oncologist wants to ensure that you have enough white blood cells and that your body chemistry is balanced enough to receive more chemotherapy. Chemotherapy will decrease your body's ability to create white blood cells. Even though my white blood cell count was consistently falling as I received more chemotherapy, it never got to the point where I needed to stop taking chemo.

My hemoglobin count also decreased with each chemotherapy cycle. It was below average, between nine and ten. The oncologist encouraged me to take vitamins B12, B-complex, and C. Likewise, the nurse offered a printout with a selection of iron-rich foods such as sweet potatoes, dark leafy greens, dried figs, raisins, dried apricots, beans, almonds, broccoli, artichokes, peaches, red meat, pumpkin seeds, green peas, beets, apples, lentils, nettle tea, chicken liver, and canned clams and oysters. If your hemoglobin drops below seven, you may need a blood transfusion.

Patients who have taken more chemotherapy than I did wanted you to know that people can receive a shot to boost their white blood cell count. One of those drugs is Neulasta. Often patients give themselves the shot. Patients shared that Neulasta produces painful body and bone ache side effects. Sometimes doctors prescribe Claritin to offset the bone pain as it decreases inflammation and swelling. One patient mentioned Claritin helped a little, but she still got three-day headaches that nothing helped. Her doctor put her on a lower dose of Neulasta, but her bones still ached.

Two women said that strong chemo was fatiguing. One wanted you to know that the fatigue you get from chemo differs from normal tiredness. She said living in yoga pants and T-shirts while on chemo is okay. Another woman slept 20 hours daily. She seconds how cancer fatigue differs from regular fatigue. It doesn't respond to a caffeine pick-me-up. Sometimes she would pass out without any recollection of having gone to sleep. Her advice: after chemo infusion day, go straight to bed. She also mentioned that as chemo accumulates, the side effects may worsen. After her last treatment, within two weeks, she was okay; not back to how she felt before, but she could stay awake. Other patients found it took a full year for the side effects of chemotherapy to abate.

I had chemo fatigue to a lesser degree than that patient. When I finished chemo, I was still lethargic. My energy improved a year after chemo. Four years after finishing chemo treatment, my energy has not returned to the same level it was before treatment. Most patients report feeling the same way- more sluggish than before treatment. The few people who told me their energy was great were involved in daily high-intensity exercise such as running, cycling, aerobic dancing, or swimming long distances.

Another patient said to eat what sounds good because it most likely will not stay down with chemo. She recommends Nuun electrolyte tablets for hydrating. I used coconut water or water with maple and lemon for electrolytes.

Several patients recommended asking for hydration after chemo infusions. One woman shared that she received hydration on her chemo Monday. Then, when she returned for her other chemo formula pack on Wednesday, she would be hydrated again. She said that hydration requires patients to stay an extra hour, for about five hours, but it made a huge difference in her side effects.

Another patient said she was part of a study. She received an infusion of calcium-magnesium before her chemo and said she had very little neuropathy, which disappeared after her treatment.

Some patients report feeling nauseous with the stronger chemo. One woman wished she had searched harder for a better anti-nausea medicine. She was offered a couple but still felt sick. She seconds the advice about having IV hydration after the chemo treatment. It was helpful to feel better quicker. At the doses I took, I never experienced nausea with Xeloda, but two women on the Facebook page told me they had nausea with Xeloda.

Some people receive FOLFOX chemotherapy. It is composed of 5-FU Xeloda, Oxaliplatin, and Leucovorin calcium. One woman mentioned that FOLFOX caused neuropathy and fatigue. Medications controlled her nausea. Although it was temporarily horrible, it was precisely that – temporary. She trusts you'll be able to cope with whatever comes your way. This treatment is a moment in life, and it will pass.

I have two friends, a man and a woman, who underwent stage III rectal cancer treatments. The man handled Oxaliplatin infusions five times. The sixth time, the doctor reduced his dosage. My woman friend received one Oxaliplatin treatment, and after the first infusion, she ended up in the hospital with a severe reaction. Your doctor will work with you. Most likely, you'll be able to tolerate chemotherapy. If you're taking only Xeloda, you'll likely be fine unless you're allergic to it. If you receive the more potent chemo treatments, you and your doctor will work out if you need a lower dose or change to another chemotherapy agent. Often, it's a trial-and-error process.

One patient suggested going to the dentist to buff your teeth before you start chemotherapy. Chemo can cause mouth sores. The smoother your teeth, the fewer sores. She also said that ice helps to reduce terrible chemo side effects. She now has ice in her socks, ice packs around her legs, in her mittens, around her arms, and on top of her head when she receives IV treatment. She has ice chips that she sucks on throughout the process. She says the ice constricts the blood vessels, and she has less neuropathy.

When healing from cancer, there are choices, and you get to take care of yourself. It helps when you know what you're going into. Most likely, these treatments are short-term therapy in the scope of your life. Rest, sleep, take care of yourself, and go for walks. Short walks are fine.

Some people diagnosed with stage III later discovered that cancer was actually stage IV. These patients may be dealing with a much longer and varied course of chemotherapy treatments, more radiation treatments, ablation therapy, or immunotherapy with chemotherapy treatments. Several stage IV patients advocate for themselves by getting second, third, or fourth opinions. If you're in the same boat, consider asking until someone gives you a creative solution. There are options, and some doctors don't know them all. Consider asking questions on the colorectal Facebook pages.

There are also clinical trials that you might be interested in joining. You can find them at clinicaltrials.gov or ask an oncologist at a major hospital. I have three friends living with stage IV rectal cancer for over ten years, with chemo and radiation combinations on and off. They continue to enjoy themselves, their hobbies, and their loved ones and contribute to life.

Whatever stage you are dealing with, you have the inner resources to handle it. You have wisdom and common sense to guide you to make changes. Advocate for yourself if you need to. Consider approving your taking time to slow down and relax or speed up and express yourself in the world. I'm reminding you that you are amazing. You are connected to a much bigger power than you know. You can do this. You'll be able to move through this time in your life. A field of intelligence and support is available to you if you ask for it. The rest of the people who went through this journey and I are backing you up with our energies. We are holding you with much love, tenderness, and support.

SUMMARY AND SUGGESTIONS

1. For stage II/III without genetic aberrations, the protocol may call for six more rounds of chemotherapy. Generally, you will take high-dose Xeloda pills and IV Oxaliplatin.

2. Everybody has different side effects from chemotherapy. For Xeloda, people may experience headaches and tenderness to the hands and feet with touching hot or cold temperatures or touching coarse textures.
3. You will have blood work check-ups before each chemotherapy cycle. The oncologist wants to check your white blood count and hemoglobin levels and ensure your body is balanced enough for more chemotherapy.
4. Your hemoglobin count will most likely reduce. Add vitamin C, B12, and B complex to your daily routine to aid in iron absorption. Eat iron-rich foods. If your hemoglobin drops to seven, you may need a blood transfusion.
5. Hydration is of utmost importance when taking more potent chemotherapy. See if you can have hydration right after your chemo infusion. You can also add Nuun electrolytes, coconut water, or water with maple and honey to your daily routine. Hydration with calcium-magnesium before chemotherapy may reduce your neuropathy.
6. People report good energy levels after engaging in high-intensity sports after chemotherapy.
7. Consider allowing yourself to slow down. I'm reminding you that you are resilient. You will move through this time in your life. The rest of the people who went through this journey and I are backing you up with our energies. We all are holding you with love, tenderness, and support.

Chapter Twenty Four

TO REVERSE OR NOT TO REVERSE?

Most likely, when you live with a stoma, you get used to it. You become comfortable with its care. You use an ostomy belt, a wrap, or a stealth belt to keep the bag close to the body when exercising, dancing, and socializing. You can go anywhere and do anything. Your stoma supplies are always nearby. Your quality of life is good, for the most part.

Then your surgeon says you can reverse your stoma, and you're facing yet another decision: to reverse or not. Some of you clearly want your stoma gone, while others are undecided about it. I once spoke with a physician's assistant. She met patients with sincere bowel challenges after the reversal surgery and was certain she would not reverse her ileostomy.

I was undecided and needed more information. Eight months after the LAR surgery, I could do almost everything with the stoma. I ate whatever I wanted. I slept through the night. I danced, hiked, and practically led a normal life. Yes, I had leaks occasionally, and I problem-solved them. On occasion, the skin around the stoma was allergic to the glue of the bag, and I had to deal with an itchy rash. I'd also need to be vigilant on tight seals around the stoma. However, over time these once-formidable problems had dwindled to predictable events I could handle.

I read posts on the Facebook pages by people who had their stomas reversed. They complained of problematic bowel issues. They needed to go to the bathroom up to thirty times a day. They had gas and consistency issues with food that turned to diarrhea or constipation. They couldn't run because of leaks. One man described sitting on the toilet and feeling like glass shards passed through his anus. Another guy described tiny turds coming out as a bowel movement for hours. I felt concerned. It seemed that staying with the stoma would have issues with raw skin, leaks, and carrying stoma supplies, and reversing the stoma would entail problems with constant bathroom issues.

I wanted to have a good quality of life after cancer. I asked on the colorectal Facebook pages: "Is there any woman with a very low reconnection with no rectum or sigmoid colon on this site who has a great quality of life post-reversal?"

Two women replied. One said she doesn't eat raw vegetables or fruit; the other eats everything. I spoke with both women on the phone and consulted with Penny, who eats everything. She said her surgeon told her that after this surgery, she should not take anything to control the flow of feces through her altered colon: no Imodium or fiber. He said the body needs to learn to heal on its own and not to take anything to control the excrement.

The surgeon further instructed her to train her bowels: Right after the surgery, the body will want to go to the bathroom the whole day. The doctor told Penny to resist and teach her bowels to discharge feces only once or twice a day at the same time. Without a normal-sized rectum to hold feces, resisting would be difficult but could be accomplished. Penny returned to work quickly after surgery. The demands of her job forced her to control her bowel movements and not go every time her body wanted to go. She trained her body to have one bowel movement daily.

Penny said she was also terrified of the prospects of reversal. She opted to experiment with coping with the effects of the reversal for two years. Penny reasoned she could get a permanent colostomy if she suffered horribly. She suggested I might consider that possibility. She also offered that people living with an excellent quality of life after the reversal aren't spending time on Facebook pages reading and responding. She inferred that they are living their lives while those not feeling well take up space to share what is wrong. I sensed the truth in her words.

Penny was inspirational and comforting. She said, "This is a temporary phase in your life, and it will pass to the next phase. More good is coming your way, and remember that life can be good."

Penny reiterated that if I had terrible results after two years, I could ask for a permanent colostomy. She insisted that her quality of life was good and was happy she chose to reverse the stoma. She even ran a half marathon within a few months after the reversal.

Before making a final decision, I made an appointment with a pelvic floor physical therapist (PFPT). The people on the Facebook forums endorsed going to such a specialist after both surgeries. The therapist had sensors to insert into the rectal area and a computer that read if the inner and outer anal sphincters could close. She gave me Kegel exercises to hold the pelvic floor up and exercises to work on closing the sphincters. She said that both the external and internal sphincters worked. Acquiring that knowledge made me see the possibility of a reversal in a more positive light. I did the Kegel exercises religiously to strengthen the sphincter muscles.

You can keep your stoma or have a reversal. If you have a reversal and don't like it, you can have another surgery to create a colostomy. I trust that you will research and come to a conclusion that fits you. I support you in your decision-making process. Often the most challenging part of this journey is making a decision. You have my encouragement and support.

SUMMARY AND SUGGESTIONS

1. Penny said to train the bowels and not take fiber or Imodium to control the output.
2. Whether you want to stay with your stoma or have it reversed is a personal choice.
3. Often, the most challenging part of this journey is making decisions. In time, you will choose what fits you and your lifestyle. Refrain from putting unnecessary pressure on yourself.
4. It's a temporary phase in your life that will pass. More good is coming your way.
5. Consider going to a pelvic floor physical therapist to check your sphincters before choosing to have the reversal.

Chapter Twenty Five

THE RECONNECTION (REVERSAL) SURGERY

My quality of life was excellent with the stoma. Still, the irritated skin around the stoma was what pushed me to choose to reverse the stoma. I had the reversal surgery in April 2018. The surgery went well, lasting about forty-five minutes. During this surgery, Dr. Steen cut out the stoma, the part of the ileum that was pulled out of the body. Then he reattached the small intestines inside the body with tiny staples. Finally, he closed the abdominal incision with a few stitches (some surgeons glue this incision).

After the surgery, I felt abdominal pain, as expected. I had to control my laughter and asked uncle Yacov to stop being funny. For the following two days, I was on a liquid diet. For lunch on the third day, I ate hospital food that included cooked carrots, a bit of rice, and the sauce of the cooked meat. Within an hour, I burped the meat sauce and threw up twice. I had horrible intestinal cramps. I couldn't tell if the cramps were because the colon was waking up or because my body was throwing up the oily food it couldn't digest yet.

At seven in the evening, I asked for painkillers as the cramps were too painful to manage; intense contractions lasted for thirty long seconds. The following day, I had almost no cramps except light ones after dinner. And the next day, I ate the same food as the previous day, though I had cramps the whole day. I could walk around better, and some of the puffiness in my belly relaxed.

I would not be allowed to leave the hospital until I'd had a bowel movement, which so far had not happened. In the late afternoon, I remembered that pure celery juice drunk on an empty stomach is a natural laxative. I asked my friend May for it, and she arrived with fresh juice.

Later that evening, I felt mild bowel urge sensations. At first, only mucus came out. Then, the tiniest bowel movement came out with mucus and blood. It was the length of less than a pinky finger and the diameter of an earthworm. That's it? I thought. Is that a bowel movement? I called the nurse to see if what I had produced counted as a bowel movement. Before she had a chance to come, my bowels signaled again. This time a slightly longer piece with the same diameter came out, and I returned to bed. Within twenty seconds, I had another tiny bowel movement. I resisted when the next urgency occurred. I held it in as Penny had advised. The nurse confirmed that what came out was a bowel movement, and I was discharged.

Like the first time I was discharged, I became emotional about my uncle's loyal support. Likewise, I appreciated the nurses and staff taking care of patients like me at their lowest abilities, in pain, unable to care for themselves, and feeling sensitive and vulnerable. I cried from gratitude. I felt so grateful for their loving efforts that helped me and others to heal.

I was scared to leave the hospital with my habit of attaching to fearful thoughts. I couldn't fathom healing outside of the hospital without the safety net of nurses and medicines. But the next phase was calling. I returned to my uncle and aunt's home to heal from abdominal pain, cramps, a puffy belly, and a colon full of food that, so far, was not coming out with bulk.

When you have your surgery, of course, it will be different.

Some hospitals will release you when your body passes gas. Other hospitals wait until you have your first bowel movement. It might be so tiny you wouldn't believe it's a bowel movement. You might have multiple urgencies that will produce small bowel movements. Or you might have diarrhea from the get-go. I'm unsure how your journey will be as you and your body are unique. I hope you don't have painful cramps as I did, but you might. It's a more straight-forward surgery to heal from regarding pain level than the first surgery. You have my support as you move through this part of the journey if you choose a reconnection surgery.

SUMMARY AND SUGGESTIONS

1. Be careful with eating greasy food right after surgery; your body might not be ready yet to digest it.
2. You may have cramps as the colon wakes up from its long beauty sleep.
3. Walking after this surgery is easier than the LAR surgery.
4. Most people stay in the hospital until they pass gas or have a bowel movement.
5. Your first bowel movement will most likely be tiny in diameter and length.
6. You have my love and support as you move through this part of the journey if you choose to have a reconnection surgery.

Chapter Twenty Six

THE FIRST WEEK HOME AFTER THE RECONNECTION SURGERY

I had tiny bowel movements the morning after leaving the hospital. Cramps came and went throughout the day. By evening, the feces was the thickness and length of a thin finger. I felt encouraged.

However, Wednesday arrived with intense colon cramps and gas all day. The cramps lasted for thirty or forty seconds, prolonged abdominal spasms with shooting pain in the abdomen and low back. I took CBD oil which did not alleviate the pain. I went to the bathroom several times. I did my best to hold and not run to the toilet every time I experienced urgency. The cramps continued on Thursday with hardly any bowel movements, even though I ate a fair amount of food.

On Friday, I went to the toilet the whole day. The body needed to discard tiny amounts of waste, a third of a finger amount, the entire day. The day was accompanied by gas and belly cramps. Friday evening, cousin Yaeli came over, made food, warmed up a hot pack for my belly, and did the dishes. I felt grateful for her efforts. I was exhausted from going to the bathroom all day and trying to "hold some in." My bottom was sensitive and sore.

I still had about eight diminutive bowel movements in the morning on Saturday. The area around the anus felt sore and irritated by acidic stool material. The cramps and the urgency persisted all day long. In the evening of that very difficult day, I thought, *Maybe I had made a mistake. Maybe this surgery was not the right choice.* I could not imagine one more day of dealing with one paralyzing discomfort after another, capped off by the pain of cleaning the sore and delicate skin around the anus. I spoke with God: "I cannot handle any more days like these. Please, I need your help. I need a milder recovery period. I will not be able to survive another day of burning, cramping, and multiple discarding."

Sunday was a calmer morning. I experienced mild cramps of urgency. I visited my family for my brother's birthday. I ate crackers with hummus, baked vegetables, avocado, and cooked beets. Back home, I had gas and needed to go to the bathroom every fifteen minutes. I was learning from my early mistakes: the body was not ready to digest beans.

Monday brought much urgency. I was trying to hold the feces in and not go each time I had a sensation. When I did go, poop the size of half a thumb came out. It was frustrating continually running to the toilet for such a small amount. I was still cramping. I went for a walk in the morning before drinking or eating anything to see if I could manage the urges. I needed to have a bowel movement while I walked. I did my best to hold it and sat on the curb until the sensation disappeared. Waves of peristalsis came again, and I couldn't control everything. Luckily, I was wearing a pull-up diaper.

I also went for an early morning walk the following day. I couldn't hold the feces. I went in the diaper. Then I felt itching around the anus the whole way back. I applied several baby rash creams: Aquaphor, zinc oxide cream, Boudreaux Butt Paste, and Calmoseptine. The new stool was sticky and challenging to remove from irritated skin. My sister got me a bidet, and I began using it, but even water spray hurt the sensitive anus.

I learned that the colon is narrow in diameter. What makes a stool thick is the packing of the stool into the long and wide rectum. I no longer have a rectum. The size of poop now can only be the diameter of the colon stitched to the little rectal muscle; what comes out is about the diameter of a finger in short segments. Dr. Steen said that the low, reconnected, radiated tissue is narrower than previously. I understood I'd need multiple bathroom trips to add to a regular-sized poop.

Wednesday was a better day, without cramps and not as many bowel movements. Thursday was my first good day: no cramps, just body signals to go to the bathroom. I returned home. It felt like years had passed, but I had only lived through the first week after reversal surgery.

The first week after your surgery will be exhausting. By the end of the week, you will have wondered if you had made a mistake. Everyone I spoke with who had a reversal surgery had the same thought. Healing takes time, gentleness, and PATIENCE after this surgery.

While you heal, for the first six weeks, it's essential to eat a low-residue healing diet: oatmeal, bananas, avocado, toast, white rice, cooked vegetables, baked potato, yams, poultry, fish, and soups. After six weeks, you might introduce raw, peeled fruit and vegetables in small quantities. The key is to introduce small amounts of raw food gradually. If you have a high-power blender, you could make smoothies for easier digestion. See how your body works. Every body is different. Some people cannot digest raw vegetables or fruit after the reconnection for a while.

I faced many elimination challenges in the first months. The cramps subsided, but my body struggled with the urgent need to go to the bathroom. The moment I took my first bite of anything, my body gave strong signals for elimination. It would happen with the second and third bites as well.

Healing from a reconnection surgery will challenge you on all levels. Have patience. There will be low moments of going to the bathroom more than thirty times daily. The feces might be acidic, and your anus will be sore. In addition, your colon may be cramping and spasming as it wakes up. Have soothing lotions nearby. Watch movies. Use CBD oils for relaxation or sleep if it's medically legal in your state or anything else that will calm you down. Your body is going through a significant change.

Most important, be easy with yourself. Love yourself through this process. Let yourself off the hook about wanting the healing to be different than what it is. Be extra compassionate with yourself. I trust your discernment about what you need. Although this phase is painful and exhausting, you are going through it. You're doing a marvelous job. I honor you and the complex process you're going through. I acknowledge your resiliency, beauty, and strength. You have my love and support through the first week after reversal surgery.

SUMMARY AND SUGGESTIONS

1. You may experience severe cramps in the first week after having your bowels reconnected.
2. Your first bowel movement will most likely be tiny in diameter and length. Your feces will most likely grow to be the thickness of a finger.
3. You will most likely have multiple urgencies as soon as you put food in your mouth.
4. In the first week after the reconnection surgery, you'll wish you hadn't done it.

5. Consider eating a low-residue diet for six weeks as your intestines heal from the surgery. Then eat what you'd like and introduce raw food in small quantities.
6. You'll need zinc oxide, Aloe vera gel, baby wipes, and possibly a bidet. You'll also want Aquaphor, Calmoseptine, or other baby butt cream nearby. Pretty soon, you'll have them in your purse, and in each bathroom you use.
7. Have patience with your healing. Watch movies. Use medical CBD oils for relaxation or sleep if it's legal in your state. Listen to your discernment. Healing from this operation is sincerely challenging. Be extra tender with yourself. This week will challenge everything you've got.
8. Own your deep beauty when you can. I honor your beauty, efforts, love, determination, and resiliency.

Chapter Twenty Seven

WHAT'S CHEMO BRAIN?

During the six months I took oral chemo pills, I became forgetful, especially of words. I would be in conversation with someone and stop midway. The words just disappeared. It was amazing. When I started the sentence, I knew what I was about to say, but the concepts dissipated after saying a few words. Sometimes my brain had access to an image but could not connect it with the word for it.

When I forgot words during a conversation, I laughed out loud from fascination and amusement that the brain would not connect with words. I was flowing with the moment and accepted the manifestation. Because this scenario recurred, I realized this phenomenon must be related to the chemo. I jokingly said to myself and others as it was occurring, "I can't find the words I'm looking for; they disappeared...It must be chemo brain." I mean, what else could it be? It's never happened before taking chemo. It was like having dementia. I know because I work with dementia patients.

This forgetfulness happens to many people who take chemotherapy. The children of a friend of mine learned to guess what their mother meant when she said things like, "Put the whatyoumaycall it in the thingamabob" while she was going through chemo. I used to say, "I need the thing for the thing."

When this phenomenon occurred several times, I received a perspective on how words are only one of the ways to communicate. What felt important was that I was with Toby at the beach, and he was happily looking at me and laughing with me when I stopped in mid-sentence without a clue about what I wanted to say.

Chemo affects many organs in the body, and the brain is one of them. I read in a post on one of the online forums that this fuzzy, foggy thinking and a loss for words is a documented phenomenon. Many patients who take chemo experience similar symptoms. They cannot find the words to describe what they want to say, have slower verbal responses than usual, and are forgetful. When I searched online, I found many lists describing "chemo brain." The Mayo Clinic characterizes chemo brain as:

- Being unusually disorganized
- Confusion
- Difficulty concentrating
- Difficulty finding the right word
- Difficulty learning new skills
- Difficulty multitasking
- Fatigue
- Feeling of mental fogginess
- Short attention span
- Short-term memory problems
- Taking longer than usual to complete routine tasks
- Trouble with verbal memory, such as remembering a conversation
- Trouble with visual memory, such as recalling an image or list of words

For some patients, especially those who received more potent chemotherapy than I did, chemo brain is a real and severe issue. Some people have problems focusing and find they cannot work effectively. This terrible side effect can last for years after completion of chemo treatment. Forgetting words was a real struggle for one single mom supporting her family through writing. And not only did she forget words, but she would also forget tasks. She ended up keeping lists, but she also kept a list of the lists so she would know if she'd forgotten a whole bunch of stuff.

Many people – including bosses and coworkers at organizations that employ cancer patients – don't believe that chemo brain is accurate and give their workers a hard time if they don't perform at the same level as before. Two patients wrote that they lost their jobs due to their forgetfulness and inability to keep track of tasks.

I listened to talks about Alzheimer's prevention and began taking brain supplements with Bacopa, trace minerals, B-complex vitamins, and a vegan algae-based Omega 3 supplement. My chemo brain lasted for a year after chemo, and then my brain began connecting with more words during conversations. Five years after I finished chemotherapy, my brain comes up with words. If you need more support for your chemo brain, there are Facebook support pages for chemo brain issues. A recent one that I saw is called: Chemo Brain Awareness.

If you are in treatment, consider speaking with your bosses if it makes sense, so they can understand if you seem foggier, slower, forgetful, or shorter on words. You will get your functioning back at some point. Eat well, sleep adequately, exercise, enjoy your life, consider taking supplements, and be patient with yourself. Consider learning about brain health. Make lists when you need to, or lists of lists.

Remember to be easy with your lovable and precious self about your experience. You're in a temporary phase, and it will pass.

Consider letting yourself off the hook about being anything other than how you are on your treatment. Be kind and compassionate with yourself. Honor and acknowledge that chemotherapy affects the brain. You are going through a lot of changes. Consider being vulnerable with others. You might even laugh at the value that people place on being right, accurate, accomplishing "important" tasks, and using words. Of course, at work, it might affect your productivity. You have my love and support as you navigate your territory with chemo brain.

SUMMARY AND SUGGESTIONS

1. You may forget words while you are on chemotherapy and beyond. It's a known chemotherapy side effect.
2. Consider learning about brain health and taking supplements that boost brain function.
3. Eat a healthy, clean diet without additives, preservatives, processed foods and sugars.
4. Sleep adequately, exercise, enjoy your life, consider taking the right supplements, and be patient with yourself.
5. You are going through a lot of changes. Consider being easy with yourself about your experience. Be kind and compassionate with yourself. Honor and acknowledge that chemotherapy might affect your brain. You have my love, acknowledgment, and support.

Chapter Twenty Eight

LARS

After the reversal surgery that eliminates the need for a pouch, patients deal with various bowel issues. No patient will return to normal bowel function. There will be challenging and more manageable days until you understand your "new normal." It is a difficult recovery. The first surgeon I spoke with said that after the reconnection surgery, patients report a few bowel movements before breakfast, followed by five or six more after breakfast.

The patients I spoke with said two years elapsed before they healed from the reconnection surgery. They said they had "good days and bad days." It took my body two and a half years to digest all foods and five years to get to a comfortable rhythm. But each body is different. One woman cannot digest raw fruits or vegetables two and a half years after her reconnection surgery. Another woman had diarrhea for six months, followed by constipation. You will gauge your healing with your surgeon and your body. Have hope, patience, and faith in your body's healing, listen to your common sense and wisdom, and for heaven's sake, focus on having more fun with friends, hobbies, and family. It will offset the challenges. I promise.

One of the first things I became aware of was how often I'd go to the bathroom. On many days it was thirty times or more. Before having a bowel movement, the body would often signal with gas. But, as you can imagine, after thirty to forty trips to the bathroom, I was "fartigued."

"Clustering" was a challenge for me after the reconnection surgery. If I ate something this body could not digest yet, like legumes, and beans, I could count on acidic, burning, consistent gas. The gas was audible, foul-smelling, and wet. After passing gas multiple times, the area around the anus felt lightly burned. The reason it was acidic was that the colon hadn't healed yet. Usually, after each expulsion of this kind of gas, I immediately needed a bowel movement. Clustering lasted from three to five hours.

During clustering, I could not hold the feces in for long. I could eliminate fifteen or more small pieces per hour. Then the stool became soft and acidic, burning the area around the anus. During those times, I took sitz baths because the anus became so sensitive that if I wiped with a baby wipe or toilet paper, it hurt and left a reddish-pink residue on the paper. I applied fresh Aloe vera gel around the anus for best results or a zinc-oxide cream. Then I would lie down and relax, relax my breath, watch a movie to distract myself, and, ultimately, take some cannabis oil to relax the system and get me to sleep. During clustering, I was not functional. If I had morning doctor appointments, I'd tell my body to stop. Sometimes it listened, and other times I'd have soiled underwear.

I learned about Low Anterior Resection Syndrome (LARS) from the Facebook pages. LARS symptoms can include: "frequency or urgency of stools, largely due to the fact you have less space to store stool after removing part or all of the rectum; clustering of stools (many bowel movements during a few hours); fecal incontinence (lack of control over bowel movements); constipation for more than a few days, followed by multiple bowel movements a few days later; increased gas; abdominal pain; and a small risk to urinary and/or sexual function due to nerve damage."i

My healing was challenging for the first six months with clustering, the unpredictability of bowel movements, and sticky stools. But I functioned. I even went on a two-month trip to intentional communities and managed. There were "good days" and "bad days." Bad days were when I ate dinner and couldn't dance at a gathering because if I moved, I'd have to go to the bathroom. So I'd need to sit and watch others dance and not participate. "Bad days" were when I had clustering and an acidic anus.

Six months after the reconnection surgery, I ate potato salad with thawed frozen peas. I had forgotten this body could not digest peas yet. I then went to a tango dance party. In time, clustering began, and I needed to use the bathroom frequently. After an hour of expelling embarrassing, smelly gas while I danced with partners, I left.

While driving home, I felt an urgency to expel gas. I did my best to hold it in and let it out gently. Right after, I felt enormous pressure to have a bowel movement that I couldn't fight. I helplessly defecated in my underwear. Then it happened immediately later; I had more gas when I waited for the red light to change. And then, the urgency occurred for a bowel movement, and I had to defecate in my undies again. I'm thankful I was in the car alone and that the dance studio was near my home. When I arrived home, the anal area felt sore and burned from the acidic stool. Cleaning the area in my sitz bath hurt.

Periodically, I had days when I needed to change my underwear multiple times because of streaking. For instance, one day, I had my first discharge while waiting in line at the post office after breakfast. I had the urge to defecate. I did my best to hold it in, but some came out. I came back to my sitz bath and new underwear. Then I was out on a walk, and the same thing occurred. When my cousin came over to watch a movie, I didn't want to run to the bathroom each time I felt an urgency and pause the film, so I held it in. By nighttime, the anal area felt burned, and I felt exhausted. It happened often. As my friend Jay said, "You won't be wearing white underwear after this surgery."

Six months after surgery, my bowel movements, except for gluten, had little predictability. If I ate gluten, I had no bowel movement the following day. Those were my favorite days. I often had several bowel movements in the morning, probably four or five times before breakfast and maybe three to four more times after breakfast. If I ate large quantities at lunch, I had a bowel movement, or two or three, and if I ate a large dinner, I had five to six bowel movements before bedtime. If I ate anything after dinner, I would have five or six small bowel movements before bedtime.

After eating the low-residue diet, I went back to my pre-surgery diet: celery juice in the morning, then an hour or two later a fruit smoothie, followed by a big salad for lunch, then cooked vegetables and a small salad for dinner. When I ate this way, the stools had a wet consistency, and I constantly had stool streak marks on my underwear. After adding more grain to my diet, the stool became drier. The reality was that, on many days, there was underwear streaking.

Introducing Probiotics

I saw a GI doctor and asked about a probiotic called VSL#3. Six months after surgery, I had been taking two pills, 250 billion counts per day. I went out and had a salad for dinner with a piece of toast, and I felt fine after. That was a considerable improvement.

I went to the cancer center's nutritionist for vegan food advice. She suggested eating lentils but pureeing them for protein. She also suggested increasing the probiotic pills to six pills daily because of the foul gas smell. She said to be tender with my bowels as they underwent major trauma and are healing. She said there was a profound brain-gut connection, with many nerves leaving the gut and reaching the brain. She said I needed patience and compassion with my bowels as they were recovering.

I told my friend May about the daily streaks on my underwear. She informed me about a product that can harden the stool. It's called Shilajit. It's humus – a black, organic component of soil, rich with a substance called fulvic acid. It is formed by the decomposition of leaves and other plant material by soil microorganisms in the Himalayas.

The product's website informs that fulvic acid transports nutrients in and out of cells, chelates pollutants, "digests" inorganic compounds, and balances cellular electrolytes. I added Shilajit to my diet. It created a hardening of the stool and process, almost mimicking constipation by the end of the week. Since I used both products, the acidity of the feces was reduced, and when fecal matter trickled around my anus, it didn't burn like before.

Travel

I took my first trip two and a half months after surgery. I drove to New Mexico from Los Angeles. I ate very little while I drove for fear of having bowel issues. While visiting communities in New Mexico's mountains, my digestion was difficult. I had many LARS days and felt fatigued.

In March 2019, eleven months after the reversal surgery, I went on a four-day trip to Mexico. Before my trip, I did an enema to clear my bowels to avoid multiple bathroom trips. I used my old enema set, but the water would not enter my bowels after surgery. I had to use a balloon-type rectal enema. I applied consistent gentle pressure to squeeze water in. I inserted around three and a half cups of water, which flushed the colon.

I ate very little on that trip and didn't have a bowel movement for four days, which was both a miracle and a respite from my multiple daily bathroom trips. I also did an enema before my first flight after surgery to Israel to ensure I didn't have bathroom issues on the plane. I still do an enema before long trips.

A Year After the Reconnection Surgery

A year and a month after my reversal surgery, I realized I hadn't had the burning acidic gas or stool. I could have clustering and gas but without the burn. Gratitude and relief gushed from me. I could not believe my good fortune. It was a massive upgrade to my quality of life.

Colon healing from acidity took time and possibly intentional rehabilitation. After I took VSL#3, four pills a day, for three months, I added a new probiotic called Dr. Ohhira's for variety. Then I changed to Bio-Kult for one month. I also learned that good gut bacteria need fruit and vegetables to thrive, and I've been feeding my body accordingly.

Maybe the probiotics and diet helped? Perhaps, because I was born in Israel, I needed to eat Israeli food to have Israeli bacteria for my gut health to balance. Has the body matured and healed? Even when I've had "bathroom days," days where the body expels the large quantities I've eaten in previous days in a few hours, it hasn't been acidic. I haven't needed to use a calming lotion around the anus for the past month. That was miraculous!

By July, a year and three months after the surgery, I could finally eat lentils that were soaked for 24 hours with water changes.

Morning Massage

I perked up when a woman on the Facebook forum wrote she has just one significant bowel movement a day. How does she do that? It sounded miraculous to me. She went to a pelvic floor physical therapist, who gave her a sheet with a massage technique that she does every morning in bed for fifteen minutes after voiding urine. I asked for the sheet and followed the instructions for three weeks without improvement.

I asked that woman more questions. She replied that it took her some time to master the method. The key is to roll the ileocecal valve to get the process moving. The ileocecal valve should be massaged first. She uses her fingertips to dig in deeply and move her fingers on the area of the valve. Then she massages the colon near the liver – she pulls and manipulates it, really digs in. Then she massages the colon near the spleen on the left side of the body. She applies a lot of pressure with both hands and moves it around. She follows by massaging the colon from the ileocecal valve up the ascending colon, across the transverse colon, and following the descending colon about ten times. She ends by massaging the ileocecal valve again until she hears it flutter.

YouTube videos explained where the ileocecal valve could be. I used this method again. But I didn't see any decrease in trips to the bathroom. She repeated that consistency is vital. It took her a while to get it right. She waits until she feels her ileocecal valve start to work. She can feel it moving with her fingertips as a fluttering sensation. "It takes practice to get it right; just keep at it," she reassured.

She massages the colon in bed – apparently, it should be completed lying down. Within an hour, she feels the urge to go to the bathroom. Sorry to be graphic, but her poop is generally the width of a cigar and can be up to two feet long, broken into sections. She sits and waits for about fifteen minutes to empty her bowels.

I never felt the flutter. Then I moved to a new home and stopped the process. But this method may work for you. It would be amazing to have the colon emptied each morning using this technique. Then your whole day will be free, and you won't have to think about your bowel movements or the quantity of your meal each time you eat. That's a huge motivator to keep the practice until you get it.

Adding Beans, Still Healing

At the year and eight months mark after surgery, I still had multiple bowel movements a day. I learned to accept it. Eating smaller portions became a must for a sane life. I could not digest dairy, fatty, or oily foods well. When I ate any vegetable that was slightly wilted or had any brown spots, I would get terrible cramps, and my body would throw it up. I learned not to eat food from the fridge that's been there for more than three days. I also learned that when I have the urge to go to the toilet after a meal, it's most efficient when I sit on the toilet for fifteen minutes because several small pieces will empty. I am learning how to live with my body.

Two years after the reconnection surgery, I can eat and digest beans that have been soaked for more than 24 hours and whose water has been changed multiple times. I've learned my body. I won't go for a walk when it's clustering after I eat a big meal. I can't eat beans daily yet.

Clearing the Colon with Juices

Drinking two cups of warm hibiscus water in the morning on an empty stomach and following it with two cups of pure, fresh celery juice within thirty minutes to an hour clears my colon. I wait another thirty minutes to an hour to eat breakfast. After an hour or hour and a half, my body discards large amounts of feces, and I don't have bowel movements that day and often the next day. I use this method as needed. I need to be near a toilet for two to three hours.

For the hibiscus drink, I place a handful of dried burgundy petals in a cup and a half of boiling water overnight, then add a half cup of hot water in the morning. I get hibiscus from Amazon or any Latino/Hispanic market. It's called Jamaica. If I drink celery juice on an empty stomach in the morning, I also have greater emptying of the bowels but less than with the Hibiscus combination.

Healed

Two and a half years after the reconnection surgery, I could eat everything. I had salads and smoothies, lentils, and beans. I ate clean, primarily vegan, with lots of veggies, fruit, and greens, which offers regularity. I tried to eat smaller quantities, and when I didn't, I knew to stay home and be near a toilet. I still had a good amount of gas. Gas is what informed me that I needed to have a bowel movement. My friends and family knew that audible gas could come out anytime. I didn't suppress it much. I'm sure you'll find your way with your system.

My body is more resilient five years after the reconnection surgery. I can now eat food that has been in the refrigerator for more than three days without throwing up. The digestive system has gotten sturdier with time. I can eat anything. I have less gas. Clustering occurs each time I overeat, but much less than before. I've accepted it. I know when I overate, and I know to stay home.

Each person has a different reaction after the reconnection surgery. One woman wrote that her husband developed Celiac disease after his rectal resection (stage IIIb). Apparently, abdominal surgery is a known Celiac trigger, she mentions. Still, he went through two and a half years of misery and nearly died of malnutrition before getting the correct diagnosis. Her husband's GI doctor said that treating him changed his practice; he learned that Celiac disease is common. She said she learned that untreated Celiac disease puts a person at greater risk of cancer. When people have sincere GI issues after surgery, it's worth checking for Celiac disease. She says the blood test is accurate, but some GI doctors still consider a biopsy the "gold standard" for diagnosis.

A few people wrote they developed diarrhea right from surgery which lasted a long while. I did not experience that. Check that you don't have C. Diff bacteria after surgery. C. Diff will cause massive diarrhea. Some people develop C. Diff at the hospital after taking antibiotics.

Another man wrote that he's managing. Going back to the bag has its risks. He did fine with the bag, but he doesn't miss the bag explosions, the tender skin, and the mystery of not knowing if the stoma would erupt during a change. He lives daily for what it is and is glad to have time with his family.

A woman wrote that LARS was a shock, and her doctors downplayed the side effects. LARS and radiation affected her lifestyle dramatically. Another lady said she was blessed with her care and knowledgeable providers. They discussed LARS but only told her she would find a new normal. It's new, she says, but it's not normal. Once the reversal was completed, her quality of life changed drastically. She's now on disability due to the unpredictability of her movements and fatigue. She's almost 17 months after the reversal. Everyone's system is different. I know patients who went back to work after six weeks and managed.

Each person copes differently after the reconnection surgery. Some people do a daily enema before going to work. Others take Imodium or Lomotil daily to avoid bowel movements at work. One woman told me she doesn't eat until she gets home from work. Others manage by eating small meals throughout the day. Some people drink laxative tea or take rhubarb extract pills at night several times a week to facilitate a complete bowel movement in the morning. Others manage by juicing, massaging the ileocecal valve in the morning, or training their bowel to defecate once daily.

As your body heals, you'll learn your system, rhythm, and what works for you. You are intelligent, and you'll find solutions that fit you. You've done it your whole life and will find the type of management that's right for you.

I am glad I did the reversal. I had difficulty getting the proper seal on my ileostomy and was dealing with raw skin. What I have now is no less challenging but in a different way. I think about what I eat, when I eat, how much time I have for making and drinking juices to empty my bowels, and how much time I need in the morning before I can get out of the door. It's a lot of thinking. Sometimes I experiment with less thinking and planning about my eating and drinking habits in the morning, and the body works itself out. I'll continue to experiment with less thinking about what I'm experiencing.

If you're on this journey, notice how much energy you put into what you're going through. Are you giving the challenges a lot of thinking? Are you constantly analyzing and planning for the future? Notice how fatiguing it is. You're already exhausted from going to the bathroom many times. Consider trying to analyze and think less. Let go of obsessive and compulsive thinking to control your experience. Then see how your experience changes. I'm still working on mine.

I know you will have your ups and downs with the healing process, as everyone who had reconnection surgery did. It's challenging living without a rectum or living with an ostomy. I acknowledge your courage, patience, determination, resilience, loving, self-compassion, and surrender abilities. You chose to live knowing you will have physical challenges. I send you warmth and a tender virtual hug. I see you. I acknowledge your efforts. And I appreciate and support this delicate time as you learn your new system.

SUMMARY AND SUGGESTIONS

1. LARS refers to frequent and urgent stools with less storage capacity, clustering, fecal incontinence, constipation followed by multiple bowel movements, and gas increase. Each person after the reconnection surgery will experience some form of LARS that's in line with their body's constitution and rate of healing.
2. It takes at least two years to heal from this surgery. I'm finally feeling gut resiliency after five years.
3. Consider rehabilitating the gut with mega doses of probiotics and rotating different probiotics every few months. You might have some discharge a few days after taking the probiotics as they repopulate your gut, and other bacteria are discarded. Have patience.
4. Eating fruits and vegetables is essential to feed good gut bacteria, even in a smoothie.
5. Consider taking sitz-baths or having a bidet for cleaning around the anus when clustering happens.
6. My acidic gas and feces disappeared after about a year. Have patience with your body's healing.
7. Use creams to help with the burning around the anus.
8. Adding grains to your diet for the first six months will help dry your stool as it will be a wetter consistency than before the surgery (we have one foot less of a colon, which would reabsorb water. Your colon has to adjust to the new reality).
9. Consider doing an enema before long trips or flying.
10. Consider a morning massage routine with an emphasis on opening the ileocecal valve.

11. Two cups of warm hibiscus water followed by sixteen ounces of pure celery juice thirty minutes later will help clear your bowels, especially if you eat thirty minutes later. Make sure you are near a toilet for the next couple of hours. Pure celery juice will do similarly and is less potent. It will free you to go out at night without going to the bathroom.
12. You have discernment. You'll know when it's efficient to eat smaller meals and when to accept your new normal. See if less thinking and analyzing creates an easier life experience for you.
13. Each person with LARS copes differently. Everyone finds the type of management that's right for them. You will too.
14. Please have patience as you heal from this phase which might take two to five years. There will be many trying days ahead. That's our investment to live and love on planet Earth after rectal cancer treatments. Love yourself through it. You have my most profound compassion, admiration, respect, and support.

Section V

THE MIND-BODY CONNECTION, PART II

Chapter Twenty Nine

HEALING BODY IMAGE IN GROUPS

I had been dealing with cancer healing, alternative and otherwise, since September 2015, when I first saw blood on my stool and changed my eating habits. In June 2018, I needed to leave my home and travel. It had been nearly three years, and I felt exhausted with everything cancer and health-related.

Two and a half months after my reversal surgery, I took my car, equipped with a portable toilet, and drove to four intentional communities (an intentional community is a group of people who have chosen to live together or share resources based on common values) in New Mexico, Washington, and Oregon. I had two days between my stop in Boise and the third community. I chose to camp in my tent for one night in a national forest in Washington State. That morning my digestion felt fine, and I decided to hike.

I saw luscious, juicy, red, and perfectly August-ripened thimbleberries begging me to eat them. I hiked, ate, and marveled at my food fortune. But in a moment, the body signaled for a bowel movement. I hadn't yet internalized how quickly my body responds to eating anything. I found a spot in the forest and continued hiking, but the body went into clustering mode and demanded a bowel movement nearly every five minutes. I made it to the waterfall with my anxious and fatigued body. I didn't even want to look at the waterfall for too long as the body signaled again for another bowel movement. I chose to hike back with great discomfort and urgency. I felt constant acidic burning along with the fatigue of holding my sphincter muscles around the anus. Walking became painful, and I waddled like a duck.

Three-quarters of the way through the experience, I broke down. I sat on a log and cried. I couldn't walk with the burning and urgency any longer, and I didn't know what to do. I felt defeated and discouraged. I wondered how I would make it back to the car.

Desperately, I begged God for help by repeating the word "help" for two consecutive minutes. Then, I said, "God, I can't do this anymore. I can't walk any further with this burning discomfort. Please help me. This is too much for me to handle today. I can't do it. I need help. I need help." Then I surrendered, cried, surrendered, cried, surrendered, and cried some more. When I calmed down enough, I realized I had to return to the car. I got up and miraculously, there was no more urgency. The pain and burning disappeared, and I could walk normally and have a normal rest of the day. I profusely thanked the greater power.

I also had perspective shifts as I walked. Instead of being frustrated about how difficult life is for me some days after the reversal, I began opening up to the idea that thousands of others, like me, are challenged daily with the same manifestation.

In addition, I realized that some people go to war or have accidents and end up without body parts. I also don't have an internal part of the rectum or a sigmoid colon. People have issues to deal with, and they do. Everyone has to find a way to be in their new reality without resistance to make it easier mentally. I became accepting of where I was, remembering I was in good company with many more on this planet. This is a human experience in a body. Bodies are vulnerable. I calmed down and got to my car.

I drove to the Sahale Retreat Center on the Kitsap Peninsula by the Hood Canal. The retreat center belongs to the Good Enough Intentional Community. About ten residents lived in the retreat center, while most community members lived in separate dwellings in Washington state. Sahale is composed of 68 acres through which the Tahuya River runs. During the right season, salmon spawn in the river. There is a beautiful green meadow, a forest leading to the river, several wood cabins and a building with small rooms, a big white tent for retreats, a fir forest, an apple orchard, a black walnut grove under which my tent rested, berry plants, gardens, hot tubs, and a common house where meals are served.

The community said the best way to get to know them is to come to their annual Human Relations Lab. The point of this community is that people grow best in community – the personal edges, triggers, and upper limits can be seen with each other, and that is where growth opportunities occur.

The participants were assigned to small groups to process their daily learning. During this year's lab, the first day was about intentions. The second day was about freedom. The third day addressed sexuality/intimacy/orgasmic relationship with life, the fourth day addressed intimacy and upper limits, the fifth day approached the subject of vulnerability, etc. A chakra healer and a music healer were present, and we began each day by toning the chakras along with sound healing through songs, harmonies, and musical instruments.

After a full day of healing processes, people gathered at the makeshift bar. Musicians performed songs, poetry, and skits. People drank alcohol (fees went to the scholarship fund), played games, and smoked cigarettes and pot (outside). They seemed happy, joyful, creative, accepting of newcomers, and loving.

The heart of the learning is radical acceptance of the human experience. We shared our fears and limiting beliefs authentically in the small groups. We were seen, witnessed, and acknowledged in a safe space. It can be freeing when people speak their limits publicly and are accepted. When people speak their feelings instead of stuffing them, their energy can flow.

My intentions had to do with creating a new life: intending to live in a new place, getting ready to create a coaching business, and connecting with a life partner. I also wanted to leave my cancer identity behind and start being me without cancer.

The most fear and discomfort was around bringing in a life partner. With a new body, soiled underwear, much gas, and baby cream smeared on my behind, I felt embarrassed and insecure about letting a potential partner share my body.

I saw myself as damaged. I feared that men would not see me as a potential partner once they learned about my medical challenges. I spoke about this to my small group. Each time I shared, I went deeper into another layer of perceived limitations. I shed many tears.

Interestingly, the more I got to know several men in this community, the more fun I had. Both men and women in the community exhibited friendliness, caring, and curiosity about me and my life. I found myself with new attractive, present men. They had no idea what challenges I faced. They simply enjoyed my presence, and it was fun to sense it.

One day, I hurt my leg from overstretching and needed medical assistance from the nurses. It was decided that someone would go into my tent and put a heavy mattress under my mattress so that I'd have more cushion and less pain to sleep. An attractive man went into my tent and saw everything that I was afraid a man would see, soiled underwear, a syringe with cannabis oil that I use for sleep, and a dildo to stretch the vagina.

When I realized he'd be seeing all those things and I couldn't do anything about it, I had a huge internal embarrassed laugh. I chuckled to myself all evening. He returned and said, "I added a mattress to your tent. I had to take everything out of the tent. There's a lot of interesting things in there...just saying." I felt embarrassed, and all I could do was accept the embarrassment and thank him.

The following day, when it was time for the bigger group sharing about intimacy and vulnerability, I shared my experience of being embarrassed and why. I shared my fears of a man seeing my underwear smeared in baby lotion and feces, the syringes with cannabis oil lying around, and the stretching of the vagina dildo. I spoke in front of the whole group in the funniest and most matter-of-fact way. There, the secrets were out.

That day and the next day, community members, men and women alike, gave me accepting feedback, even some of the men I'd been talking with. There was positive regard and warmth for my courage and the humor with which I shared. I felt both embarrassed and grateful to be acknowledged for my vulnerability.

The last night, they held a talent show. People performed songs, music, poetry readings, and comedy. I teamed up with the musicians, and we created a belly dance piece that I performed at the bar. I was going to perform it with a shirt on, not baring my waist with surgery scars and my port, but when I consulted with the head musician, he said, "Show it. It might be healing for you."

I found clothes to create an outfit. That night, I had to go to the bathroom every five minutes, it was awful, and my anus hurt. I didn't think I could perform, but when it was time to perform, the system stopped, and I went on stage and danced - baring my belly with surgery scars...and getting people up to dance, both men and women. It felt energizing and healing.

My digestion was relatively okay here, maybe because of the diet, the elevation, or the ease in the community. I did have some uncomfortable days when I walked like a duck, but overall, it was doable. The experience was fun. I received consistent support and love. I got to express myself with scars on many levels and be accepted. I was healing my deepest perceived wounds. My intentions created the best scenarios to move through this level of limitations. I glided into confidence and a more honest acceptance of myself as I am today.

This community helped me get myself back. When I was departing from the community, saying my good-byes one by one, one community member said to me, "You know, if I were ever to draw a nude body of a woman, I would prefer drawing the body of an older woman; one that has scars and folds that shows the life she has lived rather than a body of a young woman who hasn't lived a full life. That would be much more interesting and meaningful for me." I cried. His message deeply touched and moved me. His compassion and sensitivity stay with me until this day, four years later. I'm grateful to Sahale's community and the Human Relations Laboratory for providing the space and support to see myself with fresh eyes.

Perhaps you have a community of people you can connect with and heal, maybe a support group or a men's or women's group where you can share your fears deeply and intimately. While going to such a support group over time, you get to know people, hear each other and understand where everyone is in their journey. The key to healing with groups is consistency, vulnerability, and not trying to change another person's experience. You share what you are experiencing and allow others to hold you with acceptance and appreciation for your courage to undergo a healing journey in life.

Alternatively, if you are in a loving, intimate partnership, consider sharing with your partner what you feel ashamed or embarrassed about. Once it's out in the open, and you feel accepted and loved, scars and all, you might accept yourself. You've chosen life. You did everything possible to heal from stage II/III rectal cancer. Celebrate that. Celebrate you. Celebrate your scars that show what you chose.

Celebrate that protruding port and stoma. That's what adds to your already radiant beauty. That's what adds depth to life. I honor your courage, strength, beauty, and magnificence. You have my support in healing your body image from whatever treatments you underwent.

SUMMARY AND SUGGESTIONS

1. When you eat something raw and new, you may have clustering. Consider trying new foods when you're close to a bathroom.
2. Consider the power of surrendering the thinking mind and dropping into a more expansive field of inner quiet where you can ask the divine / God / creative power for help.
3. Lots of people are being challenged on this planet at this moment when they are missing a body part. You are on par with many others and connected to them in your challenges. You are not alone in your struggles.
4. You may consider speaking any shame or insecurity about your body to a trusted friend who knows how to hold space for your experience, a coach, a therapist, or in a support group.
5. You might consider showing your body as is, scars and all, to the world. You might consider a radical acceptance of your body today. Your body displays your courage, resilience, and commitment to be in life. Consider being proud of that.
6. You may choose to share yourself with a consistent support group and receive acceptance and acknowledgment for all you are going through. The key is to be consistent and vulnerable, to allow others to see what you are going through without fixing or changing your experience. Allow them to support you. Allow yourself to accept that love.

Chapter Thirty

A "CANCER PERSONALITY?"

At the beginning of my journey with cancer, I read *The Complete Cancer Cleanse* by Cherie Calbom, John Calbom, MA, and Michael Mahaffey, PC. These authors spoke of a "cancer personality:" someone who is experiencing the loss of a loved one or faith; feeling hopelessness and despair; questioning the rightness and worthiness of living, suppressing emotions, especially anger and resentment; living in loneliness; lacking connection with one or both parents; having a tendency to carry other people's burdens and worry for others, and seeking approval. Unfortunately, before and during my diagnosis, I could relate to these observations.

But knowing that I chose to clean up everything that could contribute to cancer, including habitual unproductive thinking, meant that I would use the information above to heal. Doing the forgiveness work and questioning my stressful thinking transformed my past habits of negativity into greater awareness and lightness as my thought attachment to a painful past dissolved.

When I got to the Hope4cancer Clinic in Mexico, the clinic utilized an emotional healing method called Recall healing based partly on German New Medicine (GNM). Dr. Hamer, who created GNM, developed testicular cancer about a year after his son died suddenly in a car accident. As a healthy man all his life, Dr. Hamer got curious about how his body created cancer. Dr. Hamer wondered if his deep grief signaled his body to create cancer. Since he worked with cancer patients, he tested his hypothesis on his patients by using brain imaging.

Dr. Hamer reported that certain life events, which people registered as a shock, showed themselves in a particular part of the brain. All people who had their shock register at the same part of the brain had the same disease: breast, testicular, ovarian, rectal, brain cancer, or some other type of cancer. The same shocking event could be experienced differently by siblings and register in different parts of their brains, leading to different disease manifestations. GNM holds that once the mental-emotional shock components are resolved, the body will clear the trauma, and cancer will dissolve. In Recall Healing, they believe that the shock occurred the year before diagnosis, but I could not find any such shock the year before my diagnosis except for chronic stress about my diminishing finances.

For rectal cancer, Recall Healing lists several mental-emotional components that could contribute to the disease. One is a belief of not having a strong identity in the world, i.e., not fitting in anywhere. The second issue associated with the rectum was an inability to release judgments or resentments. The third topic was: what was so disgusting that I couldn't accept it. The fourth idea was what was difficult to digest. The fifth idea was who was sodomized in the family.

For me, all of the topics were relevant, and I addressed them during my cancer journey. I went to a recall healing therapist and examined all the topics. I grew up with different family combinations and remained single with no children. I had to question my thinking and see that I belong with all of life when I don't believe in separating thinking. "I" don't even exist as a personality when I don't believe any thinking. I saw where I was stuck in judgments of self and others and saw my innocence beyond believing thoughts. I found my light, my inner IT, over and over anytime I did The Work on any judgment. I used the information above to uncover family secrets and my emotional entanglements with the past. I freed myself.

But did I need to do all that work looking at and questioning my thinking about patterns? Everyone has had something disgusting happen in their lives, something they couldn't digest, and thinking they don't belong sometimes. Should you spend time, energy, and focus looking at all the things that shackled you, or should you trust how you are made? You have a trusted toolkit for getting into your space of quiet and mental health. It's called your emotions.

When your feelings don't feel good about anything, stop what you're doing. Check-in with yourself if you need to communicate something to another or do something to change your environment. If not, your feelings are telling you that you're misusing your gift of thought against yourself or the world. Stop the mental commentary.

Notice where you feel the feelings in the body and follow them. Place your focus on your feelings in the body and breathe. And breathe some more. There, there. Your feelings communicated to you that you were caught up in unhelpful thinking, and you followed the feeling and woke up from what the mind was doing. How grateful to have a trusted guidance system to alert you to wake up. It means that you don't have to look for your habitual "patterns". Life will show you when you're misusing the gift of thought, and you'll wake up over and over.

When thoughts and feelings do what they do, which is move, you'll be back to focusing on now, your light, your It, your goodness, loving, belonging, healthy intentions, resilience, and creative gifts and talents. Wouldn't you prefer focusing on fun and joy rather than looking at negative patterns? When you look at contracted patterns, you'll focus there. When you focus on enjoying life, being creative, loving, contributing, and appreciating life, you get more of that.

Check with your inner discernment whether you need to look at the Recall Healing themes and transform them (if you still believe those thoughts) or are ready to focus on what is healthy in you right now. The more you use your creative tool of thought to focus on what is joyous, pleasant, lovely, working well, where you already belong, what you love, and the abundance in your life, the more you'll feel your innate well-being. The more you feel your innate well-being, the more you are productive, joyful, creative, empowered, and loving. You have discernment and get to choose how to use the creative gift of thought.

Have you found your identity in the world that you are grounding in your deeper self, or are you still seeking to fit in with your work, family, or friends? Who you are is perfect, whole, and complete. The real belonging is inside of you and is eternal. You can connect with your own loving right now as you are, as life is.

I encourage you to connect with the quiet stillness that you are beyond fleeting thoughts and feelings. Your well-being and belonging reside there. That quiet is a lovely feeling available to you at all times. It's inside, and it's relaxing. You truly belong with the bigger It, and with life. You matter enormously to life. You are connected to everyone and everything. You bring your beautiful and unique gifts, which you contribute to the world. You are precious. You are connected to the whole of life. That makes you enormous and on par with everyone. Go there often.

Have you addressed what was difficult for you to release about your past? I invite you to find a way to accept what was and let go of painful judgments. Given their conditioning and awareness, everyone was doing their best to meet a basic human need with the best strategy they could find. Perhaps do a Judge-

Your-Neighbor Worksheet if you need to free your judgments.

If you still struggle with what was so disgusting in your life and what you could not digest, I invite you to resolve it through a Judge-Your-Neighbor Worksheet or through accepting yourself in the past and everyone in it. Wouldn't it be sweet if you could have a do-over and choose differently from what you know today? Wouldn't it be amazing to have that superpower? We're so smart in hindsight. Oh, the things we wouldn't do.

But since you can't roll back the time, given what you know today, you might want to connect with your right brain for support and warmth: *There, there, I love you so much. It's safe for you to release the feelings into me. You're doing so great. Release some more and some more. You're allowed to feel and release the feeling. Let's follow the feeling together in the body. Let's see where it goes. I've got you. I've got your back. It's safe to release the past. Release it into me. There you go. You're waking up to who you are beyond thinking. You're waking up to how powerful you are. You can create and then release your feelings. I'm here for you. You can release everything. Forgive yourself for your judgments of yourself and others often. Just like that. I love you so much.*

Is there a more effortless and lighter way to get the learning that life has for us? Emotional pain wakes us up to the thinking that runs the circuit of pain. We can follow the feeling, stop the story, notice the sensations in our body, and know that when the time comes, our thinking will shift. We don't have to know when.

You've learned from your experience, and I acknowledge and have compassion for what you had to go through. I honor your strength of heart. Everyone is a work in progress. I invite you to be easy with yourself and others. Everyone has limitations in listening to their thought habits instead of the quiet voice of knowing. Everyone acts from fear and conditioning sometimes, and it isn't pretty. I trust you to forgive yourself; from there, you'll nurture compassion for others' limitations.

Humanity is changing, one thought at a time. Pain teaches you to surrender judgmental thinking. Eventually, one concept at a time, you learn to for-give yourself the love and quiet you already are. Ultimately, attaching to painful thinking doesn't seem like a good idea. Then you choose more and more to live from a space of fun, love, humor, joy, goodness, lightness, gratitude, creativity, and seeing your magnificence.

Even nowadays, when someone, including yourself, says something inconsiderate, inflicts physical pain on you or others, when treatment creates physical pain, or when you don't like the heads of your government or the bureaucratic system, notice if you maintain the emotional pain circuits by recalling and repeating the story. See if retelling the story recreates and preserves the original pain.

Some stories need to be told to raise awareness. But even if you're raising awareness, can you be neutral and evaluative about it? Or do you have an unconscious habit of perpetuating pain for yourself? Accept what is, accept yourself, allow everything you're experiencing, and stop retelling stories of pain. Leave stories in the past, and when you settle down, you'll return to those good feelings again. Choose your health.

Your nature is love and is always there under the thinking. You have discernment and common sense and know what to choose, even where to focus your thinking. No matter what you or your lineage went through, you can enter a new reality right now. The past is truly gone. There's only now. Step into a lighter version of yourself by letting the past be in the past. Celebrate who you are today. Enjoy who you are. Express yourself in the world how you like. Be your creative self. The life force in you wants to be expressed in the world. It will heal the world, including yourself.

I honor your journey, resilience, love, willingness to grow, and strength of heart.

SUMMARY AND SUGGESTIONS

1. If you're not part of a community, consider finding and going to activities that seem fun or attract you. If you enjoy being in nature, check out the Sierra Club website for local hikes. If you enjoy spirituality, consider joining a spiritual center of your choice. If you enjoy a hobby and want to share it with people, see where there's a group you can join.
2. Consider looking at the "cancer personality traits" list and let go of any misidentification with painful concepts and beliefs. Question your thinking. See who you would be if you didn't believe that thought. Which feels more peaceful? Consider doing a Byron Katie Judge-Your-Neighbor Worksheet or going to the Helpline at TheWork.com. If you're having difficulty letting go of painful concepts, consider hiring a therapist or coach to help you with that process.
3. Consider giving yourself love, acceptance, approval, communion, and appreciation right now. And now. And now. And now. And now.
4. Find who you are beyond the passing thoughts and concepts. Remind yourself often that you are the magnificent, loving, powerful, capable, joyous, peaceful energy under any thinking. Consider taking three minutes daily to notice the quiet breath. Or consider putting your attention on the body, as Eckhart Tolle advises. Can you notice subtle, peaceful energy in your body, hands, arms, legs, face, and torso? There is a quiet hum in your being that is not the thinking. See if you can sense it.

5. Family secrets may affect unconscious patterns through the generations. Recall Healing therapists and Family Constellation facilitators can help contextualize things for you.
6. Consider the possibility that, as Byron Katie says, "Everything happens for you and not to you." Pain helps you wake up to your painful judgments about life. It's how you learn what you're doing so you can release it. You can cultivate, recognize, and use an experience to grow and expand into who you truly are beyond thinking.
7. This is a new moment where you can have that beautiful inner feeling. You just feel good. It's inside of you. I see your magnificence beyond any conditioning. I honor your journey, resilience, love, and strength of heart. I honor your beautiful and resilient lineage who dealt with their challenges. You are so stunning and important with your deep and meaningful lives.

Chapter Thirty One

DO YOU LOVE YOUR LIFE?

Do you wake up in the morning and love your life, and engage in creative endeavors that are fun for you? Or do you focus on what's not there, what's wrong in your life, and other unproductive thoughts that contract your energy? Are you using the power of thinking to create joy and fun for yourself? Your thoughts are constantly creating delight, expansion, fear, or contraction. Notice who you are being in life, expanded, calm, contracted, or afraid.

At the beginning of my healing from cancer, I read a book called *Cancer as a Turning Point* by Dr. Lawrence LeShan, a hospital psychologist who worked with cancer patients. Dr. LeShan affirmed that when patients align their lives with joy, creativity, and meaningful activities to support physical healing, they heal better from cancer.

"All people have a natural way of being, relating, creating; when they find it, they are using themselves in the way most fulfilling for themselves...when they become committed to finding and then to living this new way, the body's defenses increase their functioning, and they frequently begin to respond much more positively to whatever medical treatment they are on.i...

The method concerns people taking control over their own life- searching for a lifestyle especially suited for them and, when found, actively working toward living this life. For many individuals, this requires a complete restructuring of their thinking about themselves...our actions are based on "shoulds" rather than on the question of what would fulfill me—what style of being, relating, and creating, would bring me to a life of zest?"

A loving, powerful light runs you. Your inner light is bright, pure, and straightforward. It communicates clearly to you what you're interested in. Do you long to do more yoga or Qi Gong? Do you feel like dancing, knitting, living by the sea, or creating a family? If you are a beautiful, loving, powerful light that isn't attached to thinking of limitation, what do you want to express and create in the world?

While having treatments, I changed a few habits. I ate clean, detoxified my environment and personal products, and exercised daily. I spent time with family and friends when I could. I learned West Coast Swing and took Argentine Tango classes. Both allowed me to focus on something other than cancer and connect with new people. I questioned painful thinking and got to a place of love.

I also looked at my work. Before my health journey, I sporadically used my spiritual psychology skills. I supported women with their emotional journey of In-Vitro-Fertilization as a Thai Yoga Therapist at an acupuncturist's office. I ministered to patients as a per-diem hospice spiritual care provider and a volunteer hospital chaplain. I taught classes in spiritual psychology and communication skills. I continued to take Nonviolent Communication (NVC) and spiritual courses for my growth. I had a few private spiritual counseling clients. However, my work wasn't yet a career. I made a sparse effort to serve more people. I didn't trust my abilities, education, and experience. I had an idea of perfection, that if I weren't experienced, I shouldn't work with people. I didn't want to feel the angst that comes from growth by making healthy errors.

Before cancer, I sometimes felt frustrated at my lack of effort in creating a more engaged work life. I was stuck thinking that an M.A. in spiritual psychology wasn't enough. I wondered if I should study coaching or social work or become a therapist or minister. After ten years of working part-time jobs related to spiritual psychology during my cancer journey, I finally chose. I enrolled in an online coaching program to become a certified life coach. Coaching classes and practice incentivized me to recover from the reconnection surgery and diverted my attention in a direction I love.

A woman recently told me that she got a raise during her cancer healing journey, moved to a location she enjoys, and engaged in new hobbies. She's feeling jazzed up about her life.

You might want to take out a journal and answer the following questions: what changes would you like to make in your life? What would a more aligned life look like for you?

1. Are you satisfied with your creative professional expression in the world?
2. Are you working in a field that you love? If yes, fantastic.
3. Are you working at a position you love that uses skills and talents you enjoy?
4. If not, what field of work would you enjoy?
5. Do you need to learn new skills to fit a position you'd love?
6. Are you willing to put in the time to add new skills that you'd love to engage with?
7. What brings you alive? What hobbies would you like to do more of? How can you add it to your life?
8. Are you prioritizing your hobbies and exercise?
9. What do you want to do less of? How could you do less of it or stop doing it altogether?
10. What would you enjoy contributing if you had a magic wand?

11. If you're getting a second chance at life through these treatments, would you dare have a juicy, vital life? Are you willing to step toward a life you'd love? What would be the first step? And the next?

Growth means that you'll have thoughts that would feel uncomfortable. The thoughts might say that you're not good enough, who are you to do this or that, don't know how, need to be perfect, and "others can do it better." But the more you see that thought is an energy that may or may not serve you, the easier it is not to listen to discouraging thoughts and move forward with your longing. Trust your inner direction. Add aliveness for yourself despite having habitual dispiriting thoughts. Keep moving towards what's fun.

Consider steering your rudder toward an enlivening creative work expression in the world. If you're having challenges exploring this area by yourself, consider reaching out to family members or friends who are good listeners. Otherwise, you can contact a professional therapist or coach. You're worth the exploration and support. You can express yourself with your gifts and talents in a way that feels alive.

If you love your field but want to change your position, would you consider speaking with your manager or supervisor and asking to change your job to one that would fit your talents better? Consider stretching into your dreams.

How are your finances? Are you spending less than you're earning, so you have some surplus to save? If not, what do you need to change about your lifestyle? Do you need to change your position within your company to fit your family's lifestyle and earn more money, or look at your finances and spend less? Would you like to stay at the company and ask for a raise by highlighting your incredible contribution and commitment to the company and your family's needs? If your company can't increase your salary, would you consider pointing yourself toward another company and asking for compensation based on your family's needs? I invite you to use your voice and creativity to ask for what you need financially. Do you want to examine your monthly expenses and eliminate unnecessary costs?

Does living in your home make your heart sing? Are you giddy with the possibility of redecorating? Perhaps you've wanted to garden and learn to compost but haven't made the time. Consider going for it and enjoying the fruits of your labor. Do you want to live in the country on a farm, in a retreat center, or in an intentional community? Do you want to live abroad and experience a different culture while working remotely? Consider conversing with your family about this matter. I encourage you to go for what brings you alive.

How are your relationships with your romantic partner, children, and family? Are you present when you're with them? Are you focusing on joy and fun activities whenever you can? Permit yourself to enjoy your relationship with your children, partner, and friends. Consider leaving the churning, anxious, judgmental thinking about yourself or another alone unless something essential needs addressing. In your relationship with yourself, remember that who you are in this moment is spectacular, perfect, and enough. Remind yourself that it's healthy to enjoy life. The more you focus on fun activities you love, the more life force energy you bring to your healing.

Are there areas where you're holding back your expression of what you appreciate about your loved ones? Are there areas where you're holding back your expression about how you'd like to be treated by others? Do you want to take parenting or communication classes to learn to listen to others' and your needs? You might talk with your loved ones about these matters and see how your relationship deepens.

A close friend of mine was married and had a newborn. Then she was diagnosed with cancer. The large doses of chemotherapy she accepted into her body affected her mood. Her husband couldn't handle her moods, and he left. Another friend met his wife while she experienced remission from brain cancer treatments. He was so taken by her, and they married. Her cancer returned, and he supported her and her children until her passing. A cancer diagnosis will either draw your romantic partner closer to you and your love will deepen or will possibly break up the connection if it wasn't strong enough before cancer.

Also, in my life, Joe had a hard time with my "smell" when I was bleeding rectally and taking supplements. He did not consistently try to be involved in my healing journey. After five years of an on-and-off connection, I told him not to call, text, or contact me. I did so much to heal and didn't have the energy to invest in what wouldn't flourish into a mature, supportive romantic relationship. For two and a half years, he did not reach out. Joe and I re-met a few years later at a dance event and have maintained a supportive friendship.

By contrast, my friend Toby stepped up in every way. He wanted to be as involved with my journey as I would let him. He offered to drive me to doctors and be a listening ear whenever I wanted. He donated over $7,000 to my journey when I went to Mexico and needed funds. Cancer will show you what your partner is capable of. However, Toby wanted what I couldn't give him. After he read an earlier version of my book chapters, he realized he could not be just my friend. Toby wanted me as a wife. I did not share his wish, and he chose to part ways.

A cancer journey might change other relationships. Some

friends will want to help you, call you, bring you food, or drive you to doctor appointments. Your bond will deepen. Other friends will disappear. They might be afraid to speak with you or think you need privacy for your journey. Some family members will be closer. Some new friends will enter your life and join you on this journey for a short or long time. They might understand what you are going through.

When people pull away, it's about them. They're uncomfortable, scared, busy, unable, or unwilling to receive someone's pain, physical or emotional. They might think they're intruding. If you feel hurt, accept it. You don't need to change the feelings or fix them or yourself. In time, the thinking will move along. But if you're hurt, you've personalized something you didn't need to. You may question your thoughts by doing Byron Katie's inquiry process or leave the thoughts alone, knowing it's not the purity of who you are.

You are resilient even when partners or friends pull away. You've gone through life until this moment. You've moved through other challenges. You can handle this. Trust life. When one door closes, another opens. Others will step in to fill a supportive role for you. I know the journey can feel lonely at times. I invite you to consider giving yourself love and appreciation right now. Love yourself. Accept yourself now. You're going through a journey of metamorphosis. You will not be the same after this journey. You are made amazingly. There is no one else like you. You are incredibly gifted. It's safe for you to settle into your sense of well-being.

You might not be able to make many changes while on treatments. But little tweaks can make a big difference. Doing more of your hobbies could light you up. Changes to your workload or asking a friend to cook for you once a week could make a big difference. Even resting more could help. If you keep your rudder on joy, other changes will unfold one step at a time.

SUMMARY AND SUGGESTIONS

1. It's vital for your healing that you create a life with zest.
2. Are you working in a field that you love? If not, explore what would light your heart with family, friends, or professionals. Consider taking steps toward creating work for yourself that you enjoy.
3. Do you need to ask your company for a raise? Do you want to change position at your company to have enough finances for your family? Have you created a budget to see your monthly outflow and inflow? Are you spending a bit less than what's coming in?
4. Do you love where you're living? Would you like to move somewhere during or after treatment plans? Can you change anything about the place where you are currently living to fit your needs? Do you need to request something from someone about your living situation?
5. Are you enjoying your primary relationships? Do you need to learn intimate speaking skills? Do you need not to crit icize yourself or those around you? Do you want to know more about sexuality with your partner? What resources are available for you to learn these skills? Tantra classes? Nonviolent Communication (NVC) classes online?
6. Some relationships will terminate while on a cancer journey, while others will bring people closer. When relationships fall apart, and you're feeling low, notice your feeling in the body. Allow the thoughts and feelings to be. Allow yourself to be as you are. Consider giving yourself love, approval, and appreciation as you find your place in the world again.

Be extra tender with yourself. The thoughts will move along in time. You might want to reach out to the Facebook pages for support.

7. Pain about a breakup is made of thoughts about the situation, not the situation. You'll feel this way as long as you believe the thoughts. Have compassion for yourself. Have patience for your process. You are a beautiful and loving being. When one door closes, another opens. If you're feeling pain, you might want to do a Byron Katie JYN Worksheet or wait until your thinking settles. You have been through many challenges in your life. You are resilient. You are the loving energy through which those thoughts pass.
8. Consider making time for what lights you up.
9. Sometimes, you only need to rest more and do less.
10. Do you remember how magnificent, loving, and gifted you are? Are you reminding yourself of your goodness? I invite you to be kind, considerate, and compassionate with yourself as you move through this journey and create a life of joy and meaning for yourself.

Chapter Thirty Two

PEOPLE-PLEASING, SAYING NO

When I was a child, my dad told me to keep secrets, and I did. Then I felt guilty and fearful about what would happen when others found out. I followed parental and step-parental rules. If I didn't follow the rules, the consequences might have been being hit, taunted, getting a stern, disapproving look, or losing a parent's approval.

I played small to avoid repercussions and changed myself. I played to the adults' wishes. On the few occasions when I spoke out about what I thought was dysfunctional, I was dismissed. I was told I was wrong when I disagreed with some adults. I gave up voicing myself and became a people-pleaser as a coping mechanism. I developed a habit of fearing people and feeling uncomfortable saying no, thereby being dishonest. It's been a long and painful learning curve to say no and be okay with disappointing others.

People-pleasing presented itself as fear of disagreeing with doctors. When my labia buzzed during radiation, it took inner resolve to tell the technician. Logically I knew the buzzing shouldn't be happening. But my trauma brain said, *What if they dismiss your complaint? What if they act as if it weren't true? What if they say our calculations are correct? What would you do then?* It took every ounce of courage from me to resolve to express my symptoms and insist on being heard. I was lucky the radiation technician took my complaint seriously, and my radiation oncologist agreed to look at the calculations. That past conditioning moves with me everywhere I go, and I've learned to see it as another habitual fearful thought, not reality.

One of the former students from the Essence of Spiritual Counseling class I ran at the cancer center at St. John's Hospital in Oxnard said she was a people-pleaser due to early fears of punishment. Before her diagnosis, she couldn't breathe. At the emergency room (ER), she asked for an X-ray fearing she had pneumonia. The doctors dismissed her request and sent her home, saying she had bronchitis. She told the doctors that she felt fluid around her heart. She said they listened to her heart for one second.

She left upset at herself because she didn't stand up for herself. She wished she had demanded an X-ray but was scared to speak up. She didn't know how to talk nicely and affirmatively. She returned to the ER three more times because she couldn't breathe. She even explained to the doctors that she had to sleep sitting up. She didn't get an X-ray. Finally, after four months, she got an X-ray which showed that she had aggressive and advanced lung cancer. Please follow your inner hunches and take care of yourself. Cancer is a journey of empowerment, and it's up to you to speak up with doctors and ensure you're heard.

One attribute of the "cancer personality" is empathic people who have developed people-pleasing coping mechanisms. According to Merriam-Webster's dictionary, a people-pleaser is "a person who has an emotional need to please others, often at the expense of his or her own needs or desire." The upshot is, "Being a people-pleaser... shows that you are a caring person who values social connections and enjoys making others happy," writes Samantha Boardman, a positive psychiatrist. And according to LCSW Meghan Fritz, "…if you grew up in a home with a difficult, emotionally unavailable parent, you may have unconsciously picked up the pattern of people-pleasing in an attempt to engage the aloof parent." In other words, people-pleasing is doing something to garner another person's attention, approval, love, or acceptance. It is also the inability to say or maintain an honest no when people you care about ask you to meet their needs, and you don't want to.

According to Psychology Today, there are more attributes to people-pleasing. These include pretending to agree with everyone, feeling responsible for how other people feel, blaming yourself excessively for something that wasn't your fault, feeling burdened by the things one has to do (not taking charge of one's time), feeling uncomfortable if someone is angry with you, acting like the people around, needing praise to feel good, going to great lengths to avoid conflict, and not admitting when your feelings are hurt.i

Questions supporting your authenticity are: How would I respond to this request if I loved myself? Taking a few moments to check in with this question will quickly give you an honest answer. Psychologist Marshall B. Rosenberg asks, "Am I feeling the joy of a child feeding a duck if I say yes to this?" as a barometer for an honest yes or no. In the coaching world, it's called a "hell, yes." If what you're feeling isn't a "hell yes," or if you're dreading or feeling neutral about it, the answer is "no, thank you." Another question that can help you decipher your answer is: am I sacrificing my needs to meet someone else's needs? If you ask yourself these questions, you'll receive an immediate inner signal of contraction or expansion. Contraction means you want to do something other than do it. Take some time to sit in silence to hear the whispers of your heart.

How do you communicate a clear and loving no that doesn't alienate your loved ones? I learned to acknowledge the request I received because others either want to give me a gift or are inviting me to provide them with a gift through their request. A boy I used to babysit taught me to say "Thank you, and no." Or "No, thanks." Saying no without explanation is one clear way to stand by your no. You can lovingly repeat the "no, thank you," as many times as it takes for the other person to hear it.

Other times, you may want to tell others your needs for a yes or no. For example, "I appreciate that you asked me to babysit, and my work schedule is full that day. I hope you'll keep me in the loop when you need support in the future." Or, "I appreciate you giving me another project to sink into at work. However, I'd like to have time, space, and focus on finishing the project I'm working on right now before I take another one. Would you be willing to wait a week, assign it to someone else, or assign someone to help me finish my current project?"

When you say no but the person doesn't hear you or ignores your "no," consider repeating it more clearly, with empowered energy. Center yourself in your deeper, wise center, talk with the person again, and tell him with a clear, neutral, or loving energy, "I said, thank you, and I'm not interested. I meant, thank you, and I'm not interested. What did you hear me say?" You can also ask, "What thought in you is choosing to ignore my no?" You can tell them, "I care about you, but it's a 'no' for me." If they don't respect your response, they may not be the listening type. You may need to take stronger measures to ensure the "no" is honored. Growth is about claiming power and being yourself, especially on a cancer journey.

Who is the most uncomfortable person to say no to? Is it with the people you live with or care deeply about? Is it your boss? Are you scared that if they knew that you didn't want to help them or attend to their emotional needs or requests, they'd stop caring about you or leave you? Your loved ones will care about you just as much if you say no. They might respect you more and know not to ask you in the future. You might have more psychological air space as you claim your power.

Being a people-pleaser has been a practice for me to undo, and it's still a work in progress. In the past, I had been in some relationships with men in which I had a partial interest. I'd tell them I had partial interest, not enough for a full relationship. They'd still pursue me for a relationship. They'd keep trying until I said yes to a partial connection. I grew to care about these men yet wasn't fully engaged in the relationship. I wasn't sticking with my clear no. The stress of being dishonest with myself and not being consistently firm took its toll on me. I felt ashamed and angry when I said yes when I meant no. Yet I am the only one that can be courageous enough to say yes to myself and disappoint another.

During my cancer journey, I felt incredibly challenged with saying no to my housemate Jake. June and Jake, a married couple, were my roommates and dear and beloved friends. June was one of my best friends. I loved her so much. Jake supported me emotionally during my cancer journey, asking what I felt and experienced. I appreciated the care and support of a close friend wanting to hear me.

Then, Jake wanted to connect daily. The emotional connection felt like we had crossed a friendship boundary, and I became anxious and stressed. But I didn't talk about it. Jake occasionally sat on the swing with me and asked to massage my calves. I felt uncomfortable with the request, but I didn't say anything. I wanted to maintain the friendship and convinced myself he does this with all his female friends.

One day, Jake said he developed an attraction to me and wanted to know if it was the same for me. I said there was an attraction, typical for masculine and feminine energies living in the same house and opening up emotionally, but I was not interested in a romantic relationship. The following day, he asked me again, sharing intimate and uncomfortable details of a dream he'd had about me. I stood my ground, "I'm not interested. Your dream is yours. I'm only your friend. I am not interested in anything other than friendship. I am only your and June's friend. I am not interested in having any more of a relationship."

Jake wouldn't stop. He walked by, seeing me sit in the kitchen holding my head, and asked how I felt. I said I had a headache. He offered to give me a massage. I felt conflicted. I didn't trust his energy or intention, and a clear voice inside wanted to say, "No, not from you." Another thought said, maybe a massage would help, and another feared his reaction if I said no. "Ummm, Okay," I said.

The massage felt uncomfortable, and I could feel icky energy coming at me. But I didn't get up and leave. At the end of the head massage, while I sat cross-legged on the floor, Jake picked my hips up without my consent and placed me on his lap, facing him. I felt frozen, unable to say anything or move. I sent a silent mental message to him; *please don't do anything to me. Please let me go.* Maybe he saw my scared eyes and immobility. He gave me a peck on the lips and placed me back down on the floor. I felt stunned and ashamed. I got up and left. I told myself something must have overtaken him and that he'll never repeat it.

Jake spoke with June, then the three of us had a conversation. I told them I was not interested in any romantic connection, and June felt like I did. But Jake continued with unsolicited attention each time June wasn't home. I told him I didn't want any touch between us. And a week later, a hand went on my shoulders. I wanted to scream, "I SAID NO," but I didn't. I let it go.

I looked to move out and contacted a social worker to find solutions, but I couldn't afford to get my own place. I stayed hidden in my room as much as possible and lived with anxiety for two years during my cancer treatments. Jake made inappropriate comments such as "Are you still getting your periods? I mean, because you lost a lot of weight." I felt uncomfortable with that inquiry, imagining where his mind went with that question, but I answered.

The day I came home from the second surgery, June was on a retreat. Jake walked by, put a hand on my shoulders in a friendly manner, and said, "Your body feels tight. Would you like a massage?"

Again, the inner conflict arose: the body needed a massage, but not from Jake. I wanted to say no. Just say no, Just say no. "Um.. okay," I said. Fear and paralysis set in each time with my old coping mechanism of pleasing others' requests. I told myself not to make it into a drama and relax with my diaper on. I was surprised I could do that. I took the massage at face value without caring where he came from. At the end of the massage, Jake said, "So, I notice you seem to enjoy the massage. Would you like a Yoni massage because I know you need to bring blood flow to the vaginal area for rehabilitation?" Yoni is the female genitalia in Sanskrit

"No," I clearly said without an explanation. This time, my no was respected.

The following morning Jake asked to give me a massage again. I could hear my inside scream at me: *NOOOOOOO, say no.* I still felt paralyzed and shocked by his unexpected request, scared of what would happen if I said no. Would he do underhanded things to me while I lived there? I replied, "Um....Okay." I felt angry with myself.

Later, I spoke with my brother about my challenges in saying no to Jake. My brother advised, "If you don't say a firm no to him, he won't get it. Some men just don't get it. You need to repeat yourself clearly and strongly until he hears you."

I would sit in my car each time I pulled up to the house and practice repeating an imaginary conversation in my head: "Do you want a massage?" "No." "Do you want a massage?" "No." "Do you want a massage?" "Nooo!!!" The third time that Jake asked to massage me when June wasn't there, I said, "No, I'm busy."

"Really? What are you doing tonight?"

"I have a deadline for visiting the intentional communities, and it takes hours to go through the website. I have to finish that as I'm leaving soon," I said. Then, Jake offered to sit with me while I researched. Anything that didn't involve touch would be fine, I reasoned.

The fourth time he asked, I said "no" without an excuse. And the fifth time he asked to give me a massage, I said "no," without an explanation. He returned a couple of hours after I said no and asked if he should stop asking. I managed, "Yes. Stop asking."

Finally, my distress was so great I shared it with June, "I feel creeped out by Jake. He often asks to give me massages when you're not here. He's so creepy. I am so uncomfortable around him."

"You need to tell him that; spell it out for him; he needs to hear it," she said. Yet, I was scared of him. Jake tended to get aggressive at times.

June confronted her husband, telling him what I had said. He stormed in, full of painful and angry energy, telling me we needed to talk.

"I'm guessing June told you that I said you were creepy?" I said.

"Yes," he replied.

"I'm guessing you're upset because you would have appreciated hearing it from me and not her, right?"

"Yes," he replied again.

"And now you're wondering why it seems we're friends one moment, and then you hear that I'm uncomfortable and call you creepy? Well, let me tell you what I call creepy," I said. "When you ask to give me massages when June's not home, I'm uncomfortable with that. It freaks me out. It would be less creepy if you asked to give me massages when she is home to observe. Why do you only request a physical connection with me when she's not home? And you do this, again and again, whenever she's not home. You talk to me for hours when she's not home, but not when she's there. What's underneath that you are not admitting to yourself? Are you lying to yourself about your true intentions? Can you see how creepy this is?"

After this conversation, Jake mostly stopped paying attention to me. I still lived in the house and scurried to my room as much as possible. I spoke with Jake as little as possible until I could move out. Carrying this fear and anxiety inside me during a cancer journey was stressful. I couldn't say a firm no all the time to a person I cared for as a dear friend.

Judith Lewis Herman, in her book Trauma and Recovery: The Aftermath of Violence - From Domestic Abuse to Political Terror, writes: "Many survivors have such profound deficiencies in self-protection that they can barely imagine themselves in a position of agency or choice. The idea of saying no to the emotional demands of a parent, spouse, lover, or authority figure may be practically inconceivable. Thus, it is not uncommon to find adult survivors who continue to minister to the needs of those who once abused them and who continue to permit major intrusions without boundaries or limits. Adult survivors may nurse their abusers in illness, defend them in adversity, and even, in extreme cases, continue to submit to their sexual demands."

When I left June and Jake's home, I had recurring thoughts of self-hatred. How could I not say no sooner? How could I let this man trespass my boundaries? Why didn't I stand up for myself more? I thought about how my not saying a stronger no affected our lives. These thoughts consumed me, especially after June asked me to speak with both of them about this. I wasn't ready. The most painful part was that I didn't honor my own no each time he trespassed a line of integrity. I experienced a trauma response of cycling fast, anxious, angry thoughts during the day and night. I'd wake up at two a.m. every day with a fury of anxious and angry thoughts. I was in a nightmare and day-mare for ten days.

During that time, I listened to David Hawkins' audiobook *Letting Go: The Pathway Of Surrender.* I was reminded that underneath trauma thinking is a well of love, well-being, and calm. I was reminded that even in trauma, it's just fast thoughts, and releasing engagement with the thoughts is okay. The past is in the past. Holding on to the trauma thinking is keeping the trauma alive; it brings the past into the present. In addition, engaging with traumatic thoughts is a barrier to connecting with my ever-present loving nature. I'm resisting my own loving. I couldn't afford to continue trauma thinking while healing from cancer.

I needed to let go of the thoughts about the past, forgive myself, and find compassion. I reminded myself that maturing is a process and that it's okay to falter. Coach Michael Neill reminded me that fear is a thought, just a thought. I had a fearful thought about Jake that I believed in and attached to. Michael reminded me that I said a firm "no" to the important stuff; the other stuff was the "gray zone" and not as important.

I can't be perfect all the time. I unconsciously believed a fearful thought, and Jake unconsciously believed a fantasy thought. Likewise, June unconsciously chose not to hear me speak about her husband because she believed an "I don't need to be involved" thought. The power of believing thoughts created our reality based on our conditioning.

A year after I left, I contacted June. She and Jake read the first version of this chapter. June was horrified. Jake owned up to everything and said it was true. June sent me a link about the stages of sexual harassment. What Jake did was considered sexual harassment. The three of us scheduled a Zoom call to talk about it.

It was important for me to confront Jake from a place of neutrality and honesty. Jake apologized for his behavior and its impact on June and me. I wanted to highlight that he needs to respect the word no. I mentioned to Jake that he has a tendency not to hear women's no and wanted to ensure he realizes it about himself. I took responsibility and apologized for not saying a firmer no each time he trespassed a boundary. Perhaps he would have heard me. I apologized to June, as well, about my fear of saying a firm no, thinking I might be kicked out of the house and not have a place to live during cancer treatment. June apologized for not hearing me when I told her what was happening.

I told June I was deciding whether to include this story in this book. June preferred that I include this story to help others who might be facing similar situations. She's amazing.

Recently I read three relevant quotes:

"Our greatest glory is not in never failing, but in rising up every time we fail." Ralph Waldo Emerson

"I dreamt - marvelous error! - that I had a beehive here inside my heart. And the golden bees were making white combs and sweet honey from my old failures." Antonio Machado

"Only when we are brave enough to explore the darkness will we discover the infinite power of our light." Brene Brown

These thoughts remind me that everyone is always on a learning curve. I'll keep working on mine.

I invite you to examine your life and your people-pleasing behaviors. Are you pretending to agree with everyone? Do you feel over-responsible for how other people feel? Do you blame yourself excessively for something that wasn't your fault? Do you feel burdened by the things you have to do (not taking charge of your time)? Do you feel uncomfortable if someone is angry with you? Are you acting like the people around you, needing praise to feel good, going to great lengths to avoid conflict, or not admitting when your feelings are hurt?

Your people-pleasing might not be as uncomfortable as the story I relayed above. But notice how you feel when you say yes when you mean no with your children, partners, friends, or with doctors. When you focus on pleasing others when you don't want to, you feel contracted in your body. It feels stressful. You suffocate your life-force energy and creative energy. You're walking with a crutch instead of sprinting forward joyfully. The other person, too, is affected by the people-pleasing. He'll figure it out at some point, and there will be more significant hurt and shame for all as he realizes that you lied.

Please consider the gains that will come from speaking your truth. You might create a better life circumstance for yourself. You might find a job that's better for you. You might stop cooking because you hate it. You might receive more appropriate cancer treatments. Your family and friends might respect you more. Your life force and healing energy might flow better through your body. You might heal faster from cancer treatments. You might have the partner you want. You might have a better relationship with your children. You might encourage the other person to take responsibility for his behavior and self-reflect. You might be a teacher to your children and partner about how to be honest. You might be happier. You might have more time and energy to focus on fun, creative endeavors.

I know the fear thoughts come from conditioning, but they're thoughts. You don't have to engage with them for too long. It will help if you become aware of them. When you stop listening to them, they'll move along, and you can speak your truth if it makes sense to you. I know you can hear your truth, your honest yeses and nos. It's safe to use your power to be you. In fact, it's crucial to your health and well-being to be yourself, claim your power, and say an honest yes and no.

You start by saying one honest no. It might feel uncomfortable when the other is disappointed and tries to convince you otherwise. Breathe through your discomfort. Accept it. It will become easier to see others' disappointment as you practice. Remember to trust their resilience. They will find solutions for themselves without you. Then repeat a clear and honest no; it will feel slightly less uncomfortable. Then you turn down someone else's request, and it feels less frightening. Then you repeat it again and again. Allow your discomfort over and over by letting it be, breathing, and not engaging with it. Stay committed to your integrity and inner guidance. You have an internal GPS that directs you. Trust your knowing about your path, as well as their resilience.

Pretty soon, you will have more breathing room. You say no some more and are thankful you're honest and living your truth. I'm still working on mine, one step at a time. My no has improved over the past few years, and my guilt and over-responsibility for others' feelings have subsided. My commitment to my integrity has become firmer. And my willingness to see others disappointed with me has grown. I'm more committed to my GPS. How about you? Try to take this pattern with case. You're learning to be yourself; it can take courage and time. Be kind to yourself as you undo mental conditioning, and chuck perfection out the door. You have my love and support.

SUMMARY AND SUGGESTIONS

1. A people-pleaser is a person who has an emotional need to please others, often at the expense of their own needs or desires. It's someone who pretends to agree

with everyone, feels responsible for how other people feel, excessively blames self when something wasn't their fault, feels burdened by the things one has to do (not taking charge of one's time), feels uncomfortable if someone is angry at them, acts like the people around, needs praise to feel good, goes to great lengths to avoid conflict, can't say an honest no, and does not admit when their feelings are hurt.

2. When changing this pattern and becoming more authentic and transparent, ask yourself: What would I do about this if I loved myself? Am I feeling the joy of a child feeding a duck if I say yes to this? Is it a "hell yes"? When I think about this matter, do I feel joy or dread? Am I sacrificing my own needs for their need?
3. To communicate an honest no, consider acknowledging the request you received first. This person is offering you a gift; you may not need or want this gift. Byron Katie suggests saying something like, "I love that you asked me, and no."
4. Another way to communicate with others is to tell them what needs of yours are met by your saying no to them and following it up with a request.
5. Whom do you need to say No to in your life? Write a list and put it where you'll see it daily until you find the courage to say no to each of these people.
6. If you say no, but the person doesn't hear or ignores you, say it more clearly, with empowered, loving energy. It's your responsibility to communicate your no clearly,

whether they choose to hear you or not. You might want to take other measures if they don't listen and respect your no. Life is about claiming your power and becoming yourself.

7. If you have a very challenging time owning your power, consider speaking with family or friends about it or hiring a life coach or a therapist to help you say a clear and consistent no. Alternatively, you can join a support group like Co-dependents Anonymous (CoDA) near you or online.
8. Consider re-reading this chapter until you muster up the courage to say no. Consider viewing this as a joyful opportunity to practice being yourself with others.
9. Own your power on a cancer journey. Being yourself will free your life-giving energy to flow and heal. I know you can say no and be yourself. You are the most powerful being. You may be a cocoon turning into a butterfly. Express Yourself! Be easy with yourself as you claim your power. You have my encouragement, love, and support.

Section VI

CLEANSING AND OTHER IMPORTANT ISSUES

Chapter Thirty Three

THE FINANCIAL JOURNEY

6/10/17: I had $300 in my bank account two and a half weeks before I receive the disability payment of $1,779. Concern set in, and I updated my GoFundMe page. Luckily, friends donated. I now have money for gas and food. For my birthday last week, I asked for gift cards to the supermarket to have money to buy food and supplements. I got two gift cards to a health food store, a chiropractic appointment to free my neck from the neck tweak, dried fruit, and $200 in cash from my family. I'm grateful! If you know someone dealing with cancer and financial struggles, find a way to GIVE money. Don't ask, "Do you need money?" It is already uncomfortable to be in the position of asking. Find a way, even lie...say, "My friend wanted to donate money to your campaign."

How are you managing finances on your cancer journey? Some of you are working through treatment and have money for your co-pays. But for others, hospital co-pays and chemo co-pays can add up even with medical insurance.

Do you have health insurance? If you don't, does the state where you live have medical insurance for people who don't have it? Social workers at every hospital and clinic can refer you to social services. One of my friends in Florida was diagnosed with uterine cancer. She had no health insurance. I encouraged her to ask the clinic that did her biopsy for referrals to insurance resources. They referred her to such a program, and she had surgery with no money out of pocket.

Sometimes I read on the Facebook pages that families used all their savings to pay for a cancer journey. Some people were laid off from work after medical treatments and consequently lost their medical insurance. One person went into bankruptcy because he didn't have the money to pay for his medical treatment. Some people have little money for follow-up scans. If this is your case, what are your options? Can you fundraise? Can a Human Services Agency refer you to temporary insurance agencies near you? And it's okay to have financial bankruptcy if you cannot find enough funding. It's more important to get the care you need.

I believe the universe takes care of us if we keep looking toward a solution and do our part. Sometimes, it takes care of us without our understanding. Two years before my diagnosis, mysteriously, all of my jobs stopped. No one called for pet sitting. The acupuncturist opened a second location, and instead of five Thai Yoga Therapy clients per Saturday, I had one or none. I didn't know why the universe was cutting my finances, but I realized I had to take a regular 9-5 job.

I found full-time work as a funeral service director at a Jewish mortuary and cemetery. There, I paid into monthly short- and long-term disability insurance. I even asked the human resources (HR) representative if I needed to pay into the insurance plans. "I don't ever get sick," I told her. Luckily, she said I had to. Remarkably, when I began the job, all my other jobs were again in demand.

When I told my job I needed time off for cancer treatments, the HR representative supplied me with family medical leave forms and instructed me how to submit them. Three months after my state disability began, the HR representative told me I was eligible for long-term disability benefits and sent me forms. After several phone interviews with the long-term disability company and six months of reviews of my medical files, the company approved my benefits. The state work disability was valid for one year after diagnosis. Once the long-term disability kicked in, it paid a monthly amount for as long as the doctors approved my disability. What a relief!

On state medical disability, I received $1,759 per month, which later rose to $1,779 and finally to $1,781. This check needed to cover rent, car payment, car insurance, phone, health insurance, food, gas, vitamins, acupuncture, chiropractor, therapists, and doctors who charged astronomical prices, like $800 for a functional medicine doctor or $600 for an integrative doctor. Of course, $1,781 was not enough, and I needed to find additional financial support.

At the beginning of this journey, I read Louise Hay's affirmation, "I trust the universe to take care of me." I didn't trust the universe to take care of me. I felt separate, alone, and scared in my financial journey. But I realized it was time to open my heart to the care of the benevolent creative energy I am a part of. I practiced opening up to goodness and receiving.

I saw that the universe always cared for me financially and otherwise, and perhaps I didn't need to fight to meet my needs. Instead, I could relax into the energy that says, *I trust the wisdom of what is occurring even when I do not understand it. I have been loved, supported, and cared for throughout my life. I'm connected to the energy that runs everything, and I can trust it. I can ask internally, tell people what I need, and follow every hunch I receive; somehow, things will work out.*

Like every physical muscle trained, I worked my confidence and trust muscles in a benevolent, supportive universe. In time, I developed unwavering confidence. I became confident that whatever new financial issue I faced would work out. In that confidence, I energetically allowed solutions to appear. I acted on whatever hunches I received that eventually led to someone coming forward with a financial solution.

My medical insurance changed several times on my cancer journey. At one time, I had state Medi-Cal insurance. This insurance paid for my pills and my first surgery. Later, the officials determined that my disability payment was too high. I changed to Covered California.

On my Covered California plan, the scan co-pays were $100, and the same for the colonoscopy and the staging endoscopies. Xeloda pills co-pay cost $150 per two-week treatment. The second surgery co-pay cost over $1,600 for three and a half hospital days, plus an extra $480 for the anesthesiologist. Every doctor appointment was between $15 and $20 co-pay. These would add up when I would visit the oncologist, endocrinologist, surgeon, gynecologist, pelvic-floor physical therapist, dermatologist, and family doctor for referrals in one month.

I went to my local Human Services Agency and asked if I qualified for food stamps. I appreciated the $15 per month I qualified for. I had shame about receiving food stamps for the first time in my life, but my brother explained to me that this is exactly the time I should be receiving help. I was learning to open my heart and receive with gratitude and humility. Later, I heard I could use EBT money at some farmer's markets in California and get double the face value. The rule at my local farmer's market was to use a maximum of $10 weekly, and the authorities matched another $10. I could buy $20 worth of fruits and vegetables for $10 of the EBT sum. I was so grateful for this generosity. If you need, consider checking if there is assistance from your local Human Services Agency.

Did you know some agencies raise funds to help cancer patients cover their chemo and surgery co-pays? I called the American Cancer Society and asked if they knew of organizations that could help me. They supplied me with four organizations that fund colorectal cancer patients. When I called in October 2017, all had exhausted their funding for the year. I couldn't think clearly enough to research while panicking – and I panicked a few times during this journey about finances. When I panicked, I knew to slow down and not do anything. I let the thinking go until I got to a place of calm. I knew things would somehow work out.

Maybe a loved one could do internet research for you to figure out which agencies can help with rectal cancer medical bills. I found a few: Fighters 4Life Cancer Financial Assistance Fund, Meredith's Miracles Colon Cancer Foundation Fund, CancerCare, Cancer Financial Assistance Coalition, HealthWell Foundation, Patient Resource, Patient Advocate Foundation Co-Pay Relief, and Needy Meds. There are more agencies out there. You can call the American Cancer Society and ask. Dealing with doctors, treatment, insurance, and finding financial resources was a full-time job.

A year after I received work-state disability insurance, I contacted the Social Security Administration about their taking over the disability portion that the state was paying. The long-term disability insurance advised me to hire a lawyer that they would recommend. I didn't, and the Social Security office denied my request for disability insurance.

At that point, my insurance agency again suggested I enlist a lawyer from their database. I contacted a lawyer, and we appealed the ruling. In 2018, I stood before a judge in Santa Barbara and answered his questions. The lawyer told me I had little to no chance of having my case reversed. But the judge awarded me Social Security disability benefits, paid retroactively for the previous year. That money sustained me through the following year.

Are there organizations in the community of family, friends, or a spiritual community that can help you if you need financial assistance? Consider speaking with friends or your house of worship group if you belong to one. Perhaps they'll fundraise for you.

In 2016, a few months after my cancer diagnosis, I set up a GoFundMe Facebook page and put it on my Facebook page. I felt embarrassed and ashamed to ask for money, but I had been doing alternative healing that came out of pocket and ran out of financial pockets. Because I committed myself to be in life and do whatever I needed to stay alive, asking for money was one of those measures.

I remember composing the GoFundMe summary and being flooded with anxious thinking: *will people donate? Will they criticize me, think of me as less than others, as having caused my cancer by my lifestyle, or will they feel sorry for me?* And still, I pressed send.

To my incredible surprise, friends came forward with tremendous support, loving comments, and donations. Some of my close friends and family forwarded my GoFundMe campaign on their Facebook pages, and their friends donated. My friends from elementary school in Israel donated. When I realized the extent of their generosity, I cried. I didn't know how much love was coming my way. So many people loved me. They wanted me to stay alive with dignity. This bounty was beyond anything that I could ever imagine. I felt deeply humbled. Moreover, people I might have had an uncomfortable relationship with donated. It was healing by itself.

Once my campaign was public, several family members sent checks to my address or gave me checks. Another dear friend, whom I had supported during her cancer journey about ten years prior, asked to meet with me several times for lunch and donated money to my journey. The journey of receiving love through finances was breaking my heart open to human kindness. Love was coming at me in many ways, and I wept with gratitude. I had to open my heart and receive love from others.

If you let people know about your situation, they might help you. Your pride or shame might hinder your willingness to publicly ask or let people know about your situation. You may have thoughts of fear of rejection and vulnerability. How will they respond? Yet I invite you to consider the possibility that people feel good about donating money to people they love and care about. Don't you love donating money to your friends when they're in a delicate moment? I bet you've donated plenty to others' journeys when they needed your time, services, or finances. Will you allow others to gift the same to you?

My sister-in-law called often and made plans to meet me at a health food store. Then she generously offered to pay for my groceries, vitamins, and fresh juice. I ran into one woman who saw my campaign on my brother's Facebook page at the farmer's market a couple of times. She insisted on paying for my groceries at one of the stands. People were generous. Moreover, people could only be helpful once they knew what I needed. I invite you to let people know about your needs, financial or otherwise. That includes cooked meals, babysitting, and house cleanings.

After my second surgery, I didn't have $2,500 for the co-pays. I felt uncomfortable asking people to donate money after they supported me with the alternative healing journey. A friend suggested I contact an Israeli-American Organization in Los Angeles called Stand By Me. This organization helps cancer patients with information, social and cultural gatherings, classes, and lectures.

Their representative read on my GoFundMe campaign that I needed funds to cover the surgery. She recommended that I contact a Jewish organization in New York called Rofeh Cholim Cancer Society which helps patients fund cancer treatments. They approved a grant for $2,500 for a year starting November 2017. With their generous assistance, I paid for all scan co-pays, my second surgery co-pays, and my heart check-ups. I am grateful for their existence, outreach, fundraising efforts, and assistance. I am likewise thankful to all those loving donors.

Are you frightened of your financial journey while having cancer? Do you have thinking about it that creates anxiety? Notice that with or without listening to the anxiety thinking, the outcome is the same. You'll still need to take steps to handle finances. One way is by listening to scary, anxious repetitive thoughts that rev you up. Another way is to know that thoughts come and go and that you don't need to attach to or control them.

Notice the thoughts and the knotted feeling in the body and be grateful that your genius machinery is at work. Keep your heart open to all of your feelings. The feelings alert you that you're listening to future fantasies. Allow yourself to have feelings without changing or fixing them. Breathe. Breathe some more. Feelings don't need to be fixed. They need to be allowed and accepted, as they're here to wake you up to what your consciousness is doing. Breathe. It's all right. The feelings will move on their own. You don't need to manipulate them or suppress your human experience. You've momentarily forgotten who you are, a powerful, creative, resourceful, immortal energy, who is innocently using the power of thought to create inner contraction for yourself right now.

When you settle down, you might realize you're resilient, and you've found solutions all your life. You've been supported financially until now and will continue to be supported. You remember there's a more profound place inside of you that is quiet and well, no matter what is occurring in your mind or with your external situation. You choose to drop into that space. You get still. You get curious.

You wonder how the universe will help you without needing to know how. Maybe you trust that whatever you need will come. You might need to let people know your needs. You might ask God/ universal intelligence/ the universe/reality to show you the next steps. Pay attention to your hunches and act on them. Keep going until solutions appear. Maybe let go of the mental struggle and be open to seeing how the universe works to help you. You'll receive ideas when you focus your brilliant mind on possibilities. You can handle anything that comes your way. You can slow things down and focus on the next step, then the next one. I know you'll be able to navigate your financial path.

When my treatments were over, I sent resumes out for one year. I had left my rental at June and Jake's and continued looking for work while living temporarily at my uncle and aunt's home for five months. Then Covid19 arrived. Pet-sitting opportunities ceased. I was teaching one class a week at the cancer center for a few months when I was finally hired to be a hospice spiritual counselor and a coach for the University of Washington School of Social Work. However, my newly hired positions stopped as the system figured out how to handle the pandemic and convert to online strategies. One month I earned $300.

At that time, my uncle said it was time for me to open my wings and fly. I packed my things and considered going to a homeless shelter as I didn't have money to pay rent. I slept in my car for a couple of days. My friend Tina called and immediately demanded that I stay with her family. After two days in the car, I went to stay with her family for ten days.

My dad stepped in and offered to pay for me to rent a room somewhere. Then I hustled with my coaching business, and things picked up. After three months, I told Dad I could pay rent, but he wanted me to have a financial cushion. He continued to pay for the rest of the year. How miraculous. How loving. I never knew the universe would provide so generously as I came out of cancer treatments, LARS, and disability during Covid times. I felt incredibly supported by my community until I stood on my financial feet.

I don't know what you are going through in your financial journey. I hope that something in this chapter helped your confidence to attract and create solutions, let people know what you need through social media or in person, and be willing to receive. I trust in your ability to focus in the direction of trust in a benevolent universe and allow it to help you. I have confidence in your wisdom and inner guidance about financial matters in this journey. I know how powerful you are when you aim at possibilities.

I wish people going through a cancer journey would have finances for their health needs and wouldn't need to wonder how they'll finance their treatments. I believe that healthcare needs to be a universal right. But this isn't the case yet. Exercise your power and do whatever you can to move through this phase of your life. Keep going. You will find a way if you keep asking. Trust yourself and the universe; you are connected to it. You are powerful, and It is taking care of you. You have my love and support.

SUMMARY AND SUGGESTIONS

1. If you don't have health insurance, can a social worker in the hospital or a Human Services Agency near you offer assistance?
2. If you need more funds, consider letting people know through social media, like GoFundMe, or an organization you belong to. Asking for financial help could be vulnerable and uncomfortable. I know you want to be self-sufficient and pay for treatment. If you've committed to healing from cancer, asking for what you need financially is part of that commitment. Please follow your guidance and press send if necessary. You may receive healing in more ways than you can imagine.

3. If you need financial assistance, you might apply for food stamps. Your county's Human Services office might help you with the proper forms.
4. You might call American Cancer Society to ask about organizations that can help rectal patients with treatment finances. Patient Assistance Programs for colon cancer | Fight CRC (fightcolorectalcancer.org) lists resources on their website.
5. Do you belong to a spiritual organization or a women's or men's organization that can help? Does your work have financial support funds, or will your co-workers fundraise for you?
6. Some drug companies (especially for the chemo you take) have funds for treatment co-pays. You might call them and ask for support.
7. Consider trusting that you can handle your financial journey. Consider reassuring yourself that you are resilient. Remember that you have wisdom and inner guidance communicating with you when you're quiet. You are powerful and connected to the universe. It will take care of you. You have my support to own your power and ask for whatever you need.

Chapter Thirty Four

A HEALING DIET

I love food. I treasure fruits and vegetables, their colors, tastes, textures, and smells. I get excited when I see fresh, crispy vegetables. I adore spices and herbs, especially when I learn about their healing properties. My maternal grandmother taught me to cook and cut when I was seven and eight, and my father took over cooking lessons when I was ten. It was a source of joy and independence. I cooked from scratch and ate everything in moderation, except for my occasional sweet chocolaty obsession.

My family showed love with food. They cooked and baked for their loved ones and took great pride in their creation. Food was a source of nourishment, creativity, comfort, and a coping mechanism to calm stress and anxiety. I still overeat when unconsciously caught up in stressful thoughts, although that has subsided markedly.

On my healing journey, I heard people speak of food as medicine and how some diets alone helped them heal from cancer. I read about the macrobiotic diet, Budwig Diet, Gerson Therapy diet, Ayurvedic diet, low-fat raw vegan diet, juicing therapy, and the ketogenic diet for healing from cancer. In addition, I learned about vegan, vegan ketogenic, and paleo diets. Some books and lectures I listened to spoke about food cleansing the body from the toxicity that creates disease. One person on the Facebook page wrote that her husband immediately started drinking pure celery and wheatgrass juices after diagnosis, and his rectal tumor shrunk considerably in two months.

In addition, I watched an interview with a man in *The Truth About Cancer* docuseries. This man wondered how to heal his skin cancer. He prayed to God and then was guided to take chili peppers and ginger. He boiled them and made a "kick-em-juice" that he drank throughout his days. The heat from this juice might have raised his body temperature and killed off his cancer cells. His cancer slowly receded until it was gone. I also read a book about Hazel Parcells, who healed herself from tuberculosis when there was no cure when she lived. She was guided to spinach. She ate spinach raw and boiled for a few weeks until her body healed. Hazel lived to be 106 years old. We are connected to an intelligent field and can ask and hear it for help. We also have discernment and determination to see it through when the stakes are high enough.

To clean my body, I took a regimen of herbs and teas from Dr. Schulze's liver, kidney, and bowel cleanses, which included four three-day juice fasts in four weeks. I also ate raw vegan meals while doing these cleanses. A month later, I drank only vegetable juices for one week. I took detoxifying herbs and mainly ate organic fruit and vegetables from my local farmer's market. As a result, in the first six months of cleaning the body, I experienced detoxifying headaches from sugar, caffeine, and other toxicities in the body that lasted one week, two weeks, and even one month. After those early six months, the headaches stopped. I never took medication to alleviate the pain.

When I went to an integrative doctor, he asked me to do a provoked toxic heavy metals panel test. I took a pill that encouraged heavy metals to be dumped into the body and collected urine over eight hours. The test showed I had astronomically high lead levels, high mercury, and thallium. In Dr. Hulda Clark's book, *The Cure for All Diseases with Many Case Histories,* she writes that every person she tested with colon cancer had high lead levels. I proceeded to do a suppository chelation therapy regimen and change my mercury fillings with biological dentistry. A year later, I followed Anthony William's recipe for a heavy metal detox smoothie outlined in his first book, *Medical Medium.* I did not retest as the cost of the test was high. I also did a few parasite cleanses.

One of my early healer guides asked me to do a vitamin D OH- blood test, and my levels were low. I learned that most people have low vitamin D OH-. Since then, I've taken vitamin D3, K2 (which helps D3 absorb into the body), vitamin B12 in drops, B complex, vegan algae-derived omega-3 DHA-EPA oil capsules, magnesium glycinate, and zinc drops. I take dulse flakes as an iodine supplement to feed my thyroid. For selenium, I eat two Brazil nuts a day.

I read several accounts of people who healed from cancer just by eating a specific raw vegan diet. I could not imagine eating raw vegan food, so I did my best to become a vegan eater. I didn't know how to eat a balanced vegan meal, and after six months, I switched to the paleo diet for four months as I was craving protein. Then I changed to a raw vegan, low-fat diet for three months, followed by a raw vegan ketogenic diet for three months. Nothing that I ate or drank regressed my tumor for the length of time that I tried it. It did, however, clean up the body. I stopped ingesting caffeine, gluten, processed sugar, corn, soy, and canola oil.

I'm neither a doctor nor a nutritionist, and I know there are many ways to use food as medicine. There are herbalists, naturopaths, nutritionists, the Optimum Health Institute, your own wisdom and connection to an intelligent field, and a plethora of books and blogs that offer guidance. Each patient chooses what feels right for them to eat.

In addition, every body is different. I can eat most greens, but other people cannot. I can eat the Brassica family (broccoli, Brussels sprouts, cabbage, cauliflower, collard green, kale, and turnips), which are regarded as anti-cancerous, but others cannot. I can eat grains and legumes, but my nephew's body has pain after he eats grains and legumes. My niece is allergic to peanuts, and I'm not. A breast cancer survivor told me she took four turmeric pills throughout the day for a month, and her cancer disappeared. I took four turmeric pills a day and developed an allergic reaction after a few days. Everyone has different gut bacteria and different nervous systems. Both influence how well we digest food.

In addition, coach Chana Studley's experience showed her that chronic anxiety thinking influences food digestion. She saw how perfectionistic thinking, PTSD, fear thinking, putting pressure on oneself, and comparing herself to an "ideal" created stressful thinking. She learned that chronic anxiety dysregulates the nervous system. Her food allergies, hormonal imbalances, and chronic pain reversed when she learned to let go of listening to and believing her stressful thinking habits. She learned to slow down and focus on peace. Her trusted feelings alert her to slow down again and let go of engaging in stressful thinking. Miraculously, even her body seizing up and going into occasional paralysis stopped when she learned to slow down and focus on the innate quiet and well-being.

There are different nutritional healing paths. I read research from Dr. Nicholas Gonzales, which said that people with solid tumors do better on a vegan or vegetarian diet, and people with blood tumors do better with meat in every meal and a whole set of different supplements. You'd need to find what makes sense to you.

Every health institution that I went to said to chew food thoroughly. The digestive system works hard to break food down. It takes energy that could be used for healing. My teachers at OHI asked everyone to chew each bite thirty times before swallowing the food. Smoothies are gentler on the digestive system's work load.

While healing from cancer, you may help your body by eating good food. In addition, juicing is a great way to introduce nutrition. Think about it; I do not eat one celery bulb a day. But I juice one bulb once or twice weekly or two bulbs daily when cleansing.

On the micro-physical level, it's important to note that the large intestine has more bacterial cells than your own body cells. Gut bacteria are enormously vital to your health. The bacteria in your gut digest food, create B vitamins and give you immunity against diseases. There is a gut-brain connection where bacterial digested substances travel to the brain from the gut and enhance your well-being. A healthy microbiome keeps you healthy.

Most people have experienced bacterial food poisoning, which happens when you ingest spoiled food with "bad bacteria." When your gut microbiome is compromised, the ratio of health-promoting to not health-promoting bacteria, viruses, and fungi changes, and this causes changes to your gut lining, your ability to digest food, and your overall health.

Eating fresh fruit and vegetables promotes healthy gut bacteria. When you eat whole foods with fiber, your good gut bacteria flourish. And when you eat processed foods, the not-so-healthy gut bacteria thrive. You can choose which bacteria you'd like to feed for good health.

In recent years, experiments have been done with fecal implants: taking feces from a healthy individual (there is a screened fecal bank) and transferring it to another person's digestive tract who isn't healthy. For example, when patients experience an outbreak of the Clostridium Difficile (C. Diff) bacteria, a fecal implant can cure the patients in a day or two. When patients take antibiotics to treat the outbreak, they must take about a month or six weeks of strong antibiotics, which also kill good gut bacteria. Some sources mention that fecal implants can help with obesity, diabetes, depression, arthritis, IBS, and eczema.i It seems that gut bacteria are vital to overall health.

Food can also manage weight. If you want to increase weight, fruit can help you. When I eliminated all sugar from my diet for five months, including all fruit and high glycemic vegetables, my weight dropped to 110-113 pounds. When I added fruit to my diet, my weight went up to 120 rapidly. If your weight is dropping, consider having smoothies. You can use fruit, fresh or frozen, greens like spinach, kale, power mix, lettuce, peanut or almond butter (without sugar or added oils), avocado, coconut water, and any alternative milk or water.

I'm a proponent of eating clean food. If food can be grown without pesticides and herbicides, as claimed in farmers' markets, I buy it. My diet consists of fruit smoothies with greens, oatmeal with fruit and nuts/nut butter, garbanzo-flour omelets, home-baked bread, fruit salads, fresh raw vegetable juices, herbal teas, salads, soups, legumes, and cooked vegetables and whole grains. I heard Dr. Joel Fuhrman say that in America, people eat a salad with a meal, and people need to eat one salad a day as a meal. Five years after the end of chemo, I didn't want to have as many fruits. I stopped drinking my smoothies. My body signaled to me that it had enough sugar. Your body is speaking to you too. Listen to what it says.

I avoid dairy products. I mostly use water instead of frying oil because oil can become rancid and hurt rather than enhance the microbiome when heated. I learned about the "clean fifteen" fruits and vegetables that can be eaten not organically and the "dirty dozen" foods that need to be eaten organically from the Environmental Working Group's website (EWG).ii The EWG is an independent testing facility whose mission is, "To empower you with breakthrough research to make informed choices and live a healthy life in a healthy environment." I eat a primarily vegan diet, and when I eat animal products, I look for wild-caught small fish with less mercury than large fish and organic, grass-fed animals walking the pastures and not eating grain.

What about drinks? Most people wake up and drink coffee. There are alternatives to coffee if you're open to experimentation. You can have water with a squeeze of lemon, water with lemon, raw honey, and ginger, or a water-Aloe-raw honey smoothie. Fresh vegetable juices like cucumber, celery, celery and cucumber, celery-cucumber-apple, carrot, carrot-celery-parsley, and carrot-apple-ginger beet are also refreshing. There are also organic herbal teas like ginger, ginger-turmeric, mint, spearmint, chamomile, nettle, rosemary, lemon verbena, cinnamon, diluted cranberry juice, hibiscus, milk-thistle, thyme, parsley, or oregano.

You can pour hot water over rosemary, mint, sage, oregano, dandelion leaves, or hibiscus and drink it. You can have water infused with cucumbers, mint, lemon, berries, or watermelon. Some people drink carob-based teas or mushroom-dandelion-based coffee substitutes. In the summer, I love drinking a melon or watermelon smoothie with water. All these drinks cleanse the body.

Why is it important to eat clean beyond feeding the good gut bacteria? In my diet explorations, I read about genetically modified organisms (GMOs) and avoided them when I could. Google Dictionary states, "GMOs are novel organisms created in a laboratory using genetic modification/ engineering techniques. Scientists, consumers, and environmental groups have cited many health and environmental risks with foods containing GMOs."

GMO foods such as soy, wheat, corn, rapeseed (canola oil plant), and sugar beets have a bacterial gene inserted into their genome that is herbicide resistant. Other inserted genes to those products can create an internal insecticide. GMO crops can be sprayed with an herbicide, glyphosate (also known as Roundup), that kills weeds while leaving GMO plants unharmed. Herbicides are sprayed because farmers won't need to till the soil and pick weeds by hand, which is labor-intensive, time-consuming, and costs more than spraying herbicide.

The problem with sprayed plants is that the weeds and insects have mutated to become resistant to low levels of glyphosate. Farmers use lots of glyphosate and other, more potent herbicides to eradicate weeds. A report from Harvard University states that "drawing from U.S. Department of Agriculture data on pesticide use estimated that an additional 383 million pounds of herbicides have been used than if Roundup Ready crops were never introduced. This increased use of glyphosate heightens the likelihood of higher concentrations of the chemical running off into nearby ecosystems. At these elevated concentrations, glyphosate may be capable of causing environmental damage." iii

In 2020, Bayer, which bought Monsanto, reached an agreement with a group of attorneys representing 90,000 plaintiffs that allege that using Roundup weedkiller regularly and for many years caused them to develop cancer. Roundup herbicide contains glyphosate, a chemical thought to be carcinogenic by the World Health Organization, and a surfactant that causes glyphosate to stick to the plant leaf and stem and human skin, bioaccumulating and causing cancerous lesions.iv

From the docuseries *Interconnected* by Dr. Pedram Shojai, I learned that glyphosate, the active component of Roundup, is classified as an herbicide and an antibiotic (episode 10). As glyphosate-sprayed corn, for example, is consumed, the glyphosate on the corn enters the gut and can kill the good gut bacteria. In addition, Roundup-sprayed crops are often used to feed cows, goats, sheep, and chickens. The herbicides become a part of the animal tissue, and when humans consume these cattle products, there's an impact on people's gut biome and general health.v

In addition to changing the gut microbiome balance, herbicides accrue toxicities in the human body. According to WebMD, although pesticide tolerances are assumed to be safe, these chemicals are toxic and haven't been studied directly in people. Moreover, the individual safety profiles of pesticides don't consider their combined effects. "Take a box of [cereal] off the shelf, and you can find residues from 32 pesticides...Each one is within its tolerance, but what's the effect of those chemicals acting in combination in our bodies?" vi

On my health journey, I learned that most processed food (made in a plant rather than grown) has additives, stabilizers, and preservatives for longer shelf life. Some of those additives and preservatives can be food coloring, which has been linked to ADHD, allergies, and cancer.vii

But isn't processed food so tasty? The issue is its high salt, fat, and sugar content. These concentrated substances create food addictions in the brain.viii People usually don't have an addiction to bananas, broccoli, cucumbers, lettuce, or potatoes. However, people can develop an addiction to even these foods if the foods are coated with oil, salt, sugar, and MSG.

Think about it. Can you stop eating plain baked potatoes willfully, or do you eat ten of them at a time? On the other hand, can you stop eating potato chips, or do you want to keep eating the whole bag of chips once you've started? Your body has a "stop" button when you eat a whole-food diet. You know when you are full when your body receives enough fuel. However, with added and extracted concentrated sugars, oils, and salts, the addiction overcomes the mechanism that stops you when you're full. There are food engineers who create addictive food products so consumers will buy more of them.

Although sugars, oils, and salt exist naturally, people have overused these products in the food industry. The rule I follow is: if nature makes it and my body feels good after I eat it, I eat it. If nature doesn't make it, I don't eat it.

What about sugar? According to a PubMed article, sweetness can induce reward and craving comparable in magnitude to those caused by addictive drugs like cocaine.ix A team in France published a lab rat experiment involving saccharin and cocaine. The rats were given cocaine until they became dependent on it. Then, researchers provided them with a choice – the rats could continue to have the cocaine, or they could switch to saccharin. Ninety-four percent of rats chose to make the switch. Even when they had to work hard to access the sugar, the rats were more interested in it than they were in the cocaine.x

Historically, when sugar was not as abundant in nature, sugar receptors would bind to sugar molecules and give you a happy feeling. Today, many kinds of extracted and concentrated sugars are added to processed food. As a result, the body's receptors get overloaded by processed foods, making the brain release abnormal amounts of happy chemicals called endorphins. This feeling causes people to develop sugar addictions.

Food companies often use several sweeteners in a single product. Together, the sweeteners add to the collective addiction to sugar. Some names for sugars in products are cane juice, cane sugar, caramel, corn syrup, corn syrup solids, barley malt, Barbados sugar, beet sugar, brown sugar, buttered syrup, confectioner's sugar, dextrose, diastatic malt, ethyl maltol, fructose, castor sugar, dehydrated cane juice, granulated sugar, high fructose corn syrup, lactose, malt, maltodextrin, dextran, fruit juice, fruit juice concentrate, galactose, glucose, rice syrup, sucrose, treacle, trehalose, glucose solids, golden sugar, maltose, malt syrup, mannitol, turbinado sugar.

After learning about all the sugar types in processed foods, I began reading labels better. I sweeten my drinks with dates, raw honey, or maple. I use a high-powered blender and add one Medjool date per cup as a sweetener. That way, I know the sweetness is bound with fiber, protein, vitamins, and minerals.

Choosing what you eat, which becomes your body, is essential to maintaining good health. Instead of elaborate desserts, I mostly eat fruit or frozen fruit. I sometimes choose a vegan dessert recipe made from whole ingredients, with nothing processed. Instead of oils, I prefer raw nuts and seeds and blend them into salad dressings and dates as a sweetener, herbs, and spices. I've learned not to coat vegetables with oil when I bake them.

However, learning about nutrition ignited fear thinking for me. While on my cancer journey, I became obsessive about "clean food." I refused to eat food at family functions if it wasn't organic. If food was baked on aluminum foil, I didn't touch it as I learned that aluminum leaches into food, then into our brains, and is linked to Alzheimer's disease. I would have a meltdown if someone invited me and placed processed sugar into the tomato sauce. I didn't trust anyone's cooking. Notice how much anxious thinking I created for myself. I often brought homemade food wherever I went. I wanted my body to heal and did everything I could to eat clean, and at the same time, I ran a loop of anxiety about "health food."

Of course, it's easier to have perspective in hindsight. If I could offer you words of wisdom, it's to be easy about your eating habits. Trust yourself to pick a healing diet that fits your body and lifestyle. Provide the body with nourishing foods. When you don't, accept yourself. It's okay to crave and eat something you know isn't the best choice. Show yourself compassion and acceptance. If you're inclined to self-judgment, forgive yourself often. Change takes time. Learning what's right for you can take time too. I listened to health forums about food for several years and read many blogs until health food consciousness became ingrained. Along the way, I had comfort food days.

Today I choose healthy food because I feel good when I eat it. I enjoy how my body feels when I nourish it with simple food. When I make a smoothie without greens, my body asks for greens. When I taste regular cookies or cakes, I no longer enjoy them. The food tastes too sugary and rich, and my taste buds no longer like it. And when I have indulged in rich foods, my body let me know that it was not the optimal choice. I'm learning.

Whatever diet you choose on this journey, whether you change your diet or not, be easy with yourself. Having extra stress chemicals and adrenaline in the body while going through a cancer journey isn't worth it. Do your best with clean eating, if you choose. At one health institute, the nutritionist offered patients to eat 80-20: 80 percent of the time clean and 20 percent comfort food. You get to choose, experiment and empower yourself. If you want to clean your incredible body, you can. There are numerous resources online and in books. I trust you'll find the right one for you. You are allowed to change your mind and direction at any point. Love yourself and your incredible body through your journey of food nourishment.

SUMMARY AND SUGGESTIONS

1. Consider eating a whole-food, nature-created diet as much as possible.
2. There are numerous healing diets for cancer. You get to choose how to keep your body clean.
3. Water, raw vegetable juices, fruit, detoxifying teas, and supplements can clean your body.

4. Toxic heavy metals can be gently cleansed from the body by experts who know about chelation or herbal heavy metal cleanses.
5. GMO crops might be sprayed with lots of herbicides and insecticides, which may wreak havoc with gut bacteria, affecting immunity, vitamin B production, and digestion.
6. Cattle-fed GMO meat might contain herbicides and insecticides. It may contribute to gut imbalance. You may choose organic grass-fed animals.
7. Processed foods have addictive chemicals that make you want to eat more, even though you know they're unhealthy.
8. Remember the 80-20 plan. Consider being as easy in your mind about eating habits. When you fall off the wagon, it's okay. I encourage you to give yourself love and compassion. Tomorrow is another day. Change and awareness take time and education. You have time to learn about healthy eating habits. Love yourself and your fabulous body through your journey.

Chapter Thirty Five

DETOXIFYING YOUR PHYSICAL ENVIRONMENT

When I first began reading books about people who healed naturally from cancer, there was often a section in the book about detoxifying the physical environment. The less toxicity that comes into the body, the freer the body is to heal. I gathered information from reading books, listening to lectures, and going to naturopaths, integrative doctors, and several health institutes.

I learned that conventional shampoos, soap, toothpaste, skincare, perfumes, nail polish, make-up, sunscreen, laundry detergents, dryer sheets, most air fresheners, cleaning products, and even new clothes could have toxic substances. Your skin is the biggest organ, and anything you put on it, including new clothing, gets absorbed into the bloodstream. That includes the scalp. In addition, clothing made of synthetic material often leaches particles into the water, the oceans, and fish, and then becomes your body.vi

Moreover, I learned that undisclosed fragrances placed in shampoos, conditioners, facial products, and perfumes could cause hormonal disruption. Some chemicals, such as parabens, have been linked to breast cancer. Sodium lauryl sulfate has been linked to cancer, and DMDM hydantoin releases formaldehyde. Ewg.org is an independent product testing organization. Their website provides a link to their Skin Deep Guide to Cosmetics,i which lists safe products. You can also go to your local health food store, which carries products that do not have the aforementioned toxic chemicals.

Health stores carry cleaning supplies that are less toxic to you and the environment. In addition, you can also use household ingredients. For example, you can clean floors and countertops with vinegar and dish soap.

My first healer was concerned about electromagnetic frequency (EMF) protection. Some people's bodies can be susceptible to EMF radiation. EMF comes from WiFi, smart homes, and appliances. Some people turn off their WiFi at night to sleep better. Some buy an EMF-canceling device, which they plug into an electrical outlet. I purchased a product that cancels EMF waves and couldn't feel any difference.

Mold can also create illness for sensitive bodies. My cousin moved to an apartment with mold and had a thyroid attack. She found black mold under the sink. Look around for any wet areas or leaks in your walls. Check anything wet for mold. Sometimes you can smell the mold, while other times, you cannot. You can call a professional company to evaluate a damp area in your home.

Asbestos can lead to lung cancer when inhaled repeatedly over time. Asbestos was often used in older homes up until the 1980s. The flooring could have asbestos, whether in vinyl or the glue under carpeting or hardwood floors. Some older buildings used asbestos as insulation. Asbestos is dangerous when its structure is disturbed and the particles can be inhaled.

If you need clarification on what type of insulation you have in your home, or if it's an older home that has yet to be inspected recently, consider getting it checked by an asbestos testing company. Some drywall, called Wallboard or Gypsum Board from the 1930s to the 1980s, also contains asbestos. Popcorn ceilings from the 1940s to the 1980s also contain asbestos, and it's best to leave them alone or to have them removed by professionals.

Living in a home with a carpet can also affect you if you're sensitive. According to the American Lung Association, "Carpets may trap pollutants like dust mites, pet dander, cockroach allergens, particle pollution, lead, mold spores, pesticides, dirt, and dust. Toxic gases in the air can stick to small particles that settle into carpets. These pollutants may become airborne during renovations, vacuuming, or even daily activities like walking on the carpet...Chemicals used in some new carpets, carpet pads, and the adhesives used to install them can harm your health. Some of these chemicals and glues are made with volatile organic compounds (VOCs), which emit odors and pollutants. New carpet installation also has been associated with wheezing and coughing in babies in their first year of life." ii

What can you do about your carpet? If you can afford to, remove it and install a wood or tile floor. If you want to buy an untreated, safer carpet, there is a list at mychemicalfreecarpet.net. Otherwise, consider purchasing an excellent air filter to absorb the chemicals and volatile organic compounds that are off-gassing from your carpet. Consumer Reports has an unbiased list of tested air purifiers.

I also learned that furniture made of particle board could emit gas, formaldehyde, and other toxic fumes from the glue-pressed wood particles. If you have furniture with particle board, consider changing it to wood. Or think about using a good air filter. It took me a while, but slowly I replaced my particle board furniture with solid wood used furniture.

Water quality is also important to check. Even though the U.S. Environmental Protection Agency manages tap water quality, water can still be contaminated. To find the level of contamination in your city, look it up at ewg.org/tapwater. This link will take you to a database of tested city water with a list of contaminants that are above a healthy level according to EWG's independent testing standards. Tap water could contain pesticide or herbicide runoff, lead, arsenic, bromoform, chloroform, chlorine products, or nitrates. Water filters can remove much of the toxicity. Berkey water filters can be an inexpensive option. Reverse osmosis systems with remineralization are the best, though most expensive, option.

Water bottles from filtered or spring water can leach BPA, a molecule that can mimic estrogen and bind to estrogen receptors in the body. BPA is also found in shatterproof windows, eyewear, epoxy resins that coat some metal food cans, bottle tops, water supply pipes, and paper receipts printed on thermal paper. BPA has been linked to certain cancers and reproductive issues. It can rub on your hands, penetrate the skin, and get absorbed into your bloodstream. If you place receipts in your purse or pocket, they will rub off on your clothes, money, or wallet. It's better to get your receipts emailed and to wash your hands when you get home.iii Also, consider limiting your use of canned food, or buy canned food that is BPA-free (the company Eden uses BPA-free cans).

Aluminum foil, aluminum cookware, and scratched Teflon cookware are toxic to the body. Consider changing aluminum foil with unbleached parchment paper for baking. Consider switching your aluminum and Teflon cookware to ceramic-coated, glass baking dishes or cast iron cookware. As much as possible, consider storing food in glass containers rather than plastic ones, especially if the food is hot.

There is some controversy about the safety of microwaves. I haven't used microwaves for years. Dr. Mercola's article "Convenience Poses Toxic Threat in More Ways Than One" proposes that microwaved food alters the structure of water molecules in a way that deforms them. He writes that when plastic is heated, toxic chemicals like BPA and phthalates can leach out of the containers or covers, contaminating food with endocrine and hormone disruptors and carcinogens. That includes popcorn and pizza packaging.

Moreover, in this article, Mercola discusses how microwaves create carcinogens in nearly all types of food during microwaving. Iv It's possible that Dr. Mercola's arguments and research are accurate, and it's also possible they're not. I didn't want to take a chance and avoided microwaved food.

A year before my cancer diagnosis, I heard Dr. Joel Fuhrman speak on PBS. He mentioned that in his first class in medical school, his teacher said that all manufactured drugs are toxic to the body. That's why the medication has to be disposed of in particular bins, usually collected at police stations. I follow his suggestion and use medicine as little as possible.

There is more to know about detoxifying your environment, but as mentioned in previous chapters, keeping your mind sane as you detoxify your environment is essential. Notice if you're becoming frightened and obsessive about toxicity. Then allow the feelings and know that you are experiencing habitual fear thoughts in the body. Make space for your human experience. You just experienced a scary movie made by your mind. It's okay. Remember who you are – the dimension of life beyond any thought or feeling. You are the space between words. You are the present subtle energy when you don't attach to any concept of me or I. You are eternal energy. You are calm. You are well. You are intelligent. You have common sense. You are loving and lovable.

I invite you to make changes at a leisurely and relaxing pace and not to stress about it. Over several months, I took steps one at a time and am still making changes according to time and budget. You have discernment and will choose what seems right and fits your budget. You have my love and support.

SUMMARY AND SUGGESTIONS

1. Consider looking at ewg.org's Skin Deep guide to learn about the toxicity of personal products, cleaning products, and other items. Alternatively, consider shopping at a health food store for your skincare products.
2. Consider using a water filter. Some bottled water uses plastic that leaches BPA into the water. BPA is also found in personal care products, lined tin cans, and receipts.
3. Consider changing particle board furniture to wood.
4. Consider using an air filter if you have particle board furniture or carpets, or change your carpets to hardwood floors.
5. Check your aluminum and Teflon cookware and change to ceramic, clay, cast iron, and glass. When you bake, change the aluminum foil to unbleached parchment paper.
6. Cleaning up your environment is a step-by-step process. Please don't let this add stress to your life. Take your time and make the changes that are right for you. You have my support.

Chapter Thirty Six

CAREGIVERS

I now understand the idiom, "It takes a village." My friend Dina joined me at my early doctor appointments. She made time in her schedule to support me whenever she could. I felt touched and deeply supported by her care for me. My friends Toby and Tina joined me at doctor appointments and spent time at the hospital with me at night. Tamara came over after her night shift as a nurse to give me the RigVir shots. She also went with me to the sex shop to get my first dilator. As a single woman, I felt grateful and relieved to have my friends' presence and support.

My ex-housemates, June and Jake, helped enormously. They agreed to lower my rent when I received my disability stipend. They were sounding boards. June asked me what I thought about having a colonoscopy when I was bleeding rectally, and the doctors said it was due to hemorrhoids. Her suggestion possibly saved my life. They also held space to hear what I experienced from time to time. Especially at the beginning of my journey, their assistance was tremendous. They helped by being present, inclusive, keeping me company, and inviting me to some home gatherings with their friends and family while I underwent treatments. They were great supporters and helped me grow in my power of expression and saying no.

I'm grateful to my sister Hanna for scheduling family and friends to be with me at the hospital. It took much effort. Likewise, I'm deeply thankful to my family and friends for their help at the hospital. My brother's family accepted me with open arms when I came to see them, and I felt supported when they visited me in the hospital after my surgery. My generous sister-in-law joined me at doctor appointments and often took me to food and supplement shopping. She also helped in encouraging my family to donate to my fundraising campaign to go to the clinic in Mexico.

My family and friends contributed financially, emotionally, and mentally to my alternative health journey. I would not be here without their love. They have all held me up. Their energy, love, and support helped me from staying in a lonely, fearful thought-created world. I am here because of their love. Really. I am forever grateful and humbled.

My mom called me daily from Israel for the first couple of years of my journey, which was a huge help. She caught a medical error one time when I told her the lab test results of my liver test. Her assistance, reassurance, and support were invaluable. I appreciated having her consistently on the other side of the line. I know that supporting me also took a toll on her. She experienced anxiety and restlessness with her thoughts and worries about me.

My uncle was my primary caregiver throughout my hospital stays and after discharge. He and my aunt opened their home to me to heal after both surgeries. My uncle was retired then, and I was tremendously grateful for his time and attention. It was frightening for me to be a burden on anyone, especially since I didn't have anyone who was "supposed" to help. When Yacov came forward and offered to help during the surgeries and beyond, it was a huge relief.

When I was discharged from the hospital stays, I was moved to tears when my uncle went to bring his car to the hospital's entrance.

My mom was in Israel, my dad was unwell, and everyone else was working. I didn't have a husband, a boyfriend, or kids, and everyone was busy living their lives. My uncle made time to support me with this journey. I became emotional about his efforts, commitment, and care, taking time away from his life to help me. After the surgeries, I felt vulnerable and helpless and greatly appreciated his sensitivity and understanding.

When I shared with Yacov about this chapter and how much I appreciated his help, he said, "I love you so much. And I care about you. You matter to me so much." When he says this to me, I am in shock. It's still challenging to receive so much love. I'm used to being on my own. I am so humbled. I told him I wouldn't be here without his and everyone's love. He said, "I know." Those are moving conversations for me. Consider appreciating your caregivers as much as you can.

So many people supported me through donations of money or their time. My Angel Mel came to help me with juicing, food support, and thinking things through at the beginning. Mel, you are so appreciated and I love you so much. Marina helped with vegan support meal prep and education. My cousins sometimes helped with food prep, and cousin Yaeli stayed at the hospital with me one night. My brother-in-law and sister walked with me. Marsha came to walk and listen once a week for many months. Lori brought me food occasionally and listened; Jess helped with transportation, food shopping, and companionship. Etty came to visit and walk with me and chat. My family in Israel and Joe lent a listening ear when needed. Toby, Tina, Tamara, and Dina held incredible space for me always. I am here because of their efforts and support. The outpouring of love deeply moves me.

That said, it's hard for caregivers to know what you need and what you are experiencing if you don't share. Some caregivers possess excellent communication skills and ask about what you're going through emotionally and physically. They can listen and connect with your experience. That in itself is a gift. The caregivers constantly look at you, trying to imagine what is happening to you. Consider sharing.

After my first surgery, I was prickly with pain and feeling depressed. I'm thankful my uncle and aunt were resilient and compassionate enough to understand my challenges and still care. They knew to leave me alone until the prickles passed. If you are especially prickly after some phases of this treatment, consider apologizing to the caregiver as soon as you snap out of your misery or pity thinking. Have compassion and warmth for yourself; you are undergoing a significant change and will get caught up in thinking. Have compassion and warmth for your caregivers also. They are giving their time and presence to care for you and would appreciate tenderness, warmth, and understanding from you too.

As a patient going through a healing journey, I didn't want to be pitied or treated as a victim. I also didn't want my caregivers to minimize what I felt. I wanted them to understand I was experiencing pain, itchiness, fatigue, mental fear, discouragement, or hopefulness. I didn't want my caregivers to change my experiences; I wanted them to understand. If I felt insecure, I wanted to say that I felt insecure (attached to insecure thinking). If you're a caregiver, consider asking your loved one how they'd like you to support them. Then listen to what they say. If you sense that something other than what they say will help them, your wisdom will tell you.

I also wanted to be treated as a regular person and to hear about my caregivers' lives. It took me away from focusing on treatments and how I felt. I couldn't believe I would ever have a "normal" life again while undergoing treatments. I couldn't see the light at the end of the tunnel. The process felt long, and I had low points.

If you have one primary caregiver, like a partner, a parent, or a child, please ensure they have time for themselves. Caregivers can get tired and dip low if they consistently take care of patients. Make sure to suggest they do things with their friends, exercise, enjoy their hobbies, watch a movie, or refresh and have alone time. Maybe someone else can hang out with you for a weekend, and your caregiver can go away to rejuvenate.

As a caregiver, you might feel guilty about doing fun activities while your loved one is in pain. When I cared for my grandmother after she fell, I sometimes felt guilty for going out and doing something fun when she was at home in pain with a caregiver. Even when I went out, I felt guilty until I relaxed into the activity and became absorbed. Then I came back refreshed and balanced. As a caregiver, consider taking breaks and immersing yourself in something unrelated to caregiving.

When the guilt feelings arrive, remind yourself that they're well intended. You are a loving being, and it's sane for you to care for your loved one and yourself. Allow and accept the guilt feelings. Breathe. Allow it all, both the human experience and the quiet wisdom you have when anchored in the place of being, the space beyond thought. You have a softness and discernment inside. Follow your discernment without overriding it with rationalization, if you can. And even when you override it, love and accept yourself with warmth. It's all acceptable. No one has a manual on how to be human.

Caregivers put their lives on hold to care for a loved one. That's a lot to give. Consider having several caregivers who can drop in and assist other than your main one, so your primary caregiver can have a break. Of course, they may not want to. They might want to be with you at every appointment. They might be scared that they might not have more days with you. They might give all their time to spend a few more moments with you. Gauge their mental-emotional state. If they get snappy or look fatigued, it may be time to add more caregivers. I've spoken to care recipients who tell me that their caregivers should go to support groups because they're "getting snappy" and are too worried like they carry the weight of the world on their shoulders.

Caregivers can use support from the extended social circle. If you're part of the family, call the caregivers and speak with them about how they're doing and what they're going through — without fixing them. Consider taking them out so they can refresh.

There are caregiver support groups where caregivers can share the load with others. Every Cancer Support Community has groups in person and online; the colorectal Facebook pages also do. One group recommended to me is called I Care: A Cancer Caregivers Support Group.

Your primary caregiver is going through the same ups and downs as you are. One patient suggested that when the patient feels better, make that time enjoyable with your caregiver. Try to be anchored in the present and enjoy life together as much as possible.

Whether you are a caregiver or a care recipient (and in life, you do both), remember your quiet space, the space of allowing everything. When caregivers see their loved ones suffering, they might contract internally with stress and pain. If that happens, notice your discomfort and breathe. Allow your heart to open to discomfort. Give it space.

Relax around the discomfort. Allow yourself to feel. Then relax around the thought that wants to protect your loved one or yourself. Breathe. Give the thoughts and feelings a space to be. All feelings are allowed. Maybe get curious about the sensations and where they are in the body. Allow them without needing to fix or change them. Anchor yourself in the place beyond thoughts and feelings. You are the quiet dimension of being, even while a feeling is there. Breathe from your quiet space, and go back to being with your loved one, then back to your quiet internal space, and back to being with them, allowing their human experience, allowing yours. It's a practice, but it will help you open yourself to all of life, all feelings, instead of contracting and closing around the feelings.

I appreciate my caregivers more than words can say, as do you. Caregivers, I acknowledge the tremendous depth of love you hold for your loved one. I acknowledge your strength of heart, generosity of spirit, caring, compassion, humor, dedication, humor, resiliency, and resourcefulness. You are the best example of a human being sharing love. You are love in action.

Other patients wanted me to tell you that patients wouldn't make it without you. Please take that in. Some patients asked me to convey that they realize that what the caregivers go through can be more challenging than what the patients go through. They wanted to say the hugest thank you from their big tender grateful hearts to yours. Caregivers, you are truly lifesavers. Patients love and appreciate you more than you will ever know.

SUMMARY AND SUGGESTIONS

1. Caregivers are patients' lifelines. They give so much support. I know that you are thankful to them. Appreciating them for what they do for you can be connecting and helpful to both.
2. Caregivers can shoulder your burdens and pain. Be kind to your caregiver as much as possible, and apologize when you've been snappy.
3. If you have one primary caregiver, consider suggesting that they take breaks. Ask other friends and family if they can care for you sporadically so your caregiver can refresh and rejuvenate themselves.

4. Consider asking the extended family and social circle to call the caregiver and support them. Cancer Support Communities, cancer centers at major hospitals, and online groups can also support caregivers.
5. As a caregiver, you might feel guilty about doing fun activities while your loved one is suffering or in pain. But it would help if you had rejuvenation and space for yourself also. Allow and accept the feelings. Breathe. Allow everything. When you have some time alone, anchor yourself in a space that is not thoughts and feelings. Drop into your essence of being. Breathe there for a while.
6. Whether you are a caregiver or a care-receiver (and in life, we get to do both), try as much as possible to be anchored in the space of allowing everything you're both experiencing.
7. Caregivers, your care receiver acknowledges the tremendous depth of love that you hold for them. You are the best example of a human being sharing love. Without you wonderful caregivers, patients wouldn't make it! You are so loved and appreciated.

Chapter Thirty Seven

FINAL THOUGHTS

I hope this book supported you and that you feel more connected to others who went through a journey with rectal cancer. I know that after these treatments, your life will be different. You constantly consider and deal with bathroom habits or changing your stoma bag. You need ample time in the morning before leaving to go anywhere or have your stoma supplies with you. Your issues will not be the same as mine; you'll have yours to figure out. But you are connected to the energy that creates worlds. Your wisdom and common sense will help you. You'll make the best of it. I know how grateful you are to be alive.

If you went through a journey with rectal cancer, I hope you appreciate how brave you are. You chose life and chose to do whatever it took to stay alive. I acknowledge your strength of heart. I celebrate your resilience. I honor your deep beauty with scars showing a life of courageous choices. You have more maturity and grit sprinkled with compassion and love for your journey and that of others. You are remarkable.

Although this book is mainly for stage II / III patients, some readers diagnosed with stage III underwent the treatments and discovered that cancer returned or was stage IV. If this is you, I honor you for receiving many rounds of various chemotherapy treatments and dealing with extensive side effects. You've had fear around scans and heard what you didn't want to hear, that cancer grew. You've gone to doctors and got second, third, fourth, and fifth opinions. I bow my head to you and your resilience and resourcefulness.

Some of you are NED, while others are on chemo for life. You are magnificent. Your spirit is radiant. I know many of you advocate for the ones that came after you and mentored others. I appreciate you so much. You have been some of my supporters and encouraged me with this book. You know how precious life is. Since life is taken one step at a time, I trust you'll know the next step at the right time, even if the next step is to accept that you've run out of treatment options. I've known patients who received palliative care and then hospice care with dignity, peacefulness, surrender, and transcendence.

When I was thirty, I had a mishap in a kayaking class in Nepal. I couldn't flip the kayak over. I tried but couldn't pull the skirt attached to the kayak. I kept trying to flip the kayak, but we only learned to flip it halfway. I realized that I was wasting my energy. I stayed underwater and told myself to calm down. I experienced too much panic to find solutions. I realized I could die. A thought ran through my head, "My brother would be so sad."

Then I ran out of air. There was nothing to do but accept that I would die in Nepal. I had done my best. I let go of any struggle. I accepted my imminent death and felt peaceful underwater. Just then, I felt the hands of my guide reaching mine. He helped me flip the kayak over, and I took a massive breath. I learned from this experience that as time approaches for people to let go of their bodies, they know how to do it. The process can be peaceful with acceptance and good hospice medical care.

But until that time comes, you are here and have the light of the world inside you. I invite you to shine it brightly and intently.

You are deeper than you were at the beginning of your journey. You have earned your depth of grit and compassion. Stand proud. I'm inspired by your path to empowerment, inner resolve, and compassion. You are genuinely shining brighter than before.

You'll still need to advocate for yourself and see doctors. You'll have scans and bloodwork. When you get scans, you might have scanxiety as you think about a cancer recurrence or chemotherapy treatments not working. You might be dreading the possibility of more treatment. Notice that the thoughts are creating your experience, not the experience itself. You can handle every experience just one step at a time. Notice the feelings, accept them, breathe, allow them, and create space for them to be. Maybe notice where they are expressed in the body. Be an observer of what sensations accompany a feeling. Get curious and follow them. Breathe. You just got caught up in what your consciousness is attached to. Create space for your human experience. Anchor yourself in the breath, the sensations, music, friends, the quiet space of being, or anywhere your wisdom tells you to. It knows you best.

In some ways, you will still be the same you after treatments. The same patterns, both fun and painful, will still come up for you. I still love family, friends, dance, nature, camping, spirituality, yoga, and meditation.

Likewise, my not-fun patterns, like distancing myself from others, imagining that I don't belong, feeling less than or more than, feeling insecure and anxious, judging others, then acting from insecurity, still come up. When I'm awake to it, I realize that I got caught up in habitual thinking. I notice the feelings, allow them, accept them, and relax. I anchor myself in the breath and the quiet space inside me. I breathe. I may surrender resisting thoughts to my loving quickly, or I might take time. It's all okay. I don't have to change my human experience.

I just get caught up. But I know that I am not the heavy feelings. My wisdom might tell me to do a Judge-Your-Neighbor Worksheet or not. My common sense might say to ride it out, like with a breakup. Wait until the heaviness lightens. It could take a minute, a day, or a few months. My discernment might tell me to do the opposite of what those thoughts tell me to do. You have your wisdom to guide you about your life.

What's important is that you stop engaging with the dispiriting running story. If you can do something about it, do it now. Otherwise, notice, allow, breathe, relax, then return to your quiet and joyful self. It's the game of life in a body, the human condition. You can go back to your loving again and again. You are the most magnificent light in form.

Whatever you shine your light on grows, so consider shining your light on enjoying your life. Leave the complaints behind unless you can do something about it. You have the gift of awareness. You can choose to focus on the innate quiet, the joy of being you, the joy of being alive, and living an inspired life. Since your thoughts are constantly creating with each thought you focus on, what would you like to create? What would an inspired life be for you? If you knew you loved yourself today, what would inspired and real expression look like?

Coach Steve F. Hardison reminds you that you are free to do what you want right now. The only thing holding you back is believing in thoughts that tell you otherwise. You are free to use your power in the world. You are free to create, move to another place, take a ceramics class, and create a better job situation. You are free to find the love of your life. You are free to cling to grief thoughts, sad thoughts, or loving your life thoughts. You are free. Use your thinking mechanism wisely. You are such a magnificent life in form. Use it to celebrate you and your creativity. Use it to celebrate others.

You are so important, and your life makes a massive difference in the world. You are powerful and resourceful. I believe in you.

Are you choosing healthy food or not? Are you choosing exercise or not? You are free to choose between clean beauty and cleaning products or not. You are powerful that way. You have choice and awareness. You are free to choose and accept yourself for being on a continuum of being good enough and forever improving. The most important thing is to not stress about being perfect. Enjoy your life.

You have the freedom to accept yourself daily as a beautiful and resilient being. You can love yourself right now as you are: a magnificent, brilliant, powerful, resourceful, wise, creative, free being. Accept your new, beautiful, scarred body with love. You are alive. As such, what do you want to create and express in this beautiful world?

I invite you to consider focusing on loving. Make time for fun. Pamper your body with a relaxing massage. Take those weekend trips. Take a half day off work when the weather cooperates and go to the beach with your kids. Write that novel or poetry book, take the vegan cooking class, and the camping trip to Rocky Mountain National Park. Play your guitar. Create an art class for your friends. Love others and yourself fiercely. Do the opposite of what your limiting beliefs say. Life is so precious.

I adore you. Words cannot adequately express how precious and beautiful I know you are. You are so gifted. You are more powerful than you know. You are connected to the energy that creates worlds. You are that energy. You are free. Go create your beautiful life courageously. Enjoy it as a gift. Keep going. You have my love and support.

ACKNOWLEDGMENTS

I thank Ms. Peggy Craik. Words cannot adequately describe my ocean of gratitude to you. When I wrote the first version, the memoir of my journey, you read and edited the manuscript for no pay. I was just out of cancer treatments with no money. You spent hours and hours with your immense and caring heart, reading and editing, asking questions, and putting your beautiful touches and spins on sentences and ideas. Your brilliance still shines in this updated version of the book, and I am forever grateful. Without you, I would have given up on this book. I would not have had money to pay an editor, and I would have allowed my insecurities about writing and the content to have the best of me. I would have buried the manuscript. But you came forward, an angel walking on earth, and gave your light to this light. Because of you, this book exists.

I thank Aunt Susi and Stepmom Yula, who consistently told me to write a book. You were both on my case for a long while, and I am happy that I listened after much prodding. I likewise thank all the "Seers" who encouraged me to write: Chris Brown, Ginger Quinlan, Colby Rebel, and Becky Kay Priest.

Thank you, Dr. Shawn Steen, for saving my life. Thank you for being the first doctor who listened to me and was interested in my alternative journey. You understood my examinations about not doing radiation, chemo, or surgery. You were open-minded and a down-to-earth human being. You were the first doctor that I felt comfortable with on this journey. Thank you so much for attending medical school, putting hours into learning your specialty, and becoming an excellent and experienced surgeon who saves lives. Thank you for reading the surgery chapters and giving me feedback. Thank you for seeing me, making me feel like I matter, and respecting me as a human being. My gratitude for you is so deep. I also thank my radiation oncologist and oncologist.

Thank you, Leona Byrne, who introduced me to Self Investment Publishing. As a favor to my friend, the incredibly generous owner asked three editors to read my memoir. Their feedback was to turn the memoir into a self-help Book. I had a fit, as I couldn't imagine writing a whole new book. But their genius team was correct, and I wrote this book. I thank you, Sumner and your editors, for your generosity and contribution.

Thank you so much, Diana Richardson, for reading the tantra part of the chapter and giving me feedback. Your insights and generosity are so appreciated. Because of you, I could get my sexuality back even with permanent nerve damage, and so will others. Thank you for the vital work that you do in the world.

Thank you, Dr. Jennifer Steen. I sincerely appreciate your expertise in the world of gynecology. You took time out of your day to read the gynecologic chapters to help me and others. You are incredibly generous, caring, and learned. Thank you for your invaluable feedback, for adding resources for other readers, and for cheering me on. Other patients and I are deeply grateful.

Thank you, coach Elaine Hilides from the United Kingdom, who read most of my coaching chapters and gave me vital feedback to consider in making the manuscript more accessible for the reader to understand. I have made changes and shifted the order of chapters because of you. You encouraged me to be brave and share what's essential earlier in the book. I am so appreciative and grateful for your generosity, clarity, and insight.

Thank you, Beth Leibson, for editing the manuscript. I wanted you to do it. You were kind and patient and worked tirelessly to support this project. I am deeply grateful for your love, input, insight, support, and generosity. You gave me constructive feedback and suggested structural formats in the book. Thank you so much for such helpful insight. And you were a gentle and clear editor. I sincerely appreciate your kindness and respect. Thank you so much.

The first editor I hired for a developmental edit of my first version gave me the name for this book. Thank you, Judy Katz. And thank you for loving the first version of this book and for encouraging me to keep going. Three years later, I hired Judy to help market this book. And what a great choice that was! Judy, you acted as a project manager for the later stages of this book and helped me so much with many details and nuances of publishing a book, from picking a photo, bio, and blurbs. You were my book publishing coach. I am so grateful to have had you in my court.

Thank you, Tony Iatridis from nycartdirector.com, for helping me with the cover design, formatting, and putting this book on Amazon, Kindle, and Ingram Spark. I sketched the cover, and you transformed it into the most beautifully computerized version I adore. You chose the red lettering to the title. I love the lettering you picked and the formatting you did for this book. I asked for it to look amazing, and you did that. You are such an amazing artist. I am so grateful for your expertise and assistance. Thank you for your art, care, so much time spent on tiny corrections, and flexibility.

Thank you, Dr Ralph Pearce, for reading a few chapters of my first version of the manuscript. Your feedback was valuable and much appreciated.

Thank you, Tina Paterson. You have been a friend, mentor,

and guide throughout my process. You held compassionate and loving space for me when I hurt physically and mentally and have been a steady witness and support throughout my book writing. I've shared with you my whole process and my challenges at every stage in the past six years. You've suggested ideas and given me material that is in this book from what you learned. You are an amazing heart-centered coach, and I know that all those you touch are so lucky and helped by your presence. I am lucky to call you my dear friend.

Thank you, Dr. Robin McGee, for your help with research papers and encouragement about the topic of sexuality and dilators. You've encouraged me to keep going and bring attention to this subject, and I am grateful. You are an incredible human and warrior! You've advocated so much for those who come after you. You are an inspiration.

I am deeply grateful for my mom and dad, who continue to love and support me. Even though I struggled with pain and judgment for many years until I stabilized and healed from the past, they still loved me. I'm grateful that we're maturing and growing together through the years. I love you very much. Thank you, Eema, for all the phone calls and for supporting me beautifully when I visited Israel with a stoma and taking chemo pills. Thank you for regaining trust in me through the years. Thank you, Aba and Miriam, for helping with finding alternative healers and helping to finance some of the beginning journey. I am deeply grateful.

I sincerely thank my family and friends in the United States who cared for me when I was in need: Dina and Peter, Tina and Don, Toby, Tamara, Marsha, Mel, Lori, Jess, Marina, Joe, Yacov and Susi, Gali and Ayellet, Kobi, Naomi, Ori, Yaeli, Margie, Hanna and Mark, Talia and Ryan and family, Ceevan, Yula, Etty, Neta, and Itzik and family, Maayan and Gil and family, Hadar and family, Karen and

Kobey, Bob Ginsburg and Family, Joyce Rosenblum and family, June and Jake.

Thank you, Mark Kahn and Kenneth Kron, for reading portions of the manuscript and giving me feedback and valuable content assistance.

Thank you, Kay Eames, and Natalie Jadwin, for copyediting help. You were amazing! Thank you for all the hours spent on reading this manuscript and finding errors! Thank you Dr. Rain Warren for reading a portion of the manuscript and finding corrections. You all gave me positive feedback and encouragement, and I am beyond lucky to have you in my life. Thank you, Rachel Furman and Tonya DeJuan for reading and giving me feedback. It was so valuable given all your loving and credentials.

Thank you, Tina, Tamara, Yossi, my Mom, Kobi, Yuri, Lital, my brother-in-law Mark, Hanna, cousins Shani and Hilla, Peter, Dina, Etty, Malka, Ahuva, Paul, my Dad, and Antonio, for asking me about the book for the past four to six years. You've encouraged me to keep going. In addition, many of you hired me to work for you with pet sitting, massage, or coaching when I came out of cancer treatments and didn't have a steady job. I am deeply grateful for amazing friendships, generosity, care, and support. The universe miraculously brought these caring people who helped me with insight, love, warmth, encouragement, ideas, and support.

I thank my brother, Gali, for all your love and support throughout our lives. Thanks for being so supportive of my book project and believing in me. I love your wisdom in all areas of life. You have counseled me and helped me with perspective when I was deep in my emotions our whole lives. You've helped me see what I couldn't. I love and appreciate you more than you know.

I contacted almost every person mentioned in this book and asked them to read what I wrote about them. It had to be a book of integrity. Thank you to all those I spoke with and your blessing and understanding of why the material here is relevant and healing for others. I thank you so much for your courage and feedback.

Thank you to the donors who raised money toward making this book and the people who raised a lot more to help keep me alive during the alternative phase of my life. You are the miracle; without you, I and this book would not be here. Thank you from all that I am.

I'm grateful for Amazon, which has a print-on-demand possibility.

Thank you, dear reader, for taking the time to read a creation that took countless hours of research and editing over six years. It was a huge commitment. I appreciate you and your courage to read. **Please consider adding your voice to Amazon for a review of this book.** It will help to share your feedback so others can relate. If you think the medical profession should tell women how radiation therapy affects their sexuality before they have radiation therapy, **please consider posting something on your social media pages** as a way to raise awareness about this important topic.

Thank you so much! You are the miracle.

RESOURCES

Communication

Art of Communication: NVCsantacruz.org | Communication Skills for Home & Community

NVC Academy (nvctraining.com)

NVC trainer and Resonance trainer Sara Peyton, SaraPeyton.com

Jim and Jori Manske, NVC trainers, radicalcompassion@gmail.com

Mary Mackenzie, NVC trainer, MaryMackenzie.net

The Center for Nonviolent Communication | Center for Nonviolent Communication (cnvc.org)

Shoshana Wheeler, Connectingwithcomassion.com

Life Coaches

Michael Neill, www.michaelneill.org Coaching from the inside out

Chana Studley, specialty: the mind-body-pain connection www.chanastudley.com

Tom Mattox, www.tommattox.com

Elaine Hilides, www.elainehilides.com Life Coaching from the Inside out

Steve F. Hardison, theultimtecoach.com

Rohini Ross, rohiniross.com

Dicken Bettinger, 3principlesmentoring.com

Mavis Karn, Maviskarn@aol.com

Grace Kelly, Gracefulcoaching.com
Yael Abramson, mental health, food addictions, yaelabramson83@gmail.com
Rachel Furman, 2rachelwithlove@gmail.com
Tina Marie Paterson, Tinamarietulipano@gmail.com
Marina Galan (Spanish speaking), www.marinagalan.com
Azul Leguizamón (Spanish), azulleguizamon.guia@gmail.com

Trauma Healing

Sara Peyton, at SaraPeyton.com

Manifestation

Dr. Joe Dispenza, drjoedispenza.com, plus YouTube, books
Ester Hicks, www.abraham-hicks.com

Relationships

Linda and George Pransky (they have a book called The Relationship Handbook), www.pranskyandassociates.com
Dicken Bettinger, 3principlesmentoring.com
Rohini and Angus Ross, rohiniross.com
Kathlyn and Gay Hendricks, www.hendricks.com
John Gray, MVTV www.marsvenus.com

Recall Healing Therapists

Dr. Michelle LaMasa -Schrader, recallhealingusa.com
Isabelle Benarous, BioReprogramming.net

Constellation and Compassion Facilitators

Tina Marie Paterson, Tinamarietulipano@gmail.com

Listening Coaches

Mavis Karn, Maviskarn@aol.com

Dr. Rain Warren, Rainlistens@gmail.com, Rainwarrenphd.com, Creating a World That Listens

Spiritual Counselor and Mediums/PsychicsPschics

Michael Hayes, Spiritual Counselor, Karma Reader awaketolove.com (He's my go-to for difficult interactions, past-life clearings, and readings about people's lives who have passed)

Colby Rebel, Psychic / Medium. colbyrebel.com (Colby was the psychic who kept telling me I wasn't doing enough when I was on my alternative phase)

Becky Kay Priest, Psychic / Medium, beckykay.com (Becky was the psychic who knew I was prescribed wrong medication for my thyroid. She told me to immediately stop taking it. She could also see that I had colorectal cancer).

Colleen Salomon, Psychic / Medium, www.aboutmediumship.com

Chris Brown www.sylviabrowne.com / about-chris (Chris told me to write this book)

Tantra Teachers, Groups

Diana Richardson, the Making Love Retreats loveforcouples.com

Janet McGeever, janetmcgeever.com

Charu Morgan (Los Angeles), Embodytantra.com

Amara Karuna, amarakaruna.com

www.newculturehawaii.org (groups)

Tantra Teachers, Groups

Nancy Moonstar, drmoonstarr.com
Orgasmic Meditation, onetaste.us

Online Sexual Healing Resources

ROSY, meetRosy.com
The North American Menopause Society, Menopause.org
Dr. Laura Berman, drlauraberman.com
Gay and Kathlyn Hendricks, hendricks.com

Spiritual Teachers

Byron Katie
thework.com
thework.com/the-judge-your-neighbor-worksheet
www.vtw-the-work.org/the-work/the-work-helpline
thework.com/school-for-the-work-byron-katie
YouTube: Byron Katie
Books: Loving What Is, A Mind At Home with Itself, A Thousand Names for Joy: Living in Harmony with the Way Things Are

Eckhart Tolle
YouTube Eckhart Tolle
School of Awakening through Sounds True
Books by Eckhart: The Power of Now, Stillness Speaks, A New Earth: Awakening to Your Life's Purpose

Sydney Banks, sydneybanks.org
Three Principles Global Community 3pgc.org
YouTube: Sydney Banks, 3PGC

Nutrition: Vegan Teachers and Supplements

Ocean and John Robbins: foodrevolution.org

Kris Carr kriscarr.com

Dr. Joel Fuhrman www.drfuhrman.com

www.forksoverknives.com

Supplements from Anthony William's website:
www.medicalmedium.com/preferred/supplements

Support Groups

Colontown - Here With You. | Facebook

Blue Hope Nation | Facebook

https://imermanangels.org

Cancer Support CommunityCommuity:
www.cancersupportcommunity.org

United Ostomy Associations of America www.ostomy.org

Independent Consumer Guides

Environmental Protection Group ewg.org (for beauty products, chemicals, water quality, food products)

Consumer Reports consumerreports.org

Water Filtration Systems

Nevin Eckert, True Spring Water Quality Solutions,
Truespring.wordpress.com

BIBLIOGRAPHY

Break The Code of Your Illness, The Link Between Emotional Distress and Health Disorders, Isabelle Benarous, Bioreprogramming Press, 2010

Cancer as a Turning Point: A Handbook for People with Cancer, Their Families, and Health Professionals, Lawrence LeShan, Ph.D. A Plume Book, 1994

Cancer: Discovering Your Healing Power Audio CD by Louise Hay, Hay House, 2004

Conscious Loving: The Journey to Co-Commitment, Gay and Kathlyn Hendricks, Bantam, 1992

Dying To Be Me: My Journey from Cancer, to Near Death, to True Healing, Anita Moorjani, Hay House Inc. 2012

Letting Go: The Pathway of Surrender, David R. Hawkins M.D. Ph.D, Hay House, 2013

Love, Medicine and Miracles: Lessons Learned about Self-Healing from a Surgeon's Experience with Exceptional Patients, Bernie S. Siegel, HarperCollins Publishers, 1986

Loving What Is: Four Questions That Can Change Your Life, Byron Katie with Stephen Mitchell, Harmony, 2002

Nonviolent Communication: A Language of Life, Marshall B. Rosenberg, Puddledancer Press, 2003

Sex and Cancer: Intimacy, Romance, and Love after Diagnosis and Treatment, Saketh R. Guntapalli, Maryann Karinch, Rowman & Littlefield Publishers, 2017

Slow Sex: The Path to Fulfilling and Sustainable Sexuality, Diana Richardson, Destiny Books, 2011

Tantric Secrets for Men: What Every Woman Will Want Her Man to Know about Enhancing Sexual Ecstasy, Kerry Riley, Inner Traditions India, 2004

Tantric Sex and Menopause: Practices for Spiritual and Sexual Renewal, Diana Richardson, Janet McGeever, Destiny Books, 2018

The Complete Cancer Cleanse: A Proven Program to Detoxify and Renew Body, Mind, and Spirit, Cherie Calbom, John Calbom, Michael Mahaffey, Published by Thomas Nelson, 2006

The Hormone Cure – Reclaim Balance, Sleep, and Sex Drive; Lose Weight; Feel Focused, Vital, and Energized Naturally with the Gottfried Protocol, Sara Gottfried, MD, Scribner 2013

The Relationship Handbook: A Simple Guide to Satisfying Relationships, George S. Pranksy, Pransky & Associates, 2013

Woman Cancer Sex, Anne Katz RN PhD. Oncology Nursing Society, 2009

ENDNOTES

Introduction

i www.cancer.net / cancer-types / colorectal-cancer / statistics

Chapter 2

ii www.who.int / news-room / fact-sheets / detail / cancer

Chapter 8

iii Chemotherapy Ports Benefits and Risks (verywellhealth.com)

Chapter 9

iv Lynch syndrome - Symptoms and causes - Mayo Clinic

v Gene mutation profiling in Chinese colorectal cancer patients and its association with clinicopathological characteristics and prognosis - PubMed (nih.gov)

Chapter 11

I https: / / www.mdanderson.org / publications / cancerwise / 6-side-effects-of-radiation-therapy-to-the-pelvis-in-women.h00-159145245.html

ii (sex and cancer)

Chapter 12

I Sex and Cancer, p. 31

ii (Sex and Cancer, p. 31).

iii www.cancer.gov
iv Bladder Sling - What You Need to Know (drugs.com)
v Sex and Cancer, Guntupalli, MD, and Karinch, p. 33
vi https://www.webmd.com/menopause/guide/menopause-hot-flashes#1.
Vii (Sex and Cancer, p. 34).
viii www.ncbi.nim.nih.gov
ix https://www.ncbi.nlm.nih.gov/pmc/articles/PMC4708128/
X (https://www.ncbi.nlm.nih.gov/pmc/articles/PMC4708128/)
xi (https://www.ncbi.nlm.nih.gov/pmc/articles/PMC4708128/)
xii https://www.ncbi.nlm.nih.gov/pubmed/19197173

Chapter 14

I The Hormone Cure – Reclaim Balance, Sleep, and Sex Drive; Lose Weight; Feel Focused, Vital, and Energized Naturally with the Gottfried Protocol, Sara Gottfried, MD, Scribner 2013, pages 180, 199
ii https://www.medicalnewstoday.com/articles/317530.php.
Iii McGeever and Richardson p. 24).
iv https://www.lifeextension.com/Magazine/2012/6/Suzanne-Somers-Quest-to-Educate-World-About-How-to-Delay-Aging/Page-01.
V Making Sense of HRT: Bioidentical Hormones vs HRT | Early-Menopause.com
vi Vaginal Rejuvenation, Labiaplasty, and Other Female Genital Cosmetic Surgery | ACOG

Chapter 15

I (Richardson and McGeever, Tantric Sex and Menopause, Practices for Spiritual and Sexual Renewal, Destiny Books, 2018, p. 34).
ii (Richardson and McGeever, Tantric Sex and Menopause, Practices for Spiritual and Sexual Renewal, Destiny Books, 2018, p. 34).

iii (Richardson and McGeever, Tantric Sex and Menopause, Practices for Spiritual and Sexual Renewal, Destiny Books, 2018, p. 53).
iv (Richardson and McGeever, Tantric Sex and Menopause, Practices for Spiritual and Sexual Renewal, Destiny Books, 2018, p. 122).
v (www.loveforcouples.com)
vi https://janetmcgeever.com/#events.
Vii http://www.jaeminyi.com/living-in-an-orgasmic-meditation-house/

Chapter 16
I Erectile Dysfunction After Cancer Treatment | OncoLink
ii Men's sex life and fertility | Radiotherapy | Cancer Research UK
iii How does the prostate work? - InformedHealth.org - NCBI Bookshelf (nih.gov)
iv Men's Experience with Sexual Dysfunction Post Rectal Cancer Treatment: A Qualitative Study (nih.gov)
v Men's Experience with Sexual Dysfunction Post Rectal Cancer Treatment: A Qualitative Study (nih.gov)
vi Cancer treatment for men: Possible sexual side effects - Mayo Clinic
vii Alprostadil Injection and Suppository for Erectile Dysfunction (webmd.com)
viii Erectile Dysfunction After Cancer Treatment | OncoLink

Chapter 17
I https://www.ncbi.nlm.nih.gov/pmc/articles/PMC4708128/
ii https://clinicaltrials.gov/ct2/show/NCT01515787.
Iii www.ncbi.nlm.nih.gov/pmc/articles/PMC6042715/
iv www.ncbi.nlm.nih.gov/pmc/articles/PMC4976683/
v www.sciencedirect.com/science/article/pii/0167814088902198?via%3Dihub.

Vi.https://www.ncbi.nlm.nih.gov/pmc/articles/PMC2843890/
vii https://www.ncbi.nlm.nih.gov/pubmed/15496622.
Viii https://www.ncbi.nlm.nih.gov/pubmed/22529255.
Ix https://www.ncbi.nlm.nih.gov/pmc/articles/PMC2789502/.
X https://www.ncbi.nlm.nih.gov/pubmed/2425199/
xi https://www.ncbi.nlm.nih.gov/pubmed/12130870
xii https://www.ncbi.nlm.nih.gov/pubmed/11547717
xiii https://www.ncbi.nlm.nih.gov/pmc/articles/PMC4976683/
xiv https://www.ncbi.nlm.nih.gov/pubmed/20692872/
xv https://www.ncbi.nlm.nih.gov/pmc/articles/PMC4976683/#-gow017-B3.
Xvi https://www.ncbi.nlm.nih.gov/pubmed/26705854
xvii https://www.ncbi.nlm.nih.gov/pubmed/16135487
xviii https://www.ncbi.nlm.nih.gov/pmc/articles/PMC4976683/#gow017-B3
xix (https://cancer.ufl.edu/2018/07/09/younger-patients-do-not-attain-a-survival-benefit-from-current-rectal-cancer-treatment-recommendations).
Xx https://www.cancer.net/cancer-types/colorectal-cancer/statistics
xxi pubmed.ncbi.nlm.nih.gov/30309324/
xxii https://pubmed.ncbi.nlm.nih.gov/27334350/
xxiii https://pubmed.ncbi.nlm.nih.gov/22867889/
xxiv PROSPECT: Chemotherapy Alone or Chemotherapy Plus Radiation Therapy in Treating Patients With Locally Advanced Rectal Cancer Undergoing Surgery - Full Text View - ClinicalTrials.gov

Chapter 19

I — It Didn't Start with You: How Inherited Family Trauma Shapes Who We Are and How to End the Cycle by Mark Wolynn, Penguin Books, 2016

Chapter 20

I www.foodmatters.com/article/22-additives-and-preservatives-to-avoid

Chapter 23

I http://chemocare.com/chemotherapy/drug-info/Oxaliplatin.aspx

Chapter 27

I https://www.mayoclinic.org/diseases-conditions/chemo-brain/symptoms-causes/syc-20351060

Chapter 28

I www.Fightcolorectalcancer.org.
Ii https://www.ncbi.nlm.nih.gov/pubmed/29936195

Chapter 31

I Lawrence LeShan, A Plume book, 1994, p.55

Chapter 32

i10 Signs You're a People-Pleaser | Psychology Today

Chapter 34

I What is a fecal transplant? Everything you need to know (medicalnewstoday.com)
ii EWG's2020 Shopper's Guide to Pesticides in Produce | Clean Fifteen
iii http://sitn.hms.harvard.edu/flash/2015/roundup-ready-crops/
iv Monsanto/Bayer Glyphosate Cancer Settlement Agreement Reached (monsantoroundupcancerlawsuit.com)
V www.nongmoproject.org/gmo-facts.
Vi www.webmd.com/diet/features/safer-food-healthier-you#3.

Vii Food Dyes Linked to Allergies, ADHD and Cancer: Group Calls on U.S. to Outlaw Their Use - CBS News
Viii Salt, Sugar and Fat: Could You Be Addicted? - The Dr. Oz Show (doctoroz.com)
ix Sugar addiction: pushing the drug-sugar analogy to the limit - PubMed (nih.gov)
x Study Shows Sugar is More Addictive Than Cocaine! - David Avocado Wolfe (davidwolfe.com)

Chapter 35

I EWG Skin Deep® Cosmetics Database
ii Carpets | American Lung Association
iii BPA In Receipts | BPA Health Risk - Consumer Reports News
iv https://articles.mercola.com/sites/articles/archive/2010/05/18/microwave-hazards.aspx
vi The contribution of washing processes of synthetic clothes to microplastic pollution | Scientific Reports (nature.com)

ABOUT THE AUTHOR

Kineret Sherman graduated from UCLA with a Bachelor of Science degree in Biochemistry and received a Master of Science degree in Life Sciences from The Weizmann Institute of Science. In addition, she had a spiritual insight. She also holds a Master of Arts in spiritual psychology from the University of Santa Monica.

Certified as a Life Coach by The Coach Training Academy, an ICF-accredited school, Kineret has taken subsequent coach training with Michael Neill, Rohini Ross, Dicken Bettinger, Mavis Karn, and Pransky and Associates. Kineret went to Byron Katie's 9-Day School For The Work and Eckhart Tolle's School of Awakening. She studied Nonviolent Communication (NVC) for many years. She has certificates in Thai Yoga Therapy, Reiki, and Holoenergetic Healing.

Today Kineret works as a life coach and a hospice spiritual care provider. She has worked as an intervention coach for Alzheimer's patients and their caregivers for a study with the University of Washington on the LGBTQ community.

In 2015, at age 43, Kineret discovered she had Stage II rectal cancer. She used alternative healing methods for a year and a half, and the tumor developed into stage III. Dealing with this disease, she has found internal and external resources to heal her life and, in the process, help others. Patients and others with cancer-related issues often approach her for coaching, speaking, and teaching.

To learn more about Kineret go to www.kineretsherman.com

Made in the USA
Monee, IL
20 October 2026

66035288R00223